DISTINGUISHED WISDOM PRESENTS . . .

Your WEALTH *Is In Your* ANOINTING

Discover Keys to Releasing Your Potential

— PASTOR TERRANCE LEVISE TURNER, MBA —

Copyright © 2017 Pastor Terrance Levise Turner

All rights reserved. No part of this book may be used or reproduced by any means, graphic, electronic, or mechanical, including photocopying, recording, taping, or by any information storage retrieval system without the written permission of the author except in the case of brief quotations embodied in critical articles and reviews. For information or permission, write: WellSpokenInc@bellsouth.net

This is a work of creative nonfiction. The events herein are portrayed to the best of the author's memory. While all the stories in this book are true, some names and identifying details may have been changed to protect the privacy of the people involved.

Scripture quotations are taken from the King James Version (KJV) of the Bible, unless otherwise specified.

Editorial work by Eschler Editing Staff
Cover Art © 2017 Terrance Levise Turner
Cover design by Lizaa
Interior print design and layout by Eschler Editing Staff.
eBook design and layout by Eschler Editing Staff.

Published by:
Well Spoken Inc.
P.O. Box 291806
Nashville, TN. 37229

www.TerranceTurnerBooks.com

Contact Well Spoken Inc. to learn more about discounts available for buying books in bulk.

First Edition: September 2017
Printed in the United States of America

10   9   8   7   6   5   4   3   2

ISBN 978-0-9993236-0-1 (trade paperback)
ISBN 978-0-9993236-2-5 (hard back)
ISBN 978-0-9993236-1-8 (e-book)

This book is dedicated to men and women everywhere seeking godly wisdom for their financial future and the security of their family.

ALSO BY PASTOR TERRANCE LEVISE TURNER:

DISTINGUISHED WISDOM PRESENTS . . .
"LIVING PROVERBS"-VOLUME 1

DISTINGUISHED WISDOM PRESENTS . . .
"LIVING PROVERBS"-VOLUME 2

DISTINGUISHED WISDOM PRESENTS . . .
"THE DYNAMIC VICTORY CONFESSION!"

CONTENTS

Acknowledgments	1
Preface	3
Introduction	4
PART ONE: YOU WERE BORN WITH IT!	**7**
Chapter One: God Planned Your Life From The Beginning	9
Chapter Two: The Anointing Is To Make You Rich!	29
Chapter Three: God's Word Is Anointed	33
Chapter Four: The Anointed One and His Anointing	41
Chapter Five: It's In You	57
PART TWO: THE ESSENTIAL KEYS TO THE RELEASE OF THE ANOINTING WITHIN YOU	**63**
Chapter Six: Focus—The 1st Essential Key	65
Chapter Seven: Purpose:—The 2nd Essential Key	71
Chapter Eight: Passion—The 3rd Essential Key	89
The 1st Component of Passion: The Joy of Pursuit!	90
The 2nd Component of Passion: The Fight for Focus	94
The 3rd Component of Passion: Overcoming the Frustration of Perseverance	106
The 4th Component of Passion: The Fight to Finish	119
Examples of Finishers	121
Solomon: A Finisher	121
Zerubbabel: A Finisher	126
Jesus Christ: A Finisher	134
Apostle Paul: A Finisher	149

PART THREE: ANOINTED TO LEAVE A LEGACY — 179

Chapter Nine: Faithfulness—An Essential Key
to Maintaining Wealth — 181

Chapter Ten: Abraham—The Father of Faithfulness — 199

Final Words — 227

Prayer For Salvation — 229

About the Author — 231

A Special Note — 232

ACKNOWLEDGMENTS

I would like to acknowledge and thank God for my wife and partner in life, Dr. Avis Turner, for her faithful support and encouragement as I have pursued the journey of faith as a pastor, entrepreneur, writer, and recording artist. Together, we are touching the world with the love of God and with love for one another. The life of faith requires endurance and hope. I'm thankful that God has given me a faithful wife to help keep the flame of hope alive!

I thank God for my mother, Geraldine Key, for laying the foundation of my faith in the Lord Jesus Christ. Her example taught me the meaning of sincere love, faith, and determination. My grandmother, Wilma Starks, and grandfather, Clarence Young, provided solid support of love, care, and faithfulness. My life will always rest upon what I learned from my elders.

I thank God for the teachers of faith and wisdom of the Word of God, who helped to bring revelation of God's truth. The simple presentation of the gospel in the Baptist church, which I received as a child was responsible for my salvation by faith in Jesus. I received the baptism of the Holy Ghost as I grew up in a Pentecostal church. I received further revelation of the Word of Faith and doctrines of the church, as I continued my walk of faith. I am forever grateful to the pastors, teachers, and leaders that helped to influence my faith. Their guidance helped to direct my passionate pursuit of the wisdom and truth of God's word.

I acknowledge the invaluable gift gained from my academic education and personal development over the years. I thank God for each teacher, professor, and mentor that has helped to shape and enhance my inherent acumen for knowledge and wisdom. When the student was ready, God always was faithful to send the right teachers.

YOUR WEALTH IS IN YOUR ANOINTING

Thank God for Rev. Brockway, Bishop Phillip Gardner, missionary Mary Archie, Pastor Charles Cowan, Bishop TD Jakes, Joyce Meyer, Dr. Mike Murdock, and many others that has inspired my life. Thank God for inspirational and motivational teachers such as Les Brown, Brian Tracy, Dr. John Maxwell; as well as great leaders in our society such as Gen. Colin Powell. Also, I recognize the impact of great educational leaders upon my life, such as the late Dr. James A. Hefner, former president of Tennessee State University. My life has been impacted by great leaders in wisdom, instruction, and by example. My mother laid the foundation, and Jehovah God my Heavenly Father has built upon that foundation the right keystones. My prayer is that the reader of this book will benefit from those lessons learned and will profit from that pursuit.

PREFACE

Early in my ministry, my mother, Geraldine Key, asked me if I had any insights about the story in 2 Kings 4:1-7 of the widow with the "pot of oil" that came to Elisha the prophet seeking an answer for her desperate financial situation. My mother was not only seeking understanding of the scripture for theological enlightenment, but she was seeking godly wisdom, like so many single mothers have before, for her own financial needs. Her question led me on a seven-year study of meditating and preaching the answers to why this passage was placed in the scripture and what it can reveal to all of us. In only seven verses, the writer of 2 Kings 4:1-7 instilled certain core financial principles that, once discovered, will help bring financial deliverance and security to the life of all that avail themselves to these keys.

Your Wealth Is In Your Anointing will give you the impetus to seek and discover the "potential" that you have in your "house." Your body is the "house of God." The Holy Spirit lives inside of you. Your body is the "temple of the Holy Ghost" (1 Corinthians 6:19). We have a "treasure in earthen vessels" (2 Corinthians 4:7). God wants you and me to unveil and release the wealth contained inside the treasure in us. This book will lead you on a complete, extensive journey to financial deliverance. You will be inspired to take action on your God-given gifts and talents as your mind is enlightened and renewed to the wealth mentality contained in this book. Do not die with your treasure still in the "house!" Do not die with your wealth untapped. Your wealth is in your connection with the Lord Jesus Christ! Now let's go prospecting to discover and mine your wealth together. Your life will never be the same. Your wealth is in your anointing!

–PASTOR TERRANCE L. TURNER, MBA
FINANCE & SUPPLY CHAIN MANAGEMENT

INTRODUCTION

"God has given each of us a portion of Christ's anointing, by which we are to live and succeed in life."

A lot of times we walk through life and we never realize what we have on the inside of us. We never realize that we have our blessing on the inside. God has put everything you and I need on the inside of us. We are self-contained with blessing, ability, provision, and potential. Everything we need is on the inside of us. Everything that we see on the outside came from inside of somebody. This whole world that you see surrounding you came from inside of God. You came from inside of God. You were conceived in Him and He released you into the earth. So everything we see on the outside came from inside of somebody. Somebody's mind, somebody's thoughts—somebody put forth the efforts to create a plan. It came from the inside. You have the capability, as a *thinking being*, to process information and *think your way out*. You can think your way out of your financial situation. God has anointed you to *think your way out*. Proverbs 16:1 says, "The preparations of the heart in man, and the answer of the tongue, is from the Lord." The Amplified translation says, "The plans of the mind and orderly thinking belong to man, but from the Lord comes the [wise] answer of the tongue." Also, Proverbs 16:9 says, "A man's mind plans his way, but the Lord directs his steps and makes them sure." But we have to take time to plan. We have to plan our success. We have to plan our *release*. We have to plan our success and prosperity. There is a way of planning and getting information for how to *get out*. Anything that has ever been done, somebody sat down with a piece of paper, and said, "I wonder if I did this, this, and this; then maybe I could get this."

INTRODUCTION

Everything you and I need comes from the inside, and we came from inside of God. God then put Himself inside of us. We are self-contained for what we need. We are self-contained for provision, protection, prosperity, and where we live. We are self-contained, and God has given us ability to get wealth. ***Your wealth is in your anointing***.

PART ONE
YOU WERE BORN WITH IT!

And God said, Let us make man in our image, after our likeness: and let them have dominion over the fish of the sea, and over the fowl of the air, and over the cattle, and over all the earth, and over every creeping thing that creepeth upon the earth. So God created man in his own image, in the image of God created he him; male and female created he them. And God blessed them, and God said unto them, Be fruitful, and multiply, and replenish the earth, and subdue it: and have dominion over the fish of the sea, and over the fowl of the air, and over every living thing that moveth upon the earth.

–Genesis 1:26-28

CHAPTER ONE
GOD PLANNED YOUR LIFE FROM THE BEGINNING

First, let's establish that God had you on His mind before you entered earth. He had a plan for your life before you were conceived. Let's look at Jeremiah 1:4–10. First we will look at the plan of greatness God had for the prophet Jeremiah, We will then look at the foundational scripture for this message in 2 Kings 4:1–7. We first want to establish that the plan for your life has already been made. God already established you to be prosperous. He established for you to be successful in life. Poverty is not God's will. Poverty is not God's plan. He is an abundant God. He's an *extravagant* God! He has fullness of goodness and bounty. All you have to do is look at the earth and you will see how abundant God is. The oceans are filled with all types of life and an abundance of every living thing. There are multitudes of fish and marine life. God is an abundant God! Therefore, He has a plan for you and me to live in abundance. Let's read Jeremiah 1:4–10:

> *Then the word of the Lord came unto me, saying, Before I formed thee in the belly I knew thee; and before thou camest forth out of the womb I sanctified thee, and I ordained thee a prophet unto the nations. Then said I, Ah, Lord God! behold, I cannot speak: for I am a child. But the Lord said unto me, Say not, I am a child: for thou shalt go to all that I shall send thee, and whatsoever I command thee thou shalt speak. Be not afraid of their faces: for I am with thee to deliver thee, saith the Lord. Then the Lord put forth his hand, and touched my mouth. And the Lord said unto me, Behold, I have put my words in thy mouth. See, I have this day set thee over the nations and over the kingdoms, to root out, and to pull down, and to destroy, and to throw down, to build, and to plant.*

I'm establishing that everything that we need comes from the inside, and we came from inside of God. God said before He even formed Jeremiah in the belly He knew him. In other words, God fully comprehended

YOUR WEALTH IS IN YOUR ANOINTING

Jeremiah and He had a plan for Jeremiah. He had a plan for Jeremiah's fruitfulness in life. He had a plan for Jeremiah's productivity in life, and his function in life. God said He "sanctified" Jeremiah. He selected him for this purpose. There is a specific purpose God has selected you for. God also said He "ordained" Jeremiah. He empowered him. He ordered his life. God didn't say He ordained Jeremiah a prophet unto *two* people. He said He ordained him a prophet unto the "nations." Therefore, God had an expanse of people on His mind. He wanted the reach of Jeremiah's life to be expansive. God is an abundant God.

In the same way that God had an expanse of people on His mind for Jeremiah's ministry, He has a plan for your life. You are empowered to accomplish it. Your *wealth* is there. Let's also look at Jeremiah 29:11.

> *For I know the thoughts that I think toward you, saith the Lord, thoughts of peace, and not evil, to give you an expected end.*

Here we see the kind of plans God had for Jeremiah and for us, before He formed any of us in the belly. Before we were conceived in the belly, God had a plan for our abundance. God says He has thoughts of "peace" concerning us. According to Strong's Exhaustive Concordance of the Bible, the definition for peace includes *prosperity*. The Hebrew word for peace used here is *shalom*. It is definition 7999. It has the meaning of completeness, safety, soundness, welfare, health, prosperity, tranquility, quiet, and contentment. God has plans for your prosperity. The Amplified translation of Jeremiah 29:11 says, "For I know the thoughts and plans that I have for you, saith the Lord, thoughts and plans for welfare and peace, and not for evil; to give you hope in your final outcome." God has plans for your prosperity. **Your wealth is in your anointing.**

YOU ARE SELF-CONTAINED

So, we are self-contained for what we need. We are self-contained for provision, protection, prosperity, and where we live. We are self-contained and God has given us the ability to get wealth. I'm establishing this in our hearts. You have something. And you *are* something. You are somebody and you have something. You're not lacking. Don't feel poor. You're not poor. You're wealthy. **Your wealth is in your anointing.** You are wealthy. You *are* wealth. You may have been looking for something and scratching around for something on the outside, but God tells us through scripture, you are self-contained. You have wealth on the inside.

GOD PLANNED YOUR LIFE FROM THE BEGINNING

Let's look at Colossians 2:9–10.

> *For in him dwelleth all the fulness of the Godhead bodily. And ye are complete in him, which is the head of all principality and power.*

We are self-contained. According to Dictionary.com, the word self-contained means "containing in oneself all that is necessary; independent." In other words, God says, "You're not begging someone else to help you survive." God says you are self-contained. *Containing in oneself all that is necessary*. You're independent. Self-contained also means: *containing in oneself all parts necessary for completeness*. God says you are self-contained. You are complete. A lot of times we spend our whole lives struggling, trying to be something, trying to be somebody, trying to become this or trying to become that. And yes, we do have to grow, refine, and develop. You want to develop in your skills, talents, knowledge, personality, etc. Yet, God says, you are already *complete*. You already contain something.

YOU'RE ALREADY COMPLETE

Now, we're going to look at how you, as a born-again believer, already are complete. **Your wealth is in your anointing.** Your wealth is in your connection with the Anointed One. It's because you are in Him and He is in you. Christ is the Anointed One, and the source of our supernatural empowerment is the Anointing upon the Anointed One. You are connected to that anointing. That anointing is in you.

> *For in him dwelleth all the fulness of the Godhead bodily. And ye are complete in him, which is the head of all principality and power.*
>
> –Colossians 2:9-10

We are complete in Him. **Your wealth is in your anointing.** Your wealth is in your connection with the Anointed One. Just like your salvation and peace of mind is in Him, your financial wealth is in Him. Your health and healing is in Him. "For in him dwelleth all the fulness of the Godhead bodily." All the fullness of the Father, the Son, and the Holy Ghost; the Creator God, that created all the heavens and the earth, dwells in you. The God that created all the gold, silver, diamonds, and oil in the earth, lives in you. The God that created all the stars in the universe lives in you. The Creator that pulled all of that out of Him, lives inside of you. It's in Christ Jesus, with whom you are connected.

YOUR WEALTH IS IN YOUR ANOINTING

A person is an *American* because they were born in America. You are a *Christian* because you were *born again* in Christ. And Christ lives in you. "Ye are complete in Him, which is the head of all principality and power."

I'm establishing that we are self-contained and God has given us the ability to get wealth. 2 Corinthians 5:17–18 says,

> *Therefore if any man be in Christ, he is a new creature: old things are passed away; behold, all things are become new. And all things are of God, who hath reconciled us to himself by Jesus Christ, and hath given us the ministry of reconciliation.*

Therefore, if God is whole, well, full, and healthy, you are whole, well, full, and healthy—*and wealthy!* We are connected to Christ. Your wealth is in your connection with the Anointed One. Christ is the Anointed One.

It is the anointing upon the Anointed One by which you have your wealth and inheritance. Ephesians 1:15–23 begins to tell us who Jesus is, and what we have in Him:

> *Wherefore I also, after I heard of your faith in the Lord Jesus, and love unto all the saints, Cease not to give thanks for you, making mention of you in my prayers; That the God of our Lord Jesus Christ, the Father of glory, may give unto you the spirit of wisdom and revelation in the knowledge of him: The eyes of your understanding being enlightened; that ye may know what is the hope of his calling, and what the riches of the glory of his inheritance in the saints, And what is the exceeding greatness of his power to us-ward who believe, according to the working of his mighty power, Which he wrought in Christ, when he raised him from the dead, and set him at his own right hand in the heavenly places, Far above all principality, and power, and might, and dominion, and every name that is named, not only in this world, but also in that which is to come: And hath put all things under his feet, and gave him to be the head over all things to the church, Which is his body, the fulness of him that filleth all in all.*

Notice, where Paul says, "The eyes of your understanding being enlightened; that ye may know what is the hope of his calling, and what the riches of the glory of his inheritance in the saints." The word "hope" means *to anticipate with pleasure or confidence, or to look forward with joyful expectation*. In other words, God wants your eyes to be opened to the *joyful expectation* of the inheritance that He has for you in Christ. He says He wants "The eyes of your understanding to be enlightened, that ye may know what is the hope of His calling and what the riches of the glory of His inheritance in the saints." The word "riches" has this meaning from the *Strong's Exhaustive Concordance of the Bible*:

RICHES
4149-Ploutos
1. Wealth (as fullness)
2. Literally; money and possessions
3. Figuratively; Abundance, richness
4. Specifically; Valuable bestowment, riches

It's from which we get our English word "Plutocrat." The Websters New World Dictionary defines the word "plutocrat" like this:

PLUTOCRAT
1. A member of a wealthy ruling class
2. A person whose wealth gives him control or great influence

Also, we get the word "Plutocracy" from "Ploutos". This is what it means:

PLUTOCRACY
1. Government by the wealthy
2. A group of wealthy people who control the government

God says that it is a part of our inheritance to be wealthy and to rule. This is a part of our inheritance that we have in Christ. According to *Strong's*, the word "inheritance" that's used in Ephesians 1:18 has this meaning:

INHERITANCE
2817–kleronomia
1. heir-ship
2. a patrimony
3. a possession
4. inheritance

Webster's defines the word "patrimony" as "property inherited from one's father or ancestors."

We are children of God. We have received an inheritance from Him through our Lord Jesus Christ because we have been redeemed. God bought back our right to rule and to reign in the earth through the shedding of the precious blood of Jesus.

Psalms 24:1 says, "The earth is the Lord's and the fullness thereof; the world, and they that dwell therein." In Haggai 2:8, the Lord says, "The silver is mine, and the gold is mine, saith the Lord of hosts." Also, Psalms 50:10–12 says,

> For every beast of the forest is mine, and the cattle upon a thousand hills. I know all the fowls of the mountains: and the wild beasts of the field are mine. If I were hungry, I would not tell thee: for the world is mine, and the fullness thereof.

I emphasize these scriptures to show that the wealth of the world belongs to our Father. He has made us heirs to this wealth. He wants us to rule in the earth as royal sons and daughters of God. We do that through being connected with the Anointed One, Christ Jesus. Galatians 4:7 says, "Wherefore thou art no more a servant, but a son; and if a son, then an heir of God through Christ." Christ is the Anointed One. We obtain our wealth through the anointing upon and within the Anointed One. It is our inheritance. God wants us to know that we have an inheritance, which includes wealth. If you are named in an earthly last will and testament and you get an inheritance, it typically includes money, land, property, etc. We have an inheritance from God. It's not just spiritual. It includes healing, righteousness, wealth, and heir-ship. Here are some scriptures describing our inheritance:

> But he was wounded for our transgressions, he was bruised for our iniquities: the chastisement of our peace was upon him; and with his stripes we are healed.
>
> –Isaiah 53:5

> Who his own self bare our sins in his own body on the tree, that we being dead to sins, should live unto righteousness: by whose stripes ye were healed.
>
> –1 Peter 2:24

> But ye are a chosen generation, a royal priesthood, an holy nation, a peculiar people; that ye should shew forth the praises of him who hath called you out of darkness into his marvellous light:
>
> –1 Peter 2:9

GOD PLANNED YOUR LIFE FROM THE BEGINNING

> *For he hath made him to be sin for us, who knew no sin; that we might be made the righteousness of God in him.*
>
> *–2 Corinthians 5:21*

> *The Spirit itself beareth witness with our spirit, that we are the children of God: And if children, then heirs; heirs of God, and joint-heirs with Christ; if so be that we suffer with him, that we may be also glorified together.*
>
> *--Romans 8:16-17*

> *For ye know the grace of our Lord Jesus Christ, that, though he was rich, yet for your sakes he became poor, that ye through his poverty might be rich.*
>
> *–2 Corinthians 8:9*

That's your inheritance!

Your wealth is in your connection with the Lord Jesus Christ, the Anointed One. You are empowered to succeed. You are empowered to prosper greatly. However, we must *stretch forth* and give the effort in order to obtain the wealth. All the promises of God are obtained by faith. We are self-contained and empowered by God Himself to break forth and prosper greatly! Ephesians 2:4–10 helps to establish you in Christ the Anointed One. This is what it says:

> *But God, who is rich in mercy, for his great love wherewith he loved us, Even when we were dead in sins, hath quickened us together with Christ, (by grace ye are saved;) And hath raised us up together, and made us sit together in heavenly places in Christ Jesus: That in the ages to come he might shew the exceeding riches of his grace in his kindness toward us through Christ Jesus. For by grace are ye saved through faith; and that not of yourselves: it is the gift of God: Not of works, lest any man should boast. For we are his workmanship, created in Christ Jesus unto good works, which God hath before ordained that we should walk in them.*
>
> *–Ephesians 2:4-10*

When verse 7 says "That in the ages to come he might shew the exceeding riches of his grace in his kindness toward us through Christ Jesus," He is speaking of *this* time. He is speaking of this dispensation of time and in the time to come. God wants to show the exceeding riches of His grace and favor in His kindness toward you through the inheritance you have in Christ Jesus, the Anointed One. Again, the word "riches" is defined like this in the *Strong's Exhaustive Concordance of the Bible*:

RICHES

4149-Ploutos

1. Wealth (as fullness)
2. Literally; money and possessions
3. Figuratively; Abundance, richness
4. Specifically; Valuable bestowment, riches

Again, as we saw earlier, this is a word from which the English words "plutocrat" and the word "plutocracy" are derived. *Webster's New World Dictionary* defines these words like this:

PLUTOCRAT

1. A member of a wealthy ruling class
2. A person whose wealth gives him control or great influence

PLUTOCRACY

1. Government by the wealthy
2. A group of wealthy people who control the government

BLESSED TO *BE* A BLESSING

God wants to bless us, so we'll help Him accomplish His purpose in the earth. We deprive Him of pleasure and we hinder His plan when we fail to achieve. Psalms 35:27 declares, "Let them shout for joy, and be glad, that favour my righteous cause: yea, let them say continually, Let the Lord be magnified, which hath pleasure in the prosperity of his servant." If God "has pleasure in the prosperity of His *servants*," then how much more does He have pleasure in you and me, as *sons and daughters*? You are an heir of God and a joint-heir with the Lord Jesus Christ. He has pleasure in your prosperity.

Any parent has pleasure when their child prospers, in any way. If the child goes to the next grade in school, they celebrate that child. Every birthday, they celebrate that child. If the child wins a race, they celebrate that child. When the child gets their first job, they celebrate that child. When that child graduates high school, the parents celebrate that child.

GOD PLANNED YOUR LIFE FROM THE BEGINNING

When the child goes to college, the parents celebrate the child. When the child gets married, they celebrate that child. It's because that child is *prospering*! And the parents have pleasure in the prosperity of their child. *Hallelujah*!

Well, that's the way our Heavenly Father is. He has pleasure as we prosper. He has pleasure as you *step out*. He has pleasure as you go forward. Hallelujah! Look again at Ephesians 2:10, "For we are his workmanship, created in Christ Jesus unto good works, which God hath before ordained that we should walk in them."

We have been created in Christ Jesus, the Anointed One. We are the Father's *workmanship*. We have been filled with the *anointing* and empowered to bring forth *good works*. From these good works we will obtain our *wealth*. I went over those scriptures to bear out the truth that you are self-contained for prosperity. **Your wealth is in your anointing.** Now let's look at 2 Kings 4:1–7 as we continue to establish the basis for this message:

> *Now there cried a certain woman of the wives of the sons of the prophets unto Elisha, saying, Thy servant my husband is dead; and thou knowest that thy servant did fear the Lord: and the creditor is come to take unto him my two sons to be bondmen. And Elisha said unto her, What shall I do for thee? tell me, what hast thou in the house? And she said, Thine handmaid hath not anything in the house, save a pot of oil. Then he said, Go, borrow thee vessels abroad of all thy neighbours, even empty vessels; borrow not a few. And when thou art come in, thou shalt shut the door upon thee and upon thy sons, and shalt pour out into all those vessels, and thou shalt set aside that which is full. So she went from him, and shut the door upon her and upon her sons, who brought the vessels to her; and she poured out. And it came to pass, when the vessels were full, that she said unto her son, Bring me yet a vessel. And he said unto her, There is not a vessel more. And the oil stayed. Then she came and told the man of God. And he said, Go, sell the oil, and pay thy debt, and live thou and thy children of the rest.*

Your *anointing* is your ability to get wealth. Your anointing is your *ability*, your *unction*, and your *power* to get wealth. We established that you are self-contained. We established who you *are* in Christ, and that which you *have* in Christ. Your anointing is your *"power to get wealth."* Deuteronomy 8:18 says,

> *But thou shalt remember the Lord thy God: for it is he that giveth thee power to get wealth, that he may establish his covenant which he sware unto thy fathers, as it is this day.*

YOUR WEALTH IS IN YOUR ANOINTING

God has given us power to get wealth. It's your ability to do. It's power to do. The word "dominion" starts with the two letters "do." The word "domain" starts with the letters "do." God has given you *dominion* over a *domain*. In other words, He has given you a realm of *authority*, a realm of *influence*, and a realm of *responsibility*. So, He has given you dominion over a domain. And He wants you to *dominate* in that domain by operating in your dominion or authority. In order to do that, you have to *do* something! The anointing destroys the yoke, and it lifts the heavy burden. It destroys the yoke of impossibility and poverty. It lifts the heavy burdens of life. Where things were hard, the anointing destroys the yoke so that you can do what seems to be impossible. We established that you are connected to the Anointed One, Christ Jesus. He lives inside of you. The Apostle Paul said in Philippians 4:13, "I can do all things through Christ which strengthens me." In other words, "I can *do* all things through Christ (the Anointed One and His Anointing) which is strengthening me to do it." You can say the same thing because the Anointed One lives inside of you and you have His Anointing for living. Now let's look at Genesis 1:26-28. The anointing is tied in with the *"Blessing."* It is tied in with the empowerment. God gave us an empowerment in the beginning. When God created Adam and Eve, He created him from the dust of the earth. He formed him from the dust of the earth. There was no life in him, but then God breathed in him the breath of life, and man became a living soul. And with that breath of life (God is life), God's ability—God himself—was breathed into that vessel of clay. All of God's ability, all of God's power, all of God's vision was breathed into that man, Adam.

> *And God said, Let us make man in our image, after our likeness: and let them have dominion over the fish of the sea, and over the fowl of the air, and over the cattle, and over all the earth, and over every creeping thing that creepeth upon the earth. So God created man in his own image, in the image of God created he him; male and female created he them. And God blessed them, and God said unto them, Be fruitful, and multiply, and replenish the earth, and subdue it: and have dominion over the fish of the sea, and over the fowl of the air, and over every living thing that moveth upon the earth.*
>
> *–Genesis 1:26-28*

Notice, He said "over all the earth." First of all, we established that you are *self-contained* for prosperity. You have everything you need in order to succeed in life. Now we are establishing that God gave you dominion

GOD PLANNED YOUR LIFE FROM THE BEGINNING

in the beginning. He gave you dominion and the empowerment in the beginning to prosper. So you are empowered to prosper. You have every *right* to prosper. You have every *responsibility* to prosper. Now notice, God gave you and me dominion over all the earth. That includes the gold, the silver, the diamonds, the rubies, the pearls, the sapphires, the oil, etc. He said, "over all the earth." That means things on the earth and things in the earth. The wood, the timber: "over all the earth." The lakes, the oceans, and the rivers: "over all the earth." Now there are some men that have been operating in this dominion. That's why we have the things that we have on the outside right now. Someone has been taking dominion and walking in dominion, therefore we have all the industries we have in the earth now. Someone has been taking dominion and walking in dominion. Somebody understood that they had the right to rule in the earth. Well, you have that *right* as well. You and I have that right. I'm establishing this truth in us right now. We have a right to dominion. You have the right to rule. You were created with the *right to rule*. Children should be taught that they were created with the *right to rule*. Our young people should be taught that they were created with the *right to rule*. Thus, they will learn to take the responsibility necessary to manage their lives and the earth. Each one of us was created with the right and the equipment to rule in the earth. **Your wealth is in your anointing**.

TAKING RESPONSIBILITY BRINGS *PROFIT*

Everything that we have has been produced for us. You drank coffee this morning because someone took dominion over that coffee bean, and they made use of it so it could become a stimulating, refreshing drink in the morning. That's dominion. The house that you're living in represents dominion. The wood that it took to make the house: that's dominion. Someone had to cut down the trees, and process the wood for your home. Someone had to process the brick and all the other components of your home. Someone took dominion in the earth and created an industry for housing. The gold in your earrings, necklaces, bracelets, and other items, is available because someone dug in the earth to get that gold out. That's taking dominion. God has given that dominion to you. God has given that dominion to me. This is the *Blessing*. We are *empowered*. We don't have to sit on the sidelines and wait for somebody else to "hand-feed" us! "The earth is the Lord's and the fullness thereof, the world and they that dwell therein." (Psalms 24:1) "We are His people and the sheep of His pasture." (Psalms 100:3c) "The heaven, even the heavens, are the Lord's: but the earth hath he given to the children of men" (Psalms 115:16). That's you and me. And that dominion is *ours*! It was ours in the beginning, and it is ours right now. Jesus redeemed us, and made sure that we had full possession of our rights and power. It's up to us to walk in it. God wants us to learn what we need to learn in order to master our environment. God wants us to master and have dominion in the earth. This is a part of the anointing. Look at verse 27 of Genesis, chapter 1:

> So God created man in his own image, in the image of God created he him; male and female created he them.

In the beginning, God created *woman* with power, just like He created man with power, but there was godly order even from the beginning. Yet *both* have power. Both play a powerful position in the earth. Man is to have dominion. Woman is to have dominion. And their offspring is to have dominion. We are a people of dominion: male and female. Look at verse 28:

> And God blessed them, and God said unto them, Be fruitful, and multiply, and replenish the earth, and subdue it: and have dominion over the fish of the sea, and over the fowl of the air, and over every living thing that moveth upon the earth.

Verse 28 says, "And God blessed them . . ." "Bless" means to *empower to prosper*. God empowered them to prosper. And He made them the object of His *favor*. In other words, He was going to help them, and He is helping us. We are empowered to prosper. We are anointed to prosper. We are endued with power from *on high*. We have the ability to prosper. We have the power to get wealth. That is the "original blessing"; and it is upon us.

"And God blessed them, and God said unto them, Be fruitful . . ." Being "fruitful" means to *be productive*. Be abundantly creative. Be prolific. Produce abundantly. That's what fruitful means. What's on the inside of you, bring it out to the outside. Produce. Create. Bring forth. Come forth. Let come out of you what God has put in you. And He has empowered us to do that. Be fruitful. Then, "multiply." Multiply means to take what you have produced and created and *make more*. Make more of it. Increase in number. Increase in amount. Increase in degree. Be in authority. Enlarge

GOD PLANNED YOUR LIFE FROM THE BEGINNING

and excel at it. Become plenteous in the process of time in what you have created. Magnify it and increase in it. Become stronger in it. Become more and more. *Increase.*

After that, "replenish." In other words, *do it to the full!* Fully fill up the requirements of that area of production. Fully accomplish every aspect of what you created. Insure and confirm what you have produced. Protect and fence in what you have produced. Totally fulfill what's needed for the growth and maintenance of your production. Become fully set in it. Become the authority over it. Overflow in it. Furnish the requirements of it fully. Own it *wholly*.

Next, "subdue" it. Anything that gets out of line, you have to keep in line. You have to keep your organization, business, production, family, etc., in line. Make sure your budget is in line. You have to balance your budget. You have to watch your sales. You have to watch your marketing efforts. Subdue anything that gets out of line. Watch over your production and what you have produced. If God has given you a house, you have to subdue that. You have to trim the bushes and cut the grass. You must keep everything in good repair and operating order. You must keep termites from eating your property. You must keep the plumbing working properly. You must subdue it. If you have children, you must subdue them. If they get out of line, you have to "subdue" them. Correction has to be used to guide that child up right and keep them from getting out of line. That's a part of your kingdom that God has given you. You must subdue them.

Then it says, ". . . and have dominion . . ." In other words, God is saying, "reign in the position that I have given you." *Maintain* your position. Don't let anybody move you out of what God has given you. Have dominion over "the fish of the sea, over the fowl of the air, and over every creeping thing that moveth upon the earth." This is a part of the anointing. ***Your wealth is in your anointing.***

Let's look back at 2 Kings 4:1-7. We just looked at Genesis 1:26-28. Those scriptures describe to us our anointing which God gave us. The *blessing* of Genesis 1:26-28 is our anointing. It is the *empowerment* for wealth. It is the empowerment to prosper. The empowerment to "be fruitful, multiply, replenish the earth, subdue it, and have dominion" is in the anointing. This is what's in the anointing for us. And God's favor is upon us to help us supernaturally. It's God's grace, it's God's ability in us to do what we don't have the ability to do in our natural strength. But He

YOUR WEALTH IS IN YOUR ANOINTING

gave us the ability in the beginning when He created us from the dust of the earth and breathed in us. He empowered us.

Let's read 2 King's 4:1–7:

> Now there cried a certain woman of the wives of the sons of the prophets unto Elisha, saying, Thy servant my husband is dead; and thou knowest that thy servant did fear the Lord: and the creditor is come to take unto him my two sons to be bondmen.

The woman was in a desperate situation. She didn't see what she had on the inside. She didn't see what she had to work with. Therefore, she was in a desperate situation. She was depending on her husband when he was alive, but her husband died. So she had to discover, "What do I have now, because it's on me. My wealth is in my anointing. It's on me. What do I have to bring wealth? What do I have to bring deliverance in this situation?" So she went to the man of God. Let's go on to verses 2–6:

> And Elisha said unto her, What shall I do for thee? tell me, what hast thou in the house? And she said, Thine handmaid hath not anything in the house, save a pot of oil. Then he said, Go, borrow thee vessels abroad of all thy neighbours, even empty vessels; borrow not a few. And when thou art come in, thou shalt shut the door upon thee and upon thy sons, and shalt pour out into all those vessels, and thou shalt set aside that which is full. So she went from him, and shut the door upon her and upon her sons, who brought the vessels to her; and she poured out. And it came to pass, when the vessels were full, that she said unto her son, Bring me yet a vessel. And he said unto her, There is not a vessel more. And the oil stayed.

Now we see that she *poured* out. She poured out from what she had. She poured out from what she had in her pot of oil. That was her "pot-ential." Her *potential*. It was latent ability to get wealth. Potential is latent ability. It is great latent ability to do, to have, or to become. The pot of oil was her "pot-ential." It was in the oil. Her ability to get wealth was in the pot of oil. Her wealth was in her anointing. Her wealth was in that *oil*.

> And it came to pass, when the vessels were full, that she said unto her son, Bring me yet a vessel. And he said unto her, There is not a vessel more. And the oil stayed.

The oil didn't run out. The oil just "stayed." It just ceased from pouring, because there was nothing else to pour into. You always contain more than enough ability. And all you need is something to pour that

GOD PLANNED YOUR LIFE FROM THE BEGINNING

ability into. You always have more than enough anointing. And all you need is a vessel to pour that anointing into. For example, God has given me the ability to sing. He's given me the anointing on my singing. All I need is a song to pour that anointing into. God may have given you the ability to write. All you need is an idea to pour that anointing to write into. He may have given you the ability to sew. All you need is a pattern, and you can pour your anointing into that pattern and create wonderful dresses, pantsuits, and designs. He may have given you the ability to make handcrafted hats and curtains and all types of draperies, all you need is an idea for what type of design you want to put it in. He may have given you the ability to create scientific formulas and solutions. All you need is a problem in which to apply your formula. All we need to do is pour our anointing into these various areas and our *genius* comes alive! Look at verse 7:

> Then she came and told the man of God. And he said, Go, sell the oil, and pay thy debt, and live thou and thy children of the rest.

The oil represents the anointing. "Sell the oil." The oil represents the anointing. "Sell the oil and pay thy debt, and live thou and thy children of the rest." She said, "All I have is one pot of oil," and the man of God said, "That's all you need, child!" In that one pot of oil is your *wealth*! The oil *is* your wealth. **Your wealth is in your anointing!** The oil represents the anointing. The anointing is the most valuable thing any of us have.

When the woman came to the man of God she extended her faith out with that pot of oil. He saw what she had in the pot of oil. He saw her potential. Her "pot of oil" was her potential. Potential is latent power, latent wealth, latent ability to do, to have, or to become. When she put her potential before the man of God and added her obedience to his words, then faith, power, obedience, anointing, all came together and created a miracle for her! God came on the scene! She honored the man of God. He helped her discover her potential, and God's miracle-working power came to play. The anointing is the most valuable thing any of us have. We all have received a portion of the anointing of the Anointed One, Jesus Christ. The purpose of the anointing is to destroy the yoke and lift the heavy burden off of our lives (see Isaiah 10:27). As we employ and make use of the anointing in our lives we will prosper, live long and healthy lives, and have peace. In Matthew 11:25–30, Jesus said these words:

YOUR WEALTH IS IN YOUR ANOINTING

> *At that time Jesus answered and said, I thank thee, O Father, Lord of heaven and earth, because thou hast hid these things from the wise and prudent, and hast revealed them unto babes. Even so, Father: for so it seemed good in thy sight. All things are delivered unto me of my Father: and no man knoweth the Son, but the Father; neither knoweth any man the Father, save the Son, and he to whomsoever the Son will reveal him. Come unto me, all ye that labour and are heavy laden, and I will give you rest. Take my yoke upon you, and learn of me; for I am meek and lowly in heart: and ye shall find rest unto your souls. For my yoke is easy, and my burden is light.*

Jesus said, "Come unto me..." The widow was coming unto Elisha. He was the man of God at that time. He gave her a solution: *Take my words upon you, woman of God, and I will show you how to be prosperous.* Jesus says to us, "Come unto me all ye that labor, and are heavy laden, and I will give you rest." "Rest" represents *prosperity*. Rest represents *wholeness, soundness, wellness, safety, and blessing*. This is what Jesus said that He offers to us. He said, "take my yoke upon you and learn of me." His yoke is His *Words*. "For I am meek and lowly in heart, and ye shall find rest unto your souls. For my yoke is easy and my burden is light." Jesus came to deliver us from the "yoke" of sin, sickness, and poverty. He came to deliver us from the yoke of *hard, fruitless labor*. This is not to say that hard work is not a part of life. It's just hard work that does not gain the proper fruit from your labor—that's what Jesus came to deliver us from. Working outside of your purpose. Working outside of your anointing. Working outside of your natural abilities that God has put inside of you. Working outside of your calling. Working outside of your gifting. We're not to do that. If He made you for a specific purpose, with specific gifts and talents, you should operate in those. There is an anointing for that. And in that anointing is your wealth. In that anointing is the wealth for you and your family, and your contribution to the world.

Jesus came that we might have life, and that we might have it more abundantly. He wants us to have the very best that life yields. There is an anointing for a *fruitful life*. There is an anointing of wisdom and ability, because Jesus was made unto us *wisdom*. He was "made unto us wisdom, and righteousness, and sanctification, and redemption" (1 Corinthians 1:30). For everything that the enemy stole, Jesus was made unto us *redemption*. Jesus came so that we can have what I like to call the "Big Payback!" He said that he would "restore unto us the years that the

GOD PLANNED YOUR LIFE FROM THE BEGINNING

cankerworm, and the palmer worm, the locust, and the caterpillar" hath eaten (Joel 2:25). He will restore it back to you. He will give you the wisdom to get the Big Payback! All of this is in the anointing. Hallelujah!

There is an anointing of *know-how*. He'll teach you how to do things. He'll put it in your heart. He'll put it in your mind. He will give you the ability to do, to be, to have, and to become. There is an anointing of *favor to prosper*. Jesus came to give this to us. Luke 4:14–21 tells us why Jesus came:

> And Jesus returned in the power of the Spirit into Galilee: and there went out a fame of him through all the region round about. And he taught in their synagogues, being glorified of all. And he came to Nazareth, where he had been brought up: and, as his custom was, he went into the synagogue on the sabbath day, and stood up for to read. And there was delivered unto him the book of the prophet Esaias. And when he had opened the book, he found the place where it was written. The Spirit of the Lord is upon me, because he hath anointed me to preach the gospel to the poor; he hath sent me to heal the broken-hearted, to preach deliverance to the captives, and recovering of sight to the blind, to set at liberty them that are bruised, To preach the acceptable year of the Lord. And he closed the book, and he gave it again to the minister, and sat down. And the eyes of all them that were in the synagogue were fastened on him. And he began to say unto them, This day is this scripture fulfilled in your ears.

The whole focus of Jesus was for the restoration of everything that Adam lost. When Adam disobeyed God, and bowed his knee in obedience to Satan, he gave up man's dominion in the earth. Satan then had free reign to run rampant and "steal, kill, and destroy" (John 10:10). However, Jesus came on the scene to redeem man, and restore us back to our rightful position. He came to restore back everything Adam lost, and even to supersede the former state. Luke 4:18–19 tells us why Jesus came. It also tells how the anointing will destroy the yoke off of anyone that is bound.

> The Spirit of the Lord is upon me, because he hath anointed me to preach the gospel to the poor; he hath sent me to heal the broken-hearted, to preach deliverance to the captives, and recovering of sight to the blind, to set at liberty them that are bruised, To preach the acceptable year of the Lord.

I believe even now we are living in "the acceptable year of the Lord." We are living in a time period where the blessing of the Lord is here to make us *rich*! The blessing is here to make us prosper and to restore back everything the enemy has stolen from us. Every year that the enemy has stolen, every educational opportunity, every business opportunity, all the health, all the privileges and rights that the enemy has stolen, God is here to restore it back. This is a time of restoration. This is a *season* of restoration. Jesus came to redeem man from all that the enemy stole. He came to correct wrongs and injustices, and make things right. He came "to make the crooked places straight, and the rough places smooth" (Luke 3:5). That's what He came to do. He has given us the ability to get wealth. This is what the anointing was sent to do. The anointing was sent to deliver the poor from poverty and all the ravages of poverty and slavery. **Your wealth is in your anointing.**

EVEN THE RIGHTEOUS EXPERIENCE LACK AT TIMES

Now let's get back to the widow and the pot of oil. We see in 2 Kings 4:1-2 that the widow was a woman of God. Her husband was one of the prophets. Yet, he died, leaving her and her children with financial debt. So we see that just because you know God and are anointed doesn't protect you from financial problems. It was still the responsibility of this man of God to prepare for his family. He failed to do so. Now the woman is in a desperate situation. She is being threatened by the creditor to take her sons into slavery to pay off her husband's debt.

The widow now comes to Elisha, a leader among the prophets. She cries out to him for help. Let's look at verses 1-2 again:

> Now there cried a certain woman of the wives of the sons of the prophets unto Elisha, saying, Thy servant my husband is dead; and thou knowest that thy servant did fear the Lord; and the creditor is come to take unto him my two sons to be bondmen.

Now we see that the woman's husband was a man of God. He feared the Lord. Yet, he had debt problems and he died. And his wife and children were left with that problem. There is a song entitled, "There's Grace for That." And there is grace for our every life situation. Let's look at the grace in this story:

> And Elisha said unto her, What shall I do for thee? tell me, what hast thou in the house? And she said, Thine handmaid hath not any thing in the house, save a pot of oil.

GOD PLANNED YOUR LIFE FROM THE BEGINNING

Here's the grace. "Where sin did abound, grace did much more abound." (Romans 5:20) Where her husband's neglect did abound, God's grace did much more abound. Where he neglected to prepare for his wife, for whatever reason, God had grace for his wife and his children. The fact is many are living on the grace of God. None of us have done everything right. We are all living on the grace of God. God's grace has made up for a lot of things for each one of us, particularly in the African-American community. God's grace has made up for a lot of things for each one of us, because there were a lot of opportunities that we did not have early on in the United States. From 1619, when the Dutch slave traders brought black men and women into this nation through the slave trade, until the end of the Civil War in 1865, black men, women, and children were deprived of many of the natural privileges of humanity, which our white counterparts enjoyed in the United States and around the world. There were a lot of things that we were deprived of and did not gain along the way due to slavery, and being forbidden to learn to read and write the English language by slave owners during more than 250 years of free slave labor in this nation. Yet, God blessed us with grace to make it through *anyway*. Praise God! Now we have more and more opportunity to increase in education, skill, and access. We have the opportunity to become more knowledgeable and to take the responsibility needed to *reign as kings*, which we were destined to be from the beginning, through Jesus Christ. "If the Son therefore shall make you free, ye shall be free indeed." (John 8:36)

Now we see that the woman was left with nothing of value from her husband. The man of God asked her, "What has thou in the house?" Or in other words, "What do you have of value in the house? What do you have that you can take and multiply and sell?" He was trying to help her find what she had of value. The woman thought at first that she had nothing of value. She said to the prophet, "Thine handmaid hath not anything of value, save a pot of oil." That was her *answer!* "*Save a pot of oil.*" She was so caught up with seeing her lack and desperate situation, that she failed to see her "pot" . . . her "pot-ential" answer. Her answer was in the *pot*. It was her "pot-ential" wealth. Her "pot-ential" blessing, prosperity, and deliverance were in the "pot." Her answer was in the pot.

The woman did not see her answer at first. She needed the man of God to subdue her fears, and bring enough clarity to her mind that she

YOUR WEALTH IS IN YOUR ANOINTING

could see her "pot-ential": her potential answer. The pot of *oil* was her answer. However, all she saw was that it was just a *pot of oil*. The man of God gave her instructions to follow that would multiply her potential. Her obedience would add the *exponential* to her "pot-ential." Her obedience would add the "super" to her natural. And she would get a *supernatural* supply!

CHAPTER TWO

THE *ANOINTING* IS TO MAKE YOU *RICH!*

The word "oil" in the Bible is symbolic of the *anointing*. *The Strong's Exhaustive Concordance of the Bible* defines the Hebrew word *oil* like this:

OIL

8081–shemen

1. grease, especially liquid as from the olive or olive oil; often perfumed
2. figuratively; richness, anointing, fat things, fruitfulness, and ointment
3. to shine
4. rich, fat, lusty, and plenteous

God gives the anointing to make you and me *rich, fat, fruitful* and *plenteous* in life! He gives us the anointing to make us *shine* in life. It represents *richness, fat things,* and *fruitfulness*. There was a clothing design company called Phat Farm and Phat Caps. They spelled "phat" instead of "fat." That used to be a phrase among young people. They would say, "Man that's phat!" "That's a phat watch" or "That's a Phat suit." "Phat" means *prosperous*. It means rich. It means, "You've got it going on!" It means "that's expensive." God wants us to have a fat (Phat!) life. Hallelujah! And He gives us the anointing for the fat life. Not a slim life. Not a scanty life; but a fat life. Hallelujah! Some older persons would say, "Man you're living *high on the hog*!" In other words, you are living the *fat life*! Nehemiah 8:10–12 has this to say about the *fat life*:

> Then he said unto them, Go your way, eat the fat, and drink the sweet, and send portions unto them for whom nothing is prepared: for this day is holy unto our Lord: neither be ye sorry; for the joy of the Lord is your strength. So the Levites stilled all the people, saying, Hold your peace, for the day is holy; neither be ye grieved. And all the people went their way to eat, and to drink, and to send portions, and to make great mirth, because they had understood the words that were declared unto them.

YOUR WEALTH IS IN YOUR ANOINTING

So we see the *fat life*, which God wants us to live through understanding and applying His Word, will give you joy and make you generous. It will give strength to your life. Applying the anointing causes us to enjoy the *joy of living* and the *joy of giving*! Praise God!

The oil represents *fruitfulness*. It represents *richness*. It is the anointing. When someone is anointed they are *empowered to prosper greatly* and have a rich life. The oil of the anointing makes life easier. It is just like using oil in your car. As long as you properly keep the oil changed in your car, your car can run smoothly, mile after mile, and year after year. It is the same as any kind of oil or lubricant for any joint or machine. It preserves the life of the machine. It causes it to run smoother and longer. It causes it to run properly. The anointing takes the undue burden, work, and resistance wear and tear out of our lives. Let me say that again: *The anointing takes the undue burden, work, and resistance wear and tear out of our lives.* When you are anointed and in your proper place doing what your were born to do, the anointing causes you to prosper.

One definition of prosper is *to help along the way*. Also, prosper means *to help the progression toward the successful completion of a goal*.

God said in 3 John 2, "Beloved" (this is His goal), "I wish above all things that thou mayest prosper and be in health, even as thy soul prospereth." Above all other things, this is God's goal for us. In Romans 12:1–2, God says through the Apostle Paul,

> I beseech you therefore brethren, by the mercies of God, that you present your bodies a living sacrifice, holy and acceptable unto God, which is your reasonable service; And that you be not conformed to this world, but be ye transformed by the renewing of your mind, that ye might prove what is that good, and acceptable, and perfect, will of God.

In 3 John 2 we see what God's "good, acceptable, and perfect will" is. It says, "Beloved, I wish *above all things* that you may prosper, and be in health, even as your soul prospers," He wishes *above all things* that you prosper and be in health. He wishes that you live a long, full, and healthy life. He wishes that you think healthy thoughts, eat healthy food, exercise, and live a full, long, and prosperous life. God wishes that you be in health, even as your soul (mind, will, emotions, intellect, personality) prospers and grows and increases. This is the will of God for you and for me. One definition of prosper is *to help along the way or to help the progression toward the successful completion of a goal*. **Your wealth is in your anointing**. When you operate in life in the anointing, you can have a longer and more prosperous life.

BEING *MENTORED* TO WEALTH

Now the widow has told the man of God she has only a pot of oil. The oil is her potential wealth. He now gives her some very specific instructions. Let's look at 2 Kings 4:3–4 again:

> Then he said, Go, borrow thee vessels abroad of all thy neighbours, even empty vessels; borrow not a few. And when thou art come in, thou shalt shut the door upon thee and upon thy sons, and shalt pour out into all those vessels, and thou shalt set aside that which is full.

Elisha was *mentoring* the widow to wealth. In her moment of desperation, he began to mentor her to wealth. He was showing her how to get wealth. He was showing her how to use her *potential*, which was her pot of oil. He was showing her how to use her *power to get wealth*. He said to her, "Go! Borrow a very insignificant item from as many of your neighbors as you can . . ." After she borrowed the vessels, he told her to get her family and set up a family business. He told her to get her sons and go into her own house and start *production*. He told her to take what she currently had—the oil—and begin to pour it into the seemingly insignificant vessels she had borrowed from her neighbors. The oil represented the *anointing* her potential contained. Her wealth was in her anointing. Her wealth was in the oil.

We all have needs in this life. We live in a need-based society. We all have financial needs. At some point in every person's life there is a financial need. Whether the person is rich or whether the person doesn't have as much money as they should, we all have financial needs. Most people who are rich right now didn't start that way. Some had families that were rich, or where money was passed down to them. However, most of the wealthy today did not start life wealthy. Many are "first generation wealthy." In other words, they became wealthy during their *lifetime*. They went through a course or process of becoming wealthy. They went through development. They *sold* what they had and became wealthy. Some idea, some invention, some industry was responsible for them becoming wealthy. **Your Wealth Is In Your Anointing.** In 2 Kings 4:1–7 when the prophet told the widow to go and borrow vessels and pour the oil from her one pot into those vessels, a miracle came to pass. She took what she had, and a miracle came to pass. She used what she had, and the oil began to *multiply*.

THE ANOINTING GIVES US SOMETHING *SPECIAL*

In 2 Kings 4 verse 7, the prophet Elisha told the widow to "Go, sell the oil, and pay thy debt, and live thou and thy children of the rest." Now the

YOUR WEALTH IS IN YOUR ANOINTING

oil represents the anointing. We are the *just* and we *live by our faith*, and our faithfulness to the Lord Jesus Christ. God has put something on the inside of us that's different than what the world has. The world depends on the educational system, and certain things that they have learned. They depend on the financial and economic system of this world. They depend on the stocks and bonds and other ways of trading in order to provide for them. But God gave us something *special*. He gave us the *anointing*. Hallelujah! He put an anointing on us. 1 John 2:20, 27 says:

> But ye have an unction from the Holy One, and ye know all things. But the anointing which ye have received of him abideth in you, and ye need not that any man teach you: but as the same anointing teacheth you of all things, and is truth, and is no lie, and even as it hath taught you, ye shall abide in him.

The word "unction" has this meaning in *Webster's New World Dictionary*:

UNCTION

1. a) the act of anointing, as in medical treatment or a religious ceremony
   b) the oil, ointment, etc. used for this
2. anything that soothes or comforts

Strong's Exhaustive Concordance of the Bible defines it like this:

UNCTION

5545-chrismaan: an ungent or smearing, endowment of the Holy Spirit, anointing

5548-chrioto: to smear or rub with oil, for example to consecrate to an office or religious service: anoint

5530-chraomai: to furnish what is needed, to give an oracle, to employ

The word "oracle" is defined like this:

ORACLE

3051–logion

    an utterance of God or the Word of God

The anointing furnishes us with what is needed. He employs us with His Word. The Word of God is anointed. The anointing destroys the yoke and lifts the heavy burden of poverty and lack. However, God does it by furnishing us with what we need. He employs us to release the anointing within us through the use of the gifts and talents He has placed within us. ***Your wealth is in your anointing.***

CHAPTER THREE
GOD'S *WORD* IS ANOINTED

Romans 3:1–3, Hebrews 5:12–14, and 1 Pet 4:10–11 has this to say about the importance of the anointed *oracle* or Word of God for our success:

> *What advantage then hath the Jew? or what profit is there of circumcision? Much every way: chiefly, because that unto them were committed the oracles of God. For what if some did not believe? shall their unbelief make the faith of God without effect? God forbid: yea, let God be true, but every man a liar; as it is written, That thou mightest be justified in thy sayings, and mightest overcome when thou are judged.*
>
> *–Romans 3:1-4*

> *For when for the time ye ought to be teachers, ye have need that one teach you again which be the first principles of the oracles of God: and are become such as have need of milk, and not of strong meat. For every one that useth milk is unskilful in the word of righteousness: for he is a babe. But strong meat belongeth to them that are of full age, even those who be reason of use have their senses exercised to discern both good and evil.*
>
> *–Hebrews 5:12-14*

> *As every man hath received the gift, even so minister the same one to another, as good stewards of the manifold grace of God. If any man speak, let him speak as the oracles of God; if any man minister, let him do it as of the ability which God giveth: that God in all things may be glorified through Jesus Christ, to whom be praise and dominion for ever and ever. Amen.*
>
> *–1 Peter 4:10-11*

These scriptures show the importance of the Word of God or "oracles" of God to the release of the anointing in us. The Word of God gives us the advantage because it is the living, active, authoritative,

YOUR WEALTH IS IN YOUR ANOINTING

anointed Words, which God inspired. It is the anointing that destroys the yoke. Wherever God's Word is, the anointing is. The Word releases the anointing from within us when we hear and apply it. Through obedience to the Word, the anointing within us is released. There is always power available when God's Word goes forth. Luke 5:15–17 has this to say about the power of God's Word:

> But so much the more went there a fame abroad of him: and great multitudes came together to hear, and to be healed by him of their infirmities. And he withdrew himself into the wilderness, and prayed. And it came to pass on a certain day, as he was teaching, that there were Pharisees and doctors of the law sitting by, which were come out of every town of Galilee, and Judea, and Jerusalem: and the power of the Lord was present to heal them.

First of all, we see Jesus spent time in prayer to the Father. This is where He found out what He was to say in His teaching. He said that he never said any thing of His own. He only said what the Father said, and He only did what He saw His Father do. He received what His Father said and saw what His Father did during times of fellowship. Therefore, our first place to the release of the anointing of God within us is to spend ample time in fellowship with the Father. In those times of fellowship we will receive the wisdom of God to release the anointing. Also we will receive the know-how for doing the miraculous. Whether you need a business miracle, a miracle in your family life, or on the job: time spent with God is the first step.

Next, we see in verse 17 that Jesus was *teaching*. As the Word went forth, the scripture says, ". . . the power of the Lord was present to heal them." Anytime the Word of God is on the scene, the anointing to do whatever needs be done is there. We release that anointing through our faith. Verses 18–20 show how the faith of a paralyzed man and his four friends released the anointing for healing from the Words that Jesus taught:

> And, behold, men brought in a bed a man which was taken with a palsy: and they sought means to bring him in, and to lay him before him. And when they could not find by what way they might bring him in because of the multitude, they went upon the housetop, and let him down through the tiling with his couch into the midst before Jesus. And when he saw their faith, he said unto him, Man, thy sins are forgiven thee.
>
> –Luke 5:18-20

GOD'S WORD IS ANOINTED

As we see here, it's faith that releases the anointing of God in our lives. Faith makes impossible situations possible. Faith releases the supernatural. Faith comes by hearing and hearing by the Word of God (Romans 10:17).

So we see, first of all, the man's sins were forgiven because of his faith. He was coming for his healing. However, Jesus first dealt with the sin problem. Sin is the original cause of sickness and disease entering into the world. (The first man, Adam, bowed his knee to Satan by disobeying God's Word and allowed Satan to have dominion in the earth. Sin introduced death, sickness, disease, poverty, and all forms of destruction. It allowed Satan to do what he only knows how to do—"steal, kill and destroy" [John 10:10]. This is the original cause of man's disease.) After the man was forgiven, the religious crowd began to criticize Jesus for saying He could forgive the man's sins. This is how Jesus responded:

> *And the scribes and the Pharisees began to reason, saying, Who is this which speaketh blasphemies? Who can forgive sins, but God alone? But when Jesus perceived their thoughts, he answering said unto them, What reason ye in your hearts? Whether is easier, to say, Thy sins be forgiven thee; or to say, Rise up and walk? But that ye may know that the Son of man hath power upon earth to forgive sins, (he said unto the sick of the palsy,) I say unto thee, Arise, and take up thy couch, and go into thine house. And immediately he rose up before them, and took up that whereon he lay, and departed to his own house, glorifying God. And they were all amazed, and they glorified God, and were filled with fear, saying, We have seen strange things to day.*
>
> –Luke 5:21-26

So we see, the faith, which the paralyzed man received from hearing the teaching of Jesus, manifested his healing. He *heard* and *acted on what he heard,* and it produced a miracle healing for him. In this same way, the Word of God contains the power to release the potential of the anointing resting in each one of us.

THE WIDOW *HEARD* THE ANOINTED WORD

Now let's look further at the benefits of God's Word to the release of the anointing in us. The widow with the pot of oil heard the word of the man of God. The Word and her obedience to that word released the power that was present in her oil. Her oil was her *anointing to get wealth*.

YOUR WEALTH IS IN YOUR ANOINTING

She had the potential all the time, yet it was not released until she received the Word from the man of God. Let's look at the earlier scriptures on the Word and let's see how they relate to the release of the anointing. Again, Romans 3:1–4 says,

> What advantage then hath the Jew? or what profit is there of circumcision? Much every way: chiefly, because that unto them were committed the oracles of God. For what if some did not believe? Shall their unbelief make the faith of God without effect? God forbid: yea, let God be true, but every man a liar; as it is written, That thou mightest be justified in thy sayings, and mightest overcome when thou art judged.

In looking at this scripture, in relation to the anointing, we see the Word of God is a great *advantage*. It says, "What *advantage* then hath the Jew? or what profit is there of circumcision? Much every way: chiefly, because that unto them were committed the oracles of God." An *advantage* puts you ahead of others. Everyone has potential. Every person born into the earth was born with potential. However, those who ascribe to a lifestyle guided by God's Word are able to truly release that potential to its fullest. Also, there is a difference in succeeding in accomplishing your goals, as many in the world system have done, versus having "good success." Good success, according to the Word of God, is success that is won through following after God's Word or *oracles*. Jesus said, "What does it profit a man to gain the whole world and lose his own soul?" (Matthew 16:26) However, Joshua 1:8 shows how to gain *good success*. It shows us the advantage of God's Word to the release of the anointing within us. This is what it says:

> There shall not any man be able to stand before thee all the days of thy life: as I was with Moses, so I will be with thee: I will not fail thee, nor forsake thee. Be strong and of a good courage: for unto this people shalt thou divide for an inheritance the land, which I sware unto their fathers to give them. Only be thou strong and very courageous, that thou mayest observe to do according to all the law, which Moses my servant commanded thee: turn not from it to the right hand or to the left, that thou mayest prosper whithersoever thou goest. This book of the Law shall not depart out of thy mouth; but thou shalt meditate therein day and night, that thou mayest observe to do according to all that is written therein: for then thou shalt make thy way prosperous, and then thou shalt have good success. Have not I commanded thee? Be strong and of a good courage; be not afraid, neither be thou dismayed: for the Lord thy God is with thee whithersoever thou goest.
>
> –Joshua 1:5-9

GOD'S WORD IS ANOINTED

The Word is an advantage, and it is the source of great *profit*. Joshua 1:8 says, "This book of the law shall not depart out of thy mouth: but thou shalt meditate therein day and night, that thou mayest observe to do according to all that is written therein: for then thou shalt make thy way prosperous, and then thou shalt have good success." Through meditating Gods Word and keeping His Word in your mouth, you are transformed. God's Word is *truth*. As you speak and meditate on truth continually, you can't help but prosper. That is the advantage of God's Word. That advantage is what releases the anointing that is inside of you. That advantage releases your wealth. **Your wealth is in your anointing.**

WISDOM TO PROSPER

God's Word is His wisdom. If you fill your heart and mind with the wisdom of God by keeping it going in your mouth and hearing yourself speak it, you will prosper. Elisha gave the widow with the pot of oil wisdom to prosper. He gave her wisdom to release the *wealth* that the pot of oil contained. Her obedience to the Word, released that anointing and that wealth. Elisha was the prophet and he spoke for God. The word coming out of his mouth was the same as the Word coming out of God's mouth. He was God's *spokesman*. When the woman obeyed Elisha's Word, she was obeying God's Word. When she heard Elisha's wisdom, she was hearing God's wisdom. Because she respected the anointing on Elisha's life, she was able to receive the miracles the anointing on his life produced. What you respect will *produce* for you. If you respect money, money will produce for you. If you respect your job and diligently work at it with excellence, your job will produce raises and bonuses and promotions for you. If you respect your marriage, your marriage will produce comfort, respect, and happiness for you. If you respect your parents, that respect will produce long life and it will go well for you, according to the first commandment with a promise. If you respect the anointing on a man of God, whatever that man of God is sent to do for you will produce in your life. If you respect your pastor and support your church with tithes and offerings, freewill offerings, and service, the blessing of God will rest on your home and family. The woman respected the Word of God coming out of Elisha's mouth, and it produced a miracle of *debt deliverance* for her. It provided for her family for the rest of her life.

YOUR WEALTH IS IN YOUR ANOINTING

Let's look back at Romans 3:1–4. It helps to establish the importance of God's Word to the release of the anointing inside of you.

> What advantage then hath the Jew? or what profit is there of circumcision? Much every way: chiefly, because that unto them were committed the oracles of God. For what if some did not believe? Shall their unbelief make the faith of God without effect? God forbid: yea, let God be true, but every man a liar: as it is written, That thou mightest be justified in thy sayings, and mightest overcome when thou are judged.

Let's look at the word "advantage" again.

Strong's Exhaustive Concordance of the Bible defines "advantage" like this:

ADVANTAGE

4053–perissos

1. superabundant in quantity or superior in quality
2. excessive
3. violently advantageous

["The kingdom of heaven suffereth *violence* and the violent *take it* by force" (Matthew 11:12). What you are going to have in life, you are going have to take by *force*. The Word of God is your *advantage*.]

4. preeminence
5. exceedingly abundantly above
6. more abundantly
7. advantage
8. beyond measure
9. more
10. superfluous
11. vehemently

4052–perisseuo

1. to super-abound in quantity or quality
2. be in excess
3. be superfluous
4. to cause to super-abound or excel
5. have more abundance

6. be the better

7. have enough and to spare

8. exceed

9. excel

10. increase more and more

11. have some left over

12. remain over and above

This is the *advantage* of God's Word and the anointing within you! As you feed upon God's Word by actively, intentionally using it as a tool to advance in life, you will discover new levels of productivity. The wealth that you contain will be released in its truest and fullest measure.

Romans 3:1 also asks "What profit is there of circumcision?" *Circumcision* speaks of a lifestyle of being "cut off" from the world's way of doing and thinking. The Jew in the Old Testament used the circumcision of the foreskin of the male children as a sign that they would be separate from the world. It was a sign of sanctification and distinction from the defilements and ways of a life lived according to the flesh. However, for us in the New Testament, our circumcision comes from our cutting away the fleshly, worldly life from our *hearts* and *minds*. Romans 12:1–2 has this to say about the life we as Christian believers have been called unto:

> I beseech you therefore, brethren, by the mercies of God, that ye present your bodies a living sacrifice, holy, acceptable unto God, which is your reasonable service. And be not conformed to this world: but be ye transformed by the renewing of your mind, that ye may prove what is that good, and acceptable, and perfect will of God.

God asked us to live a *sanctified* life. He wants us to live a life for Him. He wants us to live a holy life that is acceptable to Him. That is the only way He will be able to pour out the blessing He has in store for us. He wants us to live a life of *distinction*. He wants us to live a life that is *above*. That is sanctification. That is the circumcision of the heart with the Word. He says in verse 2 of Romans 12, "And be not conformed to this world: but be ye transformed by the renewing of your mind, that ye may prove what is that good, and acceptable, and perfect will of God."

What is the "good, and acceptable, and perfect will of God?" In 3 John 2 we learn what it is: "Beloved, I wish above all things that thou mayest prosper and be in health, even as thy soul prospereth."

YOUR WEALTH IS IN YOUR ANOINTING

It is God's will for you and me, above every thing else, "to prosper, be in health, even as our souls prospers." Our soul is our *mind* (so that we can think the right thoughts), our *will* (so that we can desire the right things and the right way of doing things), our *emotions* (so that we can be stable emotionally and not out of control, angry, depressed, blaming other people for our lives), and our *personality* (so we can be the unique, free, beautiful people God made us to be; so we can be ourselves, because no one else is as qualified). As we prosper in these key areas, we will prosper in our health and financially, materially, and socially as well. That is the *profit* of circumcision. Or rather that is the profit of living a life governed by the principles of God's Word. As we do this, the anointing that is in us, which is the Spirit of God, will help cause us to prosper. **Your wealth is in your anointing.**

CHAPTER FOUR

THE ANOINTED ONE AND HIS ANOINTING

Jesus Christ is called the Anointed One. He is the Messiah. He is the One that was chosen and anointed to do what only He could do. In 1 Samuel 16:1-13, David was anointed king of Israel. Samuel, the prophet, went looking for a king. He went looking to anoint one of Jesse's sons. He went into Jesse's house and looked at all of his sons. Some of them were big and strong. They were tall and strapping. Eight sons Jesse had, but they did not consider David. David was still out in the sheepfold. He was still out taking care of the sheep. The sons passed by Samuel, the prophet. Samuel thought, "Surely this big, strong one is the king." He was tall. He was strong. He *looked* like a king. But God said, "I have rejected him. You look on the outward appearance, but I look on the heart." Hallelujah! So all of Jesse's sons passed by Samuel, the prophet. And Samuel said to Jesse, "God has not chosen any of these. Do you have any other sons?" Jesse said reluctantly, "Well, I do have one. He is out in the sheepfold taking care of the sheep." Samuel said, "Go get him! We will not sit down until you go get him." So Jesse sent for David. And David came out of the sheepfold from taking care of the sheep. And he stood before Samuel. And God said, "That's him. I have chosen him. Anoint him." So Samuel took the oil, and poured it over David's head. And it just flowed all down David's clothes, from the top of his head. The Bible says, "From that point on the Spirit of God was with David." He was anointed king. David went through a lot before he sat down on the throne as king of Israel, but he was anointed from the point Samuel poured the oil over his head. We as believers are anointed. And we may go through a lot before actually *reigning* in life as kings or queens, but when we received Jesus Christ we were chosen to be *kings and queens*. God chose us before the foundation of the world to be saved. He destined our deliverance and redemption. He destined for us to be free. He destined for us to be anointed and chosen as His special people. He chose us to be sanctified. He chose us to be a "royal priesthood" and a "chosen generation." (1 Peter 2:9) He chose us to be anointed. He already called us. The Lamb was slain before the foundation of the world. (Revelation 13:8) He had our redemption in mind before we ever got here. Hallelujah!

Now we have gone through a process. And, at first, though you may not have seen yourself as reigning as royalty, you already have been anointed to reign in life as royalty through Jesus Christ. David did not reign right away. He went through a process. However, he was king all the time. He was anointed all the time. And that anointing kept producing for David while he was in process. It shielded him from dangerous situations. The anointing protected him, because he was anointed king.

Jesus is the Messiah. He is the One that was chosen. He was the One that was destined to come to be the Savior of the world. All of Israel waited for the Messiah. The world waited for the Messiah to come. However, when the Messiah did come, Israel did not recognize Him as being the Messiah. And many of them still do not. However, to those that have believed, He has given them the "power to become the sons of God, even to those that believe upon His name" (John 1:12). Hallelujah! That's who we are as the *Believers*.

Just like with Jesus, those who were looking for a king did not recognize David. They did not even call him to the anointing. They thought someone else was the king. Jesse had his other sons pass by, thinking they were the king. However, David was chosen. And he was the only one the oil would *flow* for. Jesus Christ is the only one anointed to be the Savior of the whole world. He was the only one born of a virgin. He was the only one who came into this world without the seed of sin planted in His blood. He was the only one to live in the world without sin. He was the only one chosen to carry and take upon Him the sins, sicknesses, diseases, and poverty of all mankind. He took all lack upon Himself. He "became poor that we through His poverty might be rich" (2 Corinthians 8:9). Praise God! He took it for us because He was *anointed* for that. Only He could do it. He was anointed for it.

So we see, Jesus was and is the Anointed One, and it is the Anointing upon the Anointed One that empowers us to prosper. It is the empowerment and the grace. There was a certain grace that empowered Jesus to finish the work of Redemption. Jesus had to have a certain *grace* to go

THE ANOINTED ONE AND HIS ANOINTING

to the cross. He had to have a certain grace to take the sins of the whole world upon Himself. He *became* our sin. He did not just take our sin upon Himself. He *became* our sin. The Bible says in 2 Corinthians 5:21, "For he hath made him *to be* sin for us, who knew no sin; that we might be made the righteousness of God in him." He was made to be sin for us, that we may be made the righteousness of God in Him. Our spiritual *DNA* changed. Our identity changed, and we are the righteousness of God in Him. Furthermore, only He was chosen to do this for us. He is the Anointed One. He is anointed to do what no one else could do.

Christ is the Anointed One, and it is the *anointing* upon the Anointed One that delivered us. He was anointed to redeem us. Now we, as believers, are *Christians*. He is Christ, the Anointed One. And we are *Christians*. We are *anointed ones*. We are born of Him, and therefore, that makes us *anointed ones*. We are anointed because He is the Anointed One. We are anointed because we are *in Him*. For example, we are in America. America is our country. We live in this country. We have citizenship in this country. Thus, that makes us *Americans*. This is the country we live in. He is Christ. We are *in Christ*. We have been made the righteousness of God *in Him*. Thus, that makes us *Christians*. He is the Anointed One. And that make us *anointed ones*. Hallelujah! This is the anointing I am talking about. Thus, **Your wealth is in your anointing!** I have expounded and explained that point so you could see the significance of the anointing we have.

YOU ARE FILLED WITH POTENTIAL

Let's look at 2 Kings 4:1–7 again, which is the basis for the message of this book:

> *Now there cried a certain woman of the wives of the sons of the prophets unto Elisha, saying, Thy servant my husband is dead; and thou knowest that thy servant did fear the Lord: and the creditor is come to take unto him my two sons to be bondmen. And Elisha said unto her, What shall I do for thee: tell me, what hast thou in the house? And she said, Thine handmaid hath not any thing in the house, save a pot of oil. Then he said, Go, borrow thee vessels abroad of all thy neighbours, even empty vessels; borrow not a few. And when thou art come in, thou shalt shut the door upon thee and upon thy sons, and shalt pour out into all those vessels, and thou shalt set aside that which is full. So she went from him, and shut the door upon her and upon her sons,*

> who brought the vessels to her; and she poured out. And it came to pass, when the vessels were full, that she said unto her son, Bring me yet a vessel. And he said unto her, There is not a vessel more. And the oil stayed. Then she came and told the man of God. And he said, Go, sell the oil, and pay thy debt, and live thou and thy children of the rest.

What did the woman have in the house? She had the *pot of oil*—the *anointing*. The anointing was in the house. She said she had nothing in the house "save a pot of oil." The woman's desperate situation helped her discover her "pot." It helped her to discover her "pot-ential." The anointing for her family's debt deliverance and financial freedom was in the pot of oil. Her wealth was in her anointing.

In 2 Corinthians 4:7, the Apostle Paul said these words: "But we have this treasure in earthen vessels, that the excellency of the power may be of God, and not of us."

Our body is the temple of the Holy Ghost. Our body is the home of God. His Spirit lives inside of us. His potential or *potency* lives in us. His anointing lives in us. It is the ability to do, to have, to be, and to become. We can decide what type of vessel we are by our lifestyle. We can be a vessel of honor, who lives so the treasure or anointing is released; or, we can live dishonorably, and not release the potential God put inside of us. Again, in Romans 12:1-2, the Apostle Paul exhorts us with these words:

> I beseech you therefore, brethren, by the mercies of God, that ye present your bodies a living sacrifice, holy, acceptable unto God, which is your reasonable service. And be not conformed to this world: but be ye transformed by the renewing of your mind, that ye may prove what is that good, and acceptable, and perfect will of God.

And again, *what is the will of God*? John tells us in 3 John 2, "Beloved, I wish above all things that thou mayest prosper and be in health, even as thy soul prospereth." Our soul is our mind, will, emotions, and individual personality. God wants us to work to develop our souls so we can prosper and increase. The greater the development, increase, and progress we make in our souls, will equal greater increase in the other areas of our lives. As we prosper in our souls (mind, will, emotions, personality), our physical, social, and financial prosperity will also increase as a matter of course. The force of *inner* prosperity produces *outer* prosperity. As we intentionally work to develop our inner life and outer responses, we will determine the release of the wealth within us.

THE ANOINTED ONE AND HIS ANOINTING

In 2 Timothy 2:19-22, the Apostle Paul instructs his son in the Lord, Timothy, how to succeed in life. This is applicable to all who will live godly.

> *Nevertheless the foundation of God standeth sure, having this seal, The Lord knoweth them that are his. And, Let every one that nameth the name of Christ depart from iniquity.*
>
> *But in a great house there are not only vessels of gold and of silver, but also of wood and of earth; and some to honour, and some to dishonour. If a man therefore purge himself from these, he shall be a vessel unto honour, sanctified, and meet for the master's use, and prepared unto every good work. Flee also youthful lusts: but follow righteousness, faith, charity, peace, with them that call on the Lord out of a pure heart.*

The first thing the Apostle Paul tells Timothy is that, God *knows* him. He knows what he has put in him. And because he has called himself a Christian or "Christ-like," the Apostle Paul gave him specific instructions. Christ means the *Anointed One*. Therefore, *Christian* means an *anointed one*. Therefore, Paul was saying to Timothy, "Because you are known by God and belong to God, and because you are an anointed one, follow these instructions . . ." Number one, he told Timothy to "put away iniquity." What is iniquity? In this verse according to *Strong's Exhaustive Concordance of the Bible*, "iniquity" is defined in this manner:

INIQUITY

93–adikia
 1. legally; the quality or act of injustice
 2. morally; wrongfulness of character, life, or act
 3. unrighteousness

Therefore, the first thing Paul was telling his son Timothy was to put away any form of iniquity. He was telling him to put away any legal "quality or act of injustice." He was also telling him to put away all "moral wrongfulness of character, life, or act," and all "unrighteousness" of lifestyle. Paul was letting Timothy know that the only way for him to live his fullest and best life was for him to *refine* his life, as silver is refined. He would have to *purge* himself, as gold is refined, in order to release the *wealth* that was within him. His wealth was his *ministry*. However, each of us has a ministry. Our ministry is our *life* itself.

In 2 Timothy 2:20, the Apostle Paul begins to explain to Timothy the difference between a life containing priceless refined vessels and one containing base, earthly, carnal, and perishable vessels:

YOUR WEALTH IS IN YOUR ANOINTING

> *But in a great house there are not only vessels of gold and silver, but also of wood and of earth; and some to honour, and some to dishonour.*

He was saying the same thing that Elisha, the prophet, asked the widow when she came to him after the death of her husband. "What do you have in the house?" Let's read that portion of our focus scripture to keep the context:

> *Now there cried a certain woman of the wives of the sons of the prophets unto Elisha, saying, Thy servant my husband is dead; and thou knowest that thy servant did fear the Lord: and the creditor is come to take unto him my two sons to be bondmen. And Elisha said unto her, What shall I do for thee: tell me, what hast thou in the house? And she said, Thine handmaid hath not anything in the house, save a pot of oil.*
>
> *–2 Kings 4:1-2*

The woman of God had to *discern* what she had of value in the house that had the capacity to save her out of her financial challenge. The value of what she filled her *house* with would determine if she would be saved from her devastating situation. Her husband, in whom she was depending to take care of her, had died. Now her two sons were about to be taken into slavery to pay off the mountain of debt he left behind. She was in a *desperate* situation. The question was "what did she have in the house?"

In 2 Timothy 2:20 the Apostle Paul explains to us the importance of *what's in the house*:

> *But in a great house there are not only vessels of gold and of silver, but also of wood and of earth; and some to honour, and some to dishonour.*

First of all, Paul says the house is a "great" house. Our bodies are the *temple* or house of God. We are very valuable. David says in Psalms 139:14,

> *I will praise thee; for I am fearfully and wonderfully made: marvellous are thy works; and that my soul knoweth right well.*

He says that our very bodies and souls are a wonderful creation. Each of us is created as a *triumph* of God's handiwork. We are filled with such *potential*! However, we have a choice in what we fill the "house" with. We have a choice in how we refine the *seeds of greatness* God has put in us. The Apostle Paul says, "... in a great house there are not only vessels of gold and silver, but also of wood and of earth; and some to honour, and some to dishonour." According to our choices we can decide to make our house a "vessel of honor."

The woman in 2 Kings 4:1–7 took from the vessel she contained and began to *pour* into other vessels, thus increasing their value. Elisha told her in 2 Kings 4:3–7 to go borrow other empty vessels and to pour into them. This was the key to her success in life. The key to our success in life is to be a vessel of such honor, that we contain something of such great value that we can pour into other people's lives. That something is the *anointing*. **Your wealth is in your anointing.** 2 Kings 4:3–7 says,

> Then he said, Go, borrow thee vessels abroad of all thy neighbours, even empty vessels; borrow not a few. And when thou art come in, thou shalt shut the door upon thee and upon thy sons, and shalt pour out into all those vessels, and thou shalt set aside that which is full. So she went from him, and shut the door upon her and upon her sons, who brought the vessels to her: and she poured out. And it come to pass, when the vessels were full, that she said unto her son, Bring me yet a vessel, And he said unto her, There is not a vessel more. And the oil stayed. Then she came and told the man of God. And he said, Go, sell the oil, and pay thy debt, and live thou and thy children of the rest.

THE ANOINTING TO "DESTROY THE YOKE"

Again, your anointing is God's supernatural power within you to do, to have, to be, and to become. It is your *power to prosper*. The anointing *destroys the yoke* and *lifts the heavy burdens* of life. The anointing delivers you and me from any desperate situation. It delivers us from sickness, disease, depression, debt and poverty, and all the oppression brought on by sin entering into the world. If there is an area in your life where the *thief* has been *stealing, killing, and destroying*, the anointing will destroy that yoke. The anointing will destroy the *thief's* ability to bring destruction in your life. The *Greater One* lives within us, and He is the Anointed One. "So then faith cometh by hearing, and hearing by the Word of God" (Romans 10:17). Many times the yoke can be destroyed already in our lives, yet we'll still have to be renewed in the *spirit* of our minds in order to walk free. For example, during slavery in the United States, there were slaves that were officially set free by the Emancipation Proclamation, yet there were still many continuing to work in the fields and at the "big house" because they hadn't heard or their minds had not been renewed to freedom. Their hearts had not been encouraged and emboldened to *pursue* their freedom. They needed faith to step out into the unknown and go North or go West and step into independence. Independence means *responsibility*. So, when you and I are ready to walk into the anointing God has given us, it is a place of responsibility. It is *empowerment* to succeed. It is empowerment to determine our *own* prosperity. It is empowerment to take *leadership* in our own lives and family. It is power to determine what is supposed to come out of us as individuals, and what we can do. It is not depending on someone else. It is not someone else's *fault* or what someone else is supposed to do about our lives. It is about us taking responsibility. It takes courage to do that. "Faith cometh by hearing, and hearing by the Word of God" (Romans 10:17). The Word of God *emboldens* us to do what God has destined us to do. God marked out our destiny in Genesis 1:26–28, which says,

> And God said, Let us make man in our image, after our likeness: and let them have dominion over the fish of the sea, and over the fowl of the air, and over the cattle, and over all the earth, and over every creeping thing that creepeth upon the earth. So God created man in his own image, in the image of God created he him; male and female created he them. And God blessed them, and God said unto them, Be fruitful, and multiply, and replenish the earth, and subdue it: and have dominion over the fish of the sea, and over the fowl of the air, and over every living thing that moveth upon the earth.

This is something God has given to all of us. It takes faith, *boldness*, and courage to step out into the unknown and subdue those things that rise up against your authority. God has given us this God-given authority.

Again the anointing is God's supernatural power within you to do, to have, to be, and to become. It is your power to prosper. The anointing "destroys the yoke and it lifts the heavy burdens of life" (Isaiah 10:27). It delivers us from any of the desperate situations the enemy would try to bring against us. Psalms 107:20 says, "He sent his Word, and healed them, and delivered them from their destructions."

Whatever may be bringing destruction in your life or whatever has been holding you back or whatever you have been struggling with, the anointing will destroy that yoke! Instruction from the Word of God delivers us from the destruction of the things of "the flesh, the world, and the devil." Again, *instruction* delivers us from *destruction*. The instruction we receive and humble ourselves under, by opening our hearts and inclining our ears, will deliver us from *destruction* from Satan. It may be *tradition* or *religion* we need deliverance from. If it is not in line with the Word of God, we need deliverance from it. Or, it may be learned behaviors or erroneous family values. It's said that there are *three main determinants* in how a person acts and responds to life. One is *genetic determinism*. It says you are who you are because you were born that way. Maybe certain characteristics and traits were *passed down* to you from parents, grandparents, and other ancestors. Another is *environmental determinism*. It says you are who you are, and respond like you do, based on the environment you were raised in. Maybe you were born in the "projects," and thus you act in a certain way. Or you were born in the "country," so you have certain characteristics. Or maybe you born in a certain part of the country, thus you act in a certain way. And last, there is *psychological determinism*. It states that you are who you are based on the thoughts and images you have received in your mind. It says these thoughts determine how you act, how you respond to life, and what choices in life you gravitate toward. However, God *sent His Word* to deliver us from *all* of our destructions! Again, Psalms 107:20 says, "He sent his Word, and healed them, and delivered them from their destructions." So, whatever sickness, or disease of the spirit, soul, mind, body, social, or financial life, that is in our life, for any reason, "He sent His Word and healed us, and delivered us from our destructions." "Faith cometh by *hearing*, and *hearing* by the Word of God." Even as the Word is going forth right now there is power to "destroy the yoke." Things are being *righted* in your life as you receive the Word.

The Word of God is anointed, and wherever the Word is, there is power to "destroy the yoke." John 1:1–4, 12 has this to say:

> In the beginning was the Word, and the Word was with God, and Word was God. The same was in the beginning with God. All things were made by him; and without him was not any thing made that was made. In him was life; and the life was the light of men. But as many as received him, to them gave he power to become the sons of God, even to them that believe on his name.

JESUS IS THE "LIVING WORD"

Let's examine this for a moment. Verse 12 says, "But as many as received him, to them gave he power to become the sons of God, even to them that believe on his name." Now, Psalms 107:20 says, "He sent his word, and healed them, and delivered them from all their destructions." Again, "He sent His Word and healed them, and delivered them from all their destructions." John 1:1 says,

> In the beginning was the Word, and the Word was with God, and the Word was God. The same was in the beginning with God. All things were made by Him. And without Him was not anything made that was made. In Him was life, and the life was the light of men.

Psalms 107:20 says,

> He sent his Word, and healed them, and delivered them from all their destructions.

Jesus Christ is the *Living Word*. And John 1:12 says,

> But as many as received him, to them gave he power (or anointing or authority or enabling) to become the sons of God, even to them that believe on his name.

The anointing destroys the yoke and lifts the heavy burden off your life. Again, verse 12 says, "But as many as received him, to them gave he power to become the sons of God, even to them that believe on his name." He is the Living Word.

When the scripture says "even to them that believe on his name," it is saying they that believe on what He *has done*. It means you believe Jesus was born of a virgin without sin. You believe He walked this earth without sin. You believe He took upon Him the sin, sicknesses, disease, poverty, depression, and oppression of all mankind. It means you believe He became our sin, according to 2 Corinthians 5:21 which says, "For he hath made him to be sin for us, who knew no sin; that we might be made the righteousness of God in him."

This is what it means when John 1:12 says, "But as many as received him, to them gave he power to become the sons of God, even to them that believe on his name." It means you believe He went to the cross and became our sin, and was nailed to the cross. You believe He shed His blood for us. You believe He was pierced in His side and blood and water came gushing out for you and me. It means you believe Isaiah 53, which prophesied of Jesus's suffering and redemptive work. This is what it says:

> Who hath believed our report? and to whom is the arm of the Lord revealed? For he shall grow up before him as a tender plant, and as a

> *root out of a dry ground: he hath no form nor comeliness; and when we shall see him, there is no beauty that we should desire him. He is despised and rejected of men; and man of sorrows, and acquainted with grief: and we hid as it were our faces from him; he was despised, and we esteemed him not. Surely he hath borne our griefs, and carried our sorrows: yet we did esteem him stricken, smitten of God, and afflicted. But he was wounded for our transgressions, he was bruised for our iniquities: the chastisement of our peace was upon him: and with his stripes we are healed. All we like sheep have gone astray; we have turned every one to his own way; and the Lord hath laid on him the iniquity of us all. He was oppressed, and he was afflicted, yet he opened not his mouth: he is brought as a lamb to the slaughter, and as a sheep before her shearers is dumb, so he openeth not his mouth. He was taken from prison and from judgement: and who shall declare his generation? for he was cut off out of the land of the living: for the transgression of my people was he stricken. And he made his grave with the wicked, and with the rich in his death; because he had done no violence, neither was any deceit in his mouth. Yet it pleased the Lord to bruised him; he hath put him to grief: when thou shalt make his soul an offering for sin, he shall see his seed, he shall prolong his days, and the pleasure of the Lord shall prosper in his hand. He shall see of the travail of his soul, and shall be satisfied: by his knowledge shall my righteous servant justify many; for he shall bear their iniquities. Therefore will I divide him a portion with the great, and he shall divide the spoil with the strong; because he hath poured out his soul unto death: and he was numbered with the transgressors; and he bare the sin of many, and made intercession for the transgressors.*

Also, 2 Corinthians 8:9 says,

> *For ye know the grace of our Lord Jesus Christ, that though he was rich, yet for your sakes he became poor, that ye through his poverty might be rich.*

Believing on His name means you believe what the Word says about Him. All these things are incorporated in His name. When He shed His blood, they took Him down from the cross and buried Him. For three days He went down into the belly of the earth. He went down to Hell. And while down there, He stripped Satan of the keys of Death, Hell, and the Grave. He took back our authority, which was lost by Adam when he bowed his knee in obedience to Satan in the Garden of Eden. Jesus snatched our authority and dominion back, which Satan stole from Adam when he deceived Eve into eating the *forbidden fruit.* When the woman gave it to the man and the man did eat, and disobeyed God, he lost his dominion. This released Satan to have a right to run rampant in the earth—stealing, killing, and destroying. Jesus took back that dominion for us. "He led captivity captive, and gave gifts to men." (Ephesian 4:8) He went up to Heaven and applied His blood before the Mercy Seat for the Remission of the sins of all mankind.

John 1:12 says, "But as many as received him, to them gave he power to become the sons of God, even to them that believe on his name." It means you believe that after three days, He rose again with all power both in heaven and in earth. He then told us in Mark 16:15–18 these words:

> *Go ye into all the world and preach the gospel to every creature. He that believeth and is baptized shall be saved; but he that believeth not shall be damned. And these signs shall follow them that believe; In my name shall they cast out devils; they shall speak with new tongues; They shall take up serpents; and if they drink any deadly thing, it shall not hurt them; they shall lay hands on the sick, and they shall recover.*

This is what it means to "believe in His name." He went back to Heaven after forty days of walking with His disciples after His resurrection. He ascended back on High and sat down on the right-hand side of God the Father. The Father then gave Him a name that is above every name—that, at the name of Jesus, every knee must bow, and every tongue must confess that Jesus Christ is the Lord. He sat down on the right hand side of God the Father until His enemies be made His footstool. And the Word says in 1 John 4:15–17 these words:

> *Whosoever shall confess that Jesus is the Son of God, God dwelleth in him, and he in God. And we have known and believed the love that God hath to us. God is love; and he that dwelleth in love dwelleth in God, and God in him. Herein is our love made perfect, that we may have boldness in the day of judgment: because as he is, so are we in this world.*

Again, John 1:12 says, "But as many as received him, to them gave he power to become the sons of God, even to them that believe on his name."

YOU ARE A "SON OF GOD"

Now let's look at "sons of God." This speaks of the dominion we regained in receiving Him. We regained that power. It's in your anoint-

THE ANOINTED ONE AND HIS ANOINTING

ing. Your whole life comes out of the anointing. It is in your connection with the Anointed One. Christ is the Anointed One. It is the Anointing upon the Anointed One, which we have partaken of. Because we have taken part with the Anointed One and have it on the inside of us, we are *Christians*. It's because we are of Christ. We are "one spirit with the Lord" (1 Corinthians 6:17). That makes us "sons of God" (Romans 8:14–17). Acts 17:28 declares that we are His "offspring":

> *For in him we live, and move, and have our being; as certain also of your own poets have said, For we are his offspring.*

Also, Romans 8:14–19 speaks of us as being the "sons of God." It speaks of us *maturing* in the anointing of *son-ship*, so that we can reign in life as kings. It takes maturity to have dominion. All of the creation is awaiting the manifestation of the righteous sons of God to reign in the earth. Romans 8:14–19 says,

> *For as many as are led by the Spirit of God, they are the sons of God. For ye have not received the spirit of bondage again to fear; but ye have received the Spirit of adoption, whereby we cry, Abba, Father. The Spirit itself beareth witness with our spirit, that we are the children of God: And if children, then heirs; heirs of God, and joint-heirs with Christ; if so be that we suffer with him, that we may be also glorified together. For I reckon that the sufferings of this present time are not worthy to be compared with the glory, which shall be revealed in us. For the earnest expectation of the creature waiteth for the manifestation of the sons of God.*

The word "manifestation" in verse 19 means *to reveal, appear, or come forth, or to take off the cover*. The whole creation is waiting for us, the "sons of God," to *take off the cover* of this vessel and reveal the true anointing of the Anointed One who lives inside of us. It's more than walking in love, and being *kind*. It is a demonstration of the supremacy and rule of Christ on the earth through us. The Apostle Paul said in Philippians 4:13, "I can do all things through Christ which strengtheneth me." The world needs a demonstration of that truth in the lives of the Christians who know their anointing and authority. We have the answer to the health-care crisis. We are the answer to the need for social services. Jesus has been "made unto us wisdom" for the environmental concerns of today. He has "wisdom laid up for us the righteous." Proverbs 2:6–7 has this to say:

YOUR WEALTH IS IN YOUR ANOINTING

> *For the Lord giveth wisdom: out of his mouth cometh knowledge and understanding. He layeth up sound wisdom for the righteous: he is a buckler to them that walk uprightly.*

The Lord has laid up "sound wisdom" for us, the righteous, for this time in the world. It is in our anointing. It is in our connection with the Anointed One. It is because we are in Him, and He is in us. Proverbs 29:2 says, "When the righteous are in authority, the people rejoice: but when the wicked beareth rule, the people mourn." We are the righteous. The *anointed ones* have what it takes to govern the affairs of the earth realm. We only must realize what we have inside of us, and who is on the inside of us, and take the initiative to reign. It's *expected*. It's our responsibility. Now let's go back to John 1:14 and 16. It reads:

> *And the Word was made flesh, and dwelt among us, (and we beheld his glory, the glory as of the only begotten of the Father,) full of grace and truth. And of his fullness have all we received, and grace for grace.*

We have received of Christ's fullness. We have received of the Anointed One's *fullness*. And He has given us His grace to *receive* His grace. "Grace for grace" means He has given us the ability to *receive* His grace. Before we received Jesus Christ as Lord and Savior we did not have the ability to *receive* fully the goodness of God. He had to move on our hearts for us to have the ability to receive his grace. His Holy Spirit had to move on our hearts so we could receive the free gift of salvation. He gave us "grace for grace." For example, there are some people who have had so many challenges in life. They have had so much trouble. They have dealt with poverty and pain or rejection. And in many cases, when God sends something or someone to treat them well, they can't *receive* it. They reject the goodness of God. It's hard for them to believe that they are about to receive something good. They have been so used to pain or lack that it is hard for them to receive the goodness of God. We have to open our hearts to receive the goodness of God. God wants to give us his *free gift of favor*. He wants to give us things that we never had before. He wants to give us divine advantages, and unfair partiality. He wants to make up to you and me any pain or loss we have experienced. We must only accept the goodness of God—open up our hearts to receive it. We must empty out our pain and *make room* for His goodness. This is what we are doing today. We are continually pouring in the *clean water* of God's Word into the vessel of your heart.

THE ANOINTED ONE AND HIS ANOINTING

We are purging out the contaminated water of pain, loss, poverty, low self-esteem, and the mistakes of the past. God has good things in store for each of us. Also, as we take time to pray out the issues of our life through praying in the Holy Ghost, we can purge out the issues and entanglements we have been trying to figure out in our own natural mind. We have the mind of Christ. The Holy Spirit knows what is the mind of our born-again spirit. As we take time to pray in the Spirit, we bypass the limitations of our natural human mind and tap into the mind of the Spirit. Our prayers become elevated, and we are able to see greater effectiveness because we are praying the perfect will of God. In 1 Corinthians 14:2–4, 14–15 we read:

> *For he that speaketh in an unknown tongue speaketh not unto men, but unto God: for no man understandeth him; howbeit in the spirit he speaketh mysteries. But he that prophesieth speaketh unto men to edification, and exhortation, and comfort. He that speaketh in an unknown tongue edifieth himself; but he that prophesieth edifieth the church. For if I pray in an unknown tongue, my spirit prayeth, but my understanding is unfruitful. What is it then? I will pray with the spirit, and I will pray with the understanding also: I will sing with the spirit, and I will sing with the understanding also.*

By taking time to pray in the spirit, we can pray out the mysteries that we have been grappling with in life. We also can pray out the *will of God* for our lives. We can also build up ourselves and our families, like building up a *mighty structure*! (Jude 1:20) Praying in the Holy Ghost helps to *put things in proper order* in our lives, and it helps us to be able to *receive* or accept the grace of God. Jesus Christ gives us the "grace to receive *more* grace." Through His Spirit, He helps us receive more of Himself and His goodness. Luke 5:17 says,

> *And it came to pass on a certain day, as he was teaching, that there were Pharisees and doctors of the law sitting by, which were come out of every town of Galilee, and Judea, and Jerusalem: and the power of the Lord was present to heal them.*

The anointing was present in Jesus's teaching to bring deliverance to the people. Psalms 107:20 says, "He sent his Word, and healed them, and delivered them from their destructions." The Word did not come just to heal their physical bodies. He was there to heal their spirit, soul, body, social life, and financial situation. The Word was there to deliver them

55

YOUR WEALTH IS IN YOUR ANOINTING

in every way. "He sent His Word, and healed them, and delivered them from their destructions." That means *all* their destructions.

I focused on those scriptures momentarily to let us know that the most essential component to our faith and any grace or anointing we have inside, is Christ Jesus. He is the *Living Word*. Of His fullness have all we received. **Your wealth is in your anointing.**

CHAPTER FIVE
IT'S IN YOU

The purpose of this portion of the message is to help us fully conceive the truth that God has put what we need on the inside of us. God has put what each individual needs to prosper inside that individual. In a family, God has put what that family needs to prosper inside that family. In a church, God has put what that church needs to prosper inside that church. The Bible speaks of us being members one of another, and each member needs the other member. In a church, a pastor should not always need his *special ministry* to come from outside of that local church. He should not always have to bring an evangelist in. He shouldn't always have to bring in a special prophet. He should not always have to bring in special teachers. Those individuals should already be in that local church. They are already *there*. A part of the pastor's job is to *cultivate* these various gifts in others because God has put them there to benefit that local body. They may be there in *seed form*. They may not have discovered their gifting, or they don't know how to use it, or they have not been taught about it. Therefore, the job of the pastor is to teach individual members what their calling is and how to use it. If you are called to teach and you are a part of a church, you should have ample opportunity to exercise in your calling. Times should be made available for that. Why? It is because each individual member has a *supply* for that local body. A pastor is a *feeder*. He or she is a feeder. He or she is a covering. He or she is a guide. And he or she should be guiding each member toward the individual destiny God has for them. That's the job of a pastor. You may operate in what I call the "ministry of helps." If you don't know exactly what your gifting or calling is, the ministry of helps is a perfect place to be trained. All churches need help. All ministries need help. In the ministry of helps you learn various essentials for success in ministry and life. You learn submission. You learn how to operate with other people. You learn how to love others. You learn how to serve. One of the most important things you learn is how to submit to a Godly system. You should be learning Kingdom Rule. In order for our gifting, talents, and calling to operate effectively and efficiently we must learn how to submit to Kingdom Rule. In order for the *oil* of the anointing to flow freely out of our lives, we must be submitted to the Holy Ghost. In 2 Corinthians 3:17 we read, "Now the Lord is that Spirit: and where the Spirit of the Lord is, there is liberty." According to 1 Corinthians 14:33, "The Lord is not the author of confusion, but of peace, as in all the churches of the saints." Therefore, in order to operate successfully in the anointing we must be submitted to Godly rule. We must be in proper order for the oil to *flow*. The job of a pastor is not just to preach and teach to the people, and the people stay in the same place in life. No. Rather, the members should be discovering their purpose. They should be being prepared to actively pursue their function in the Body of Christ. The Bible says we are members "in particular" or individual. We are "compacted by that which every joint supplieth." Look at 1 Corinthians 12:4–31, and Ephesians 4:16 as it tells us about the importance of each member of the Body of Christ. These scriptures tell us we are compacted by that which every joint supplies. The reason I am able to stay with you is because you have my supply. The reason you are able to stay with me is because I have your supply. Therefore, as every person in a church gives their supply, we are compacted. That's why there is no room for *jealousy* in the church if everybody is giving their *supply*. As you give your supply and I give my supply, the church increases more and more *of itself*. The Church grows from *within* as each individual member gives their supply. They are "compacted together," and that's how we become a *strong* church. A strong local body of believers is a church where every person releases their supply of *oil* or anointing. The following scriptures emphasize the importance of each member of the local church. Understanding this is key to understanding the *release* of the wealth inside of the local church.

> *Now there are diversities of gifts, but the same Spirit. And there are differences of administrations, but the same Lord. And there are diversities of operation, but it is the same God, which worketh all in all. But the manifestation of the Spirit is given to every man to profit withal. For to one is given by the Spirit the word of wisdom; to another the word of knowledge by the same Spirit; To another faith by the same*

IT'S IN YOU

Spirit; to another the gifts of healing by the same Spirit; To another the working of miracles; to another prophecy; to another discerning of spirits; to another divers kinds of tongues; to another the interpretation of tongues: But all these worketh that one and the selfsame Spirit, dividing to every man severally as he will. For as the body is one, and hath many members, and all the members of that one body, being many, are one body: so also is Christ. For by one Spirit are we all baptized into one body, whether we be Jews or Gentiles, whether we be bond or free; and have been all made to drink into one Spirit. For the body is not one member, but many. If the foot shall say, Because I am not the hand, I am not of the body; is it therefore not of the body? And if the ear shall say, Because I am not the eye, I am not of the body; is it therefore not of the body? If the whole body were an eye, where were the hearing? If the whole were hearing, where were the smelling? But now hath God set the members every one of them in the body, as it hath pleased him. And if they were all one member, where were the body? But now are they many members, yet but one body. And the eye cannot say unto the hand, I have no need of thee: nor again the head to the feet, I have no need of you. Nay, much more those members of the body, which seem to be more feeble, are necessary: And those members of the body, which we think to be less honourable, upon these we bestow more abundant honour; and our uncomely parts have more abundant comeliness. For our comely parts have no need: but God hath tempered the body together, having given more abundant honour to that part which lacked: That there should be no schism in the body; but that the members should have the same care one for another. And whether one member suffer, all the members suffer with it; or one member be honoured, all the members rejoice with it. Now ye are the body of Christ, and members in particular. And God hath set some in the church, first apostles, secondarily prophets, thirdly teachers, after that miracles, then gifts of healings, helps, governments, diversities of tongues. Are all apostles? are all prophets? are all teachers? are all workers of miracles? Have all the gifts of healing? do all speak with tongues? do all interpret? But covet earnestly the best gifts: and yet shew I unto you a more excellent way.

–1 Corinthians 12:4-31

So we see, the Apostle Paul goes into detail to emphasize the importance of each member in the body. He also encourages us in verse 31 to "covet earnestly the best gifts." He encourages us to seek to excel spiritually in our walk with the Lord, while also at the same time pointing us to the more excellent way of love as the foundation for all spiritual release.

YOUR WEALTH IS IN YOUR ANOINTING

Ephesians 4:16 emphasizes the importance of each member releasing what God has placed within each of us:

> *From whom the whole body fitly joined together and compacted by that which every joint supplieth, according to the effectual working in the measure of every part, maketh increase of the body unto the edifying of itself in love.*

So we see that the whole body is "fitly joined together and compacted" by that which we each have received from the Anointed One, Christ Jesus. As we each release our portion or *supply* of Christ's Anointing through working it out in *practical* ways, the whole Body is increased by *building-up itself* in love.

Therefore, your wealth is in your anointing as an individual, your wealth is in your anointing as a family, your wealth is in your anointing as a church, your wealth is in your anointing as a community, your wealth is in your anointing as a city, your wealth is in your anointing as a nation. **Your wealth is in your anointing!**

PART TWO

THE ESSENTIAL KEYS TO THE *RELEASE* OF THE ANOINTING WITHIN YOU

I. FOCUS
II. PURPOSE
III. PASSION

But we have this treasure in earthen vessels, that the excellency of the power may be of God, and not of us.

–2 Corinthians 4:7

CHAPTER SIX

I. *FOCUS*: THE 1ST ESSENTIAL KEY TO THE *RELEASE* OF THE ANOINTING WITHIN YOU

In the remaining portions of this book we will be looking at the Essential Keys to the *release* of the anointing within you. The first key we will be looking at is *Focus*. "Focus" is defined by *Webster's New World Dictionary* as:

1. The point where rays of light, heat, etc. or waves of sound come together, or from which they spread or seem to spread; specifically, the point where rays of light reflected by a mirror or refracted by a lens meet
2. Any center of activity or attention
3. To adjust the focal length of (the eye, lens, etc.) so as to produce a clear image
4. To concentrate (to focus ones attention)

Let's look at John 1:1–16.

> *In the beginning was the Word, and Word was with God, and the Word was God. The same was in the beginning with God. All things were made by him; and without him was not any thing made that was made. In him was life; and the life was the light of men. And the light shineth in darkness; and the darkness comprehended it not.*
> *–John 1:1-5*

It did not grasp it. It takes faith and belief to comprehend Light. It takes faith to *receive* it.

> *There was a man sent from God, whose name was John. The same came for a witness, to bear witness of the Light, that all men through him might believe. He was not that Light, but was sent to bear witness of that Light. That was the true Light, which lighteth every man that cometh into the world. He was in the world, and the world was made by him, and the world knew him not. He came unto his own and his own received him not. But as*

> *many as received him, to them gave he power to become the sons of God, even to them that believe on his name: Which were born, not of blood, nor of the will of the flesh, nor of the will of man, but of God. And the Word was made flesh, and dwelt among us, (and we beheld his glory, the glory as of the only begotten of the Father,) full of grace and truth. John bare witness of him, and cried saying, This was he of whom I spake, He that cometh after me is preferred before me: for he was before me. And of his fullness have all we received, and grace for grace.*
>
> –John 1:6-16

In this message on *Focus*, I want to center in on a few verses from which we just read. Verses 3–5, 9, 12, and 16. They read as follows:

> *All things were made by him; and without him was not any thing made that was made. In him was life; and the life was the light of men. And the light shineth in darkness; and the darkness comprehended it not. That was the true Light, which lighteth every man that cometh into the world. But as many as received him, to them gave he power to become the sons of God, even to them that believe on his name: And of his fulness have all we received, and grace for grace.*

James 1:17 says, "Every good gift and every perfect gift is from above, and cometh down from the Father of lights, with whom is no variableness, neither shadow of turning."

MICHAEL JACKSON: AN EXAMPLE OF *FOCUS*

As we look at the subject of *Focus* as an Essential Key to th*e release* of the *anointing within you*, I'm going to look at the example of Michael Jackson. Michael Jackson's father, Joe Jackson, recognized talent in his children early on, and he began to train them in the direction they would go. Proverbs 22:6 says, "Train up a child in the way he should go: and when he is old, he will not depart from it." And though the discipline was strict in order to corral the talent of Mr. and Mrs. Joe and Katherine Jackson's children, Michael Jackson himself admitted that that discipline was the source and key to his phenomenal success. Proverbs 20:11 says, "Even a child is known by his doings, whether his work be pure, and whether it be right." The word *pure* here is defined like this in *Strong's Exhaustive Concordance of the Bible*:

PURE

2134–zak

    1. clean   2. clear   3. pure

2141–zakak

    1. to be transparent or clean

FOCUS–THE 1ST ESSENTIAL KEY

It is more of a *mining* term rather than simply morality. Solomon was a king of great wealth. His various mines were a great source of his wealth. He had access to gold and silver mines as well as other durable metals. He also had mines of other precious minerals and jewels. The gold and silver and other metals did not come out of the earth 100% pure. They usually came out dirty and containing other trace minerals and metals. In order for Solomon to obtain pure gold or silver or iron or copper, he would have to take that metal through the refiner's fire. After time in the fire, the other trace minerals or metals would separate from the desired, valuable metal. At that point it would be counted as *pure*. Then it could be used for its intended purpose. Then it would have its ultimate value.

Therefore, when Solomon speaks of "pure" in this scripture he is referring to *refinement*. Again, Proverbs 20:11 says, "Even a child is known by his doings, whether his work be *pure*, and whether it be right."

Thus, the discipline given to Michael Jackson and his siblings early on was a key to his focus, discovery of his gifts and talents, refinement of those gifts, and ultimate success.

From the age of five, when Michael Jackson began to sing and dance and show his talents in front of his class, until joining his brothers band, the Jackson Brothers in 1964, and then becoming the lead vocal of the band when the name was changed to the Jackson Five, Michael Jackson stayed in the center of his focus. He stayed in the *center* of his expertise. The training that his father and mother gave him and his siblings gave him *direction* for his life's career. For over 45 years he stayed in the center of his expertise and *excelled*.

I use Michael Jackson as an example of *Focus* because his success at remaining in the center of his expertise and excelling is phenomenal and *undeniable*! His passage through the earth is chiefly marked by his discovery of his gifts and talents at an early age—and focusing on it.

Again, James 1:17 says, "Every good gift and every perfect gift is from above, and cometh down from the Father of lights, with whom is no variableness, neither shadow of turning."

Also, Romans 11:29 says, "For the gifts and calling of God are without repentance." Therefore, the gifts and calling upon Michael Jackson was from God. How he used those gifts and whether he heeded that call was a matter a choice. However, God's purpose in giving him the gifts of song and dance, and to be an entertainer, was for His glory. Romans 9:23 says, "And that he might make known the riches of his glory on the vessels of mercy, which he had afore prepared unto glory." John 3:16–17 has this to say:

YOUR WEALTH IS IN YOUR ANOINTING

> *For God so loved the world, that he gave his only begotten Son, that whosoever believeth in him should not perish, but have everlasting life. For God sent not his Son into the world to condemn the world; but that the world through him might be saved.*

Therefore, we know it is God's will that all be saved and use their gifts and talents for His glory. However, for the basis of the subject of *Focus*, Michael Jackson's lifework and musical results are an undeniable evidence of someone focused in his endeavor.

Now let's look at the foundational passage of this entire message: **your wealth is in your anointing.** Let's look at 2 Kings 4:1–7 and let's read it once again to catch the full context:

> *Now there cried a certain woman of the wives of the sons of the prophets unto Elisha, saying, Thy servant my husband is dead; and thou knowest that thy servant did fear the Lord: and the creditor is come to take unto him my two sons to be bondmen. And Elisha said unto her, What shall I do for thee? tell me, what hast thou in the house? And she said, Thine handmaid hath not any thing in the house, save a pot of oil. Then he said, Go, borrow thee vessels abroad of all thy neighbours, even empty vessels; borrow not a few. And when thou art come in, thou shalt shut the door upon thee and upon thy sons, and shalt pour out into all those vessels, and thou shalt set aside that which is full. So she went from him, and shut the door upon her and upon her sons, who brought the vessels to her: and she poured out. And it came to pass, when the vessels were full, that she said unto her son, Bring me yet a vessel, And he said unto her, There is not a vessel more. And the oil stayed. Then she came and told the man of God. And he said, Go, sell the oil, and pay thy debt, and live thou and thy children of the rest.*

We see here that Elisha the prophet told the woman to *focus* her full attention on the *escape plan* he gave her. She had to be totally focused and dedicated to the successful outcome or it would not have happened. Even with the Word from God, she would not have gotten out of her desperate situation if she had not obeyed and focused on her own deliverance. Let's read verses 3–7 again to see how she focused:

> *Then he said, Go, borrow thee vessels abroad of all thy neighbours, even empty vessels; borrow not a few. And when thou art come in, thou shalt shut the door upon thee and upon thy sons, and shalt pour out into all those vessels, and thou shalt set aside that which is full. So she went from him, and shut the door upon her and upon her sons, who brought the vessels to her; and she poured out. And it came to pass, when the vessels were full, that she said unto her son, Bring me yet a vessel, And he said unto her, There is not a vessel*

FOCUS–THE 1ST ESSENTIAL KEY

more. And the oil stayed. Then she came and told the man of God. And he said, Go, sell the oil, and pay thy debt, and live thou and thy children of the rest.

The man of God told her to go into her own house and shut the door. He told her to focus her full effort on her deliverance and *shut out all distractions*! It was an *emergency*! It was a matter of life or death, poverty or prosperity. She had to act and she had to act fast and completely. Her obedience and ability to focus and give a concentrated effort was the key to her ultimate success and deliverance.

In that same manner, we as believers only have a certain amount of time to get out of us what God has put in us before we die. The world *needs* what you have. Your family needs what you have. Your spiritual, mental, physical, social, and financial well-being is dependent upon you *releasing* the anointing within you. *Don't die with your stuff still in you*! Through your *Focus* on a God-given goal, you can *release* it! We must make the release of the anointing within us our *number one* priority in order to successfully release the *wealth* in our anointing.

Now we understand that "faith cometh by *hearing*, and *hearing* by the Word of God" (Romans 10:17). And as the Word goes forth, there are things that are happening on the *inside* of us. We're catching an *image* of prosperity. We're catching an image of God's will for our lives. It's His will that we prosper. It's His will that we be rich. It's His will that we be debt-free. It is His will that we have more than enough for every need and desire in our lives, and have enough to spare, and enough to share. He wants us to have all our debts paid and have enough in store that we can give to any need or charitable donation. He wants us to have more than enough. He wants us to be blessed so that He can make us a blessing. That's God's will for our lives. So, that's what we are establishing in our hearts through this message: **your wealth is in your anointing**. Also, we are establishing that the wealth that we need is not coming from the outside. It's not coming from some *administration*. It's not coming from some outside social service. It's coming from what God has put on the *inside* of you, and what God has put on the inside of me. It comes from the inside of us.

You have to know what God has called you to do. You have to know what God has put inside of you. You have to know what you are going after. And then you have to *focus* in order to bring out the wealth God has placed in that thing. Previously, we looked at Michael Jackson as an example of *Focus*. For the 50 years that he lived, about 45 of those were spent in the center of his focus. From about the age of five and onward, he was completely focused

YOUR WEALTH IS IN YOUR ANOINTING

on his music. Hit after hit from a little boy, until he left this earth, he was focused on his music. Even during the week of his untimely departure from this earth, he was planning his next music tour. He had tremendous success in his career because of his focus. He discovered his talents at an early age, and he stayed focused on it all of his life. He disciplined himself to his music. It was said that he was even wondering if new instruments could be created to express new sounds. He was still innovating and thinking of different ways to improve in his gifting. He received the gifts from God. "The gifts and the calling of God are without repentance" (Romans 11:29). "Every good and every perfect gift is from above, and comes down from the Father of lights" or the Father of the spirits of men (James 1:17). God gave Michael Jackson the *gift* to sing, to dance, to *move*! God gave him that natural energy. God gave him that talent. The way he used it was a matter of his choice, but God gave it to him. God invests gifts, talents, and uncommon abilities in each of us. God is the *giver*. Satan is a taker. God is the giver of good. Satan is the thief, destroyer, and murderer. Therefore, anything good that was given came from God. Anything that was taken, such as a person's life, or the glory God meant for that gifting and talent, is due to the thief, Satan. He comes only but for to "steal, kill, and to destroy" (John 10:10). If there is something to steal, then the *thief* is coming. If there is nothing worth stealing, the thief will not come. But if there is something valuable in you, your family, or your children, the thief comes not but for to steal, kill, and to destroy. That's the only reason he will come. If there is nothing to steal, kill, or destroy, you won't have to worry about the devil, because he feels like he already has you. He feels that you don't have anything to offer. But if there is something to steal, kill, or destroy in your life, such as a gifting, a calling, an anointing, your family, etc., the thief will come after that with all he has. He will start it during your youth and he will continue throughout your life until you take authority over that devil and put him underneath your feet where he is supposed to be. Jesus said, "I am come that they might have life and that they might have it more abundantly" (John 10:10). He is the Great I AM. He is the same *I AM* that spoke to Moses and told him to tell the Pharaoh to let His people go. When Moses needed to know on whose authority He would tell the people he was coming in, God told him to tell them that "I AM" sent you. He said, "I AM that I AM" (Exodus 3:14). He is that same *I AM* and He lives inside of us. We have every right, ability, and authority to fulfill our *Purpose* and to release the anointing God has put on the inside of us. Therefore, in order to accomplish any goal or purpose, we must be focused. We must make the release of the anointing within us our *number one Focus* in order to successfully release the wealth within our anointing.

CHAPTER SEVEN

II. *PURPOSE*: THE 2ND ESSENTIAL KEY TO THE *RELEASE* OF THE ANOINTING WITHIN YOU

Now, I want to focus on *Purpose*, the second Essential Key to the *release* of the anointing within you. *Purpose* is actually the most important Essential Key to the *release* of the anointing. It is the reason *why* we are here and why God has invested Himself in us. God has a *Purpose* for each of our lives. Our main goal is to realize our *Purpose*. We should have a clear picture of what His purpose is for us. Being able to *Focus* on what He has told us in His Word will reveal that purpose. Once you and I get a clear image of that *Purpose*, we can pursue it with everything within us. Many people go through life without having an idea of what their purpose is. Some have been so *beat down* by life or by the responsibilities of life that they have lost the *zeal* to seek their *Purpose*. It's more than eating, sleeping, going to work, going to church, and taking care of the children. God has a *central purpose* for each of our lives. It is a purpose by which we are to prosper and succeed. In 3 John 2 it says, "Beloved, I wish above all things that thou mayest prosper, and be in health, even as your soul prospers."

It is God's will for you and me to prosper in life. That is His central purpose for you and me. Psalms 35:27 says, "Let them shout for joy, and be glad, that favour my righteous cause: yea, let them say continually, Let the Lord be magnified, which hath pleasure in the prosperity of his servant."

Now, that scripture says, "Let them shout for joy, and be glad, that favour my righteous cause . . ." God's "righteous cause" is *your prosperity*. The rest of the scripture says, ". . . let them say continually, Let the Lord be magnified, which hath *pleasure* in the *prosperity* of his servant."

God is always thinking about your prosperity. He says, "Let them *say continually*, Let the Lord be magnified, which hath pleasure in the prosperity of his servant." God wants words and shouts *of joy* to be continually coming out our mouths concerning Him prospering us. He wants to continually hear you speaking His *Covenant of Prosperity* concerning yourself. His Word, the Bible, is His *Covenant of Prosperity*. His Word is His Will. His Word is His *Purpose*.

You may ask, "Why is God concerned about my prosperity?" Well, the number one reason is because *you* are His child and *He loves you*. Matthew 10:29-32 says this concerning His special care of you. It lets you know He is always thinking of you:

> *Are not two sparrows sold for a farthing? and one of them shall not fall on the ground without your Father. But the very hairs of your head are all numbered. Fear ye not therefore, ye are of more value than many sparrows. Whosoever therefore shall confess me before men, him will I confess also before my Father which is in heaven.*

Also, David discovered God's personal, tender care for him and for each of us. He expresses it in Psalms 139:13-18:

> *For thou hast possessed my reins: thou hast covered me in my mother's womb. I will praise thee; for I am fearfully and wonderfully made: marvellous are thy works; and that my soul knoweth right well. My substance was not hid from thee, when I was made in secret, and curiously wrought in the lowest parts of the earth. Thine eyes did see my substance, yet being unperfect; and in thy book all my members were written, which in continuance were fashioned, when as yet there was none of them. How precious also are thy thoughts unto me, O God! how great is the sum of them! If I should count them, they are more in number than the sand: when I awake, I am still with thee.*

Again, back in Matthew 7:7-11, the Word tells us that our Father is a good God, and He wants to and *will* give us good things. This is what it says:

> *Ask, and it shall be given you: seek, and ye shall find; knock, and it shall be opened unto you: For every one that asketh receiveth; and he that seeketh findeth; and to him that knocketh it shall be opened. Or what man is there of you, whom if his son ask bread, will he give him a stone? Or if he ask a fish, will he give him a serpent? If ye then, being evil, know how to give good gifts unto your children, how much more shall your Father which is in heaven give good things to them that ask him?*

And finally, to further establish that God our Father is committed in His love to us, and to prospering us, let's look at Romans 8:28-34:

> *And we know that all things work together for good to them that love God, to them who are the called according to his purpose. For whom*

PURPOSE–THE 2ND ESSENTIAL KEY

> *he did foreknow, he also did predestinate to be conformed to the image of his Son, that he might be the firstborn among many brethren. Moreover whom he did predestinate, them he also called: and whom he called, them he also justified: and whom he justified, them he also glorified. What shall we then say to these things? If God be for us, who can be against us? He that spared not his own Son, but delivered him up for us all, how shall he not with him also freely give us all things? Who shall lay any thing to the charge of God's elect? It is God that justifieth. Who is he that condemneth? It is Christ that died, yea, rather, that is risen again, who is even at the right hand of God, who also maketh intercession for us.*

And Hebrews 4:9–11 confirms God's will for us concerning our *wealth* and *prosperity*. It calls it "rest." This is what it says:

> *There remaineth therefore a rest to the people of God. For he that is entered into rest, he also hath ceased from his own works, as God did from his. Let us labour therefore to enter into that rest, lest any man fall after the same example of unbelief.*

GOD'S PURPOSE FOR YOUR DELIVERANCE

I went through those scriptures to establish the Father's love for us and desire for us to prosper. Now let's look at the woman with the pot of oil.

We began this message looking at the story of Elisha and the widow with the pot of oil in 2 Kings 4:1–7. We saw that she was in a desperate financial situation due to her husband dying and leaving her and her children with financial debt. She came to Elisha and he gave her a divine strategy to get out of her desperate situation. We will read the passage once again to get the context of the situation. However, our main focus will be on God's purpose for the woman's financial deliverance. Elisha had a vision for more than her getting out of debt. Let's read the passage:

> *Now there cried a certain woman of the wives of the sons of the prophets unto Elisha, saying, Thy servant my husband is dead; and thou knowest that thy servant did fear the Lord: and the creditor is come to take unto him my two sons to be bondmen. And Elisha said unto her, What shall I do for thee? tell me, what hast thou in the house? And she said, Thine handmaid hath not anything in the house, save a pot of oil. Then he said, Go, borrow thee vessels abroad of all thy neighbours, even empty vessels; borrow not a few. And when thou art come in, thou shalt shut the door upon thee and upon thy sons, and shalt pour out into all those vessels, and thou shalt set aside that which is full. So she went from him, and shut the door upon her and upon her sons,*

> who brought the vessels to her: and she poured out. And it came to pass, when the vessels were full, that she said unto her son, Bring me yet a vessel, And he said unto her, There is not a vessel more. And the oil stayed. Then she came and told the man of God. And he said, Go, sell the oil, and pay thy debt, and live thou and thy children of the rest.

Notice in verse 7 what Elisha told the woman of God:

> Then she came and told the man of God. And he said, Go, sell the oil, and pay thy debt, and live thou and thy children of the rest.

It is God's will or *Purpose* for you to not only be debt-free, but to have *more than enough* for you and your family for the rest of your life. God wants to establish His *covenant* in prospering you. Deuteronomy 8:1-18 explains God's process of fulfilling His Covenant or *Purpose* for our lives. It is His *Purpose* to see you blessed so that He can establish His Covenant in you.

PURPOSE: THE *PROCESS*

In Deuteronomy 8:1-3 we begin to learn more about the *Blessing* of God to us as we see how He dealt with the children of Israel. We see the reason why He has set forth to bless us so abundantly. He has a purpose, and there is a *process* in the purpose. Let's look at this passage:

> All the commandments which I command thee this day shall ye observe to do, that ye may live, and multiply, and go in and possess the land which the Lord sware unto your fathers. And thou shalt remember all the way which the Lord thy God led thee these forty years in the wilderness, to humble thee, and to prove thee, to know what was in thine heart, whether thou wouldest keep his commandments, or no. And he humbled thee, and suffered thee to hunger, and fed thee with manna, which thou knewest not, neither did thy fathers know; that he might make thee know that man doth not live by bread only, but by every word that proceedeth out the mouth of the Lord doth man live.

Now we are going to stop for a moment and look at this verse more closely. God had a *process* in leading the Children of Israel to His purpose for prospering them. He was leading them to the Promised Land. He was leading them to the place of the *fulfilled* Promise, but there was a very important and vital lesson He wanted them to learn in the process. This lesson was crucial to their long-term survival and lasting success. It would determine if they would be able to keep the Blessing. It would determine if they would be able to stay in their Promised Land. Let's look at verses 2-3 again:

PURPOSE–THE 2ND ESSENTIAL KEY

> *And thou shalt remember all the way which the Lord thy God led thee these forty years in the wilderness, to humble thee, and to prove thee, to know what was in thine heart, whether thou wouldest keep his commandments, or no. And he humbled thee, and suffered thee to hunger, and fed thee with manna, which thou knewest not, neither did thy fathers know; that he might make thee know that man doth not live by bread only, but by every word that proceedeth out the mouth of the Lord doth man live.*

Now we see that the Lord said He "humbled" them and "proved" them. In other words, He helped them to come to a place of *dependence* on Him for their provision. He helped them to realize that their significance was based on their *relationship* with Him. He also taught them how to view their fellowman and their enemies. He wanted them to view life through the eyes of the covenant they had with Jehovah God. In other words, God wanted them to learn to view their whole existence through the eyes of His Word. They had to look at God, themselves, their fellowman, and their enemy through the lens of God's covenant, which is His Word. Verse 3 says:

> *And he humbled thee, and suffered thee to hunger, and fed thee with manna, which thou knewest not, neither did thy fathers know; that he might make thee know that man doth not live by bread only, but by every word that proceedeth out of the mouth of the Lord doth man live.*

God said He "humbled" them, and suffered them to "hunger." When He says he suffered them to hunger, He wasn't talking about for *physical* food. He suffered them to hunger for His *Word*. He suffered or allowed or caused them to come into an intense conscious awareness that they needed God's Word to live.

He could not have been talking about physical food because in the next part of the verse He said He "fed" them. Again verse 3 says:

> *And he humbled thee, and suffered thee to hunger, and fed thee with manna, which thou knewest not; neither did thy fathers know; that he might make thee know that man doth not live by bread only, but by every word that proceedeth out of the mouth of the Lord doth man live.*

So we see that the people did not hunger for *food*. God fed them with manna every day. However, He disciplined their appetite for only physical gratification, and taught them to realize their need for the "Living Bread." He said He wanted them to know "that man doth not live by

YOUR WEALTH IS IN YOUR ANOINTING

bread only, but by every word that proceedeth out of the mouth of the Lord doth man live."Jesus is the "Living Word." Jesus is the "Bread of Life." In John 6:32-51 Jesus says the following concerning Himself:

> Then Jesus said unto them, Verily, verily, I say unto you, Moses gave you not that bread from heaven; but my Father giveth you the true bread from heaven. For the bread of God is he which cometh down from heaven, and giveth life unto the world. Then said they unto him, Lord ever more give us this bread. And Jesus said unto them, I am the bread of life: he that cometh to me shall never hunger; and he that believeth on me shall never thirst. But I said unto you, That ye also have seen me, and believe not. All that the Father giveth me shall come to me; and him that cometh to me I will in no wise cast out. For I came down from heaven, not to do mine own will, but the will of him that sent me. And this is the Father's will which hath sent me, that all which he hath given me I should lose nothing, but should raise it up again at the last day. And this is the will of him that sent me, that every one which seeth the Son, and believeth on him, may have everlasting life: and I will raise him up at the last day. The Jews then murmured at him, because he said, I am the bread which came down from heaven. And they said, Is not this Jesus, the son of Joseph, whose father and mother we know? how is it then that he saith, I came down from heaven? Jesus therefore answered and said unto them, Murmur not among yourselves. No man can come to me, except the Father which hath sent me draw him: and I will raise him up at the last day. It is written in the prophets, And they shall be all taught of God. Every man therefore that hath heard, and hath learned of the Father, cometh unto me. Not that any man hath seen the Father, save he which is of God, he hath seen the Father. Verily, verily I say unto you, He that believeth on me hath everlasting life. I am that bread of life. Your fathers did eat manna in the wilderness, and are dead. This is the bread which cometh down from heaven, that a man may eat therefore, and not die. I am the living bread which came down from heaven: if any man eat of this bread, he shall live for ever: and the bread that I will give is my flesh, which I will give for the life of the world.

So we see, Jesus declared that He is the "Living Bread." We are to live through our connection and consumption of who He is. John 1:1-5 and 12-13 also helps to establish that Jesus is the "Living Word" by which we are to live. This is what it says:

> In the beginning was the Word, and Word was with God, and the Word was God. The same was in the beginning with God. All things were made by him; and without him was not any thing made that was made. In him was life; and the life was the light of men. And the light shineth in darkness; and the darkness comprehended it not. But as many as received him, to them gave he power to become the sons of

God, even to them that believe on his name: Which were born, not of blood, nor of the will of the flesh, nor of the will of man, but of God.

Also, John 15:1- 8 tells us of the importance of us abiding in Him. Jesus is the "Bread of Life," the "Word of God," and the "True Vine":

I am the true vine, and my Father is the husbandman. Every branch in me that beareth not fruit he taketh away: and every branch that beareth fruit, he purgeth it, that it may bring forth more fruit. Now ye are clean through the word which I have spoken unto you. Abide in me, and I in you. As the branch cannot bear fruit of itself, except it abide in the vine; no more can he, except ye abide in me. I am the vine, ye are the branches; He that abideth in me, and I in him, the same bringeth forth much fruit: for without me ye can do nothing. If a man abide not in me, he is cast forth as a branch, and is withered; and men gather them, and cast them into the fire, and they are burned. If ye abide in me, and my words abide in you, ye shall ask what ye will, and it shall be done unto you. Herein is my Father glorified, that ye bear much fruit; so shall ye be my disciples.

God wants us to be fully cognizant of His Word. He wants us to view our lives from the lens of His Covenant Promises. He wants us to walk in the Blessing.

"IT TOOK THE WORD TO SAVE YOU, IT WILL TAKE THE WORD TO *KEEP* YOU!"

When I was growing up in church, the older saints of God would say to those who were just getting saved, "It took the Word to save you, it will take the Word to keep you!" In other words, it was God's Word that led to our salvation and deliverance from sin, disease, addiction, depression, oppression, poverty, etc. Therefore, it would take God's Word to keep us free from those things that He delivered us from. The Word of God is essential for the Believer. It is our connection with Heaven. We are born again. We are new creatures. We are no longer only residence of the earthly realm. We are now born of Heaven. We must be sustained by *Heavenly Bread*. The Bible is our source. This is what God the Father was teaching the children of Israel in the wilderness. God's manner of dealing with them in the wilderness is an example to us. We too must live by the Word.

Now let's look back at Deuteronomy 8:2–3. We are looking at *Purpose* as one of the Essential Keys to the *release* of the anointing within us. In understanding *Purpose* we have to establish the importance of God's Word. God's Word was central to the success of the children of Israel in the Old Testament, and we have established that it is vital for our success as we walk in *Purpose*. It reads:

> And thou shalt remember all the way which the Lord thy God led thee these forty years in the wilderness, to humble thee, and to prove thee, to know what was in thine heart, whether thou wouldest keep his commandments, or no. And he humbled thee, and suffered thee to hunger, and fed thee with manna, which thou knewest not, neither did thy fathers know; that he might make thee know that man doth not live by bread only, but by every word that proceedeth out the mouth of the Lord doth man live.

God wanted the Children of Israel to be fully aware that their total provision and existence was based on His Word, which is His Covenant. God reminded them of how He took care of them in the wilderness, and taught them to obey and honor His Word. Continue and look at verses 4-6 of the same chapter:

> Thy raiment waxed not old upon thee, neither did thy foot swell, these forty years. Thou shalt also consider in thine heart, that, as a man chasteneth his son, so the Lord thy God chasteneth thee. Therefore thou shalt keep the commandments of the Lord thy God, to walk in his ways, and fear him.

God taught the Children of Israel to believe and honor His Word as they were going into the *good land*. Earlier, they walked around in the wilderness forty years, because they did not honor or believe His Word. However, during that time in the wilderness, God taught them by demonstrating His faithfulness to them. He provided for them in a desolate situation. He made sure they had what they needed to live. It wasn't "the land flowing with milk and honey," but God did keep them alive with manna. God provided water for them and kept their clothing from wearing out. It was the land of *just enough*. However, God was now taking them into the land of *more than enough*. He was taking them into the land of *abundance*. He was now reminding them how they were able to survive in the land of *just enough*. He was telling them that just as His Word was essential for them to survive in the wilderness, it would be essential in the land of abundance. Let's see how God describes the land where they were going. This is essential to understanding *Purpose* in the release of the anointing within us. Now let's move to verses 7-9:

> For the Lord thy God bringeth thee into a good land, a land of brooks of water, of fountains and depths that spring out of valleys and hills. A land of wheat, and barley, and vines, and fig trees, and pomegranates; a land of oil olive, and honey; A land wherein thou shalt eat bread

PURPOSE–THE 2ND ESSENTIAL KEY

> *without scarceness, thou shalt not lack any thing in it; a land whose stones are iron, and out of whose hills thou mayest dig brass.*

God describes to them this land of abundance. It is a land with no lack. This is what God wants to give to us as believers. He wants us to walk in a land of *no lack*. Jesus said in John 10:10, "The thief cometh not, but for to steal, and to kill, and to destroy: I am come that they might have life, and that they might have it more abundantly." Therefore, it is God's will that we live in abundance. Jesus came so we could have *life* and *life more abundantly*! He wants us to live life to the *full* and to have an overflow of abundant riches and supply. However, in Deuteronomy 8:10–18, God reveals to us the *Purpose* of such abundance. He also reveals the key to us *keeping* the abundance and the key to us maintaining the right perspective concerning it. It all goes back to His Word or His Covenant. Let's look at those scriptures:

> *When thou hast eaten and art full, then thou shalt bless the Lord thy God for the good land which he hath given thee. Beware that thou forget not the Lord thy God, in not keeping his commandments, and his judgments, and his statutes, which I command thee this day: Lest when thou hast eaten and art full, and hast built goodly houses, and dwelt therein; And when thy herds and thy flocks multiply, and thy silver and gold is multiplied, and all that thou hast is multiplied; Then thine heart be lifted up, and thou forget the Lord thy God, which brought thee forth out of the land of Egypt, from the house of bondage; Who led thee through that great and terrible wilderness, wherein were fiery serpents, and scorpions, and drought, where there was no water; who brought thee forth water out of the rock of flint; Who fed thee in the wilderness with manna, which thy fathers knew not, that he might humble thee, and that he might prove thee, to do thee good at thy latter end; And thou say in thine heart, My power and the might of mine hand hath gotten me this wealth. But thou shalt remember the Lord thy God: for it is he that giveth thee power to get wealth, that he may establish his covenant which he sware unto thy fathers, as it is this day.*

God wants us to keep our focus on the Word. He wants us to remember that our *power to get wealth* is based on His Covenant that He has made with mankind to *prosper and have dominion* in the earth. The woman with the pot of oil in 2 Kings 4:1–7 who came to Elisha in a desperate situation knew that her salvation and deliverance depended on God's Word. She knew that the Word from the man of God was the key to her financial deliverance. Her sons were about to be taken into slavery. Her future survival and provision was hanging in the balance. The only thing she had was a Word from a man of God. As Deuteronomy 8:3 convinced us "man doth not live by bread only, but by every word that proceedeth out of the mouth of the Lord doth man live."

THE *ORIGIN* OF PURPOSE

In exploring *Purpose*, we must know why God made us, and what His intent is for us. Our true *Purpose* is based on what God the Father intended when He made us in the beginning. In looking at *Purpose*, let's revisit Genesis 1:26–28:

> *And God said, Let us make man in our image, after our likeness: and let them have dominion over the fish of the sea, and over the fowl of the air, and over the cattle, and over all the earth, and over every creeping thing that creepeth upon the earth. So God created man in his own image, in the image of God created he him; male and female created he them. And God blessed them, and God said unto them, Be fruitful, and multiply, and replenish the earth, and subdue it: and have dominion over the fish of the sea, and over the fowl of the air, and over every living thing that moveth upon the earth.*

After God created mankind in His own image, it was His *Purpose* for us to have rulership and dominion over the earth. We were created to reign over the works of His hands. Some have already learned to walk in dominion in the earth. However, God wants each of us to walk in dominion in our specific sphere of influence. He wants us to develop the area of responsibility He has given us and "be fruitful, multiply, replenish the earth, subdue it, and have dominion" in it. Therefore, in understanding your *individual Purpose* you must grasp God's *over-arching purpose* for mankind. If you and I fully comprehend God's purpose, we will refuse to live *below* our God-given potential and responsibility.

The Book of Ephesians, in the New Testament, begins to further explain God's original intent for us as His people. From the beginning, the Father purposed for us to reign with Him. Paul explains God's *Purpose* for us:

> *Blessed be the God and Father of our Lord Jesus Christ, who hath blessed us with all spiritual blessings in heavenly places in Christ:*
>
> *–Ephesians 1:3*

> *For we are his workmanship, created in Christ Jesus unto good works, which God hath before ordained that we should walk in them.*
>
> *–Ephesians 2:10*

PURPOSE–THE 2ND ESSENTIAL KEY

This lets us know that God blessed us with everything needful, or that could be desired, in Christ Jesus. Our entire destiny is in Christ, the Man, and in the Anointing upon Christ. Our *Purpose* is hid in heavenly places. It is brought out into material reality through our faith. Hebrews 11:1 lets us know of the material "substance" of our faith. It says, "Now faith is the *substance* of things hoped for, the evidence of things not seen." This lets us know that in order for our hope or desire to materialize, we have to use our faith. In order for the *Purpose*, which God has for us to materialize, we have to use our faith. Hebrews 11:1-3 tell us how the saints of old, as well as God Himself was able to bring the things that were in the heavenly places, which they hoped for or desired, into material reality. It says:

> Now faith is the substance of things hoped for, the evidence of things not seen. For by it the elders obtained a good report. Through faith we understand that the worlds were framed by the word of God, so that things which are seen were not made of things which do appear.

As you continue to follow through Hebrews 11, you will see how men and women of God in the Old Testament brought their purpose into reality. I recommend that you read this chapter in its entirety so you can see how *Purpose* caused these elders of the faith to accomplish their assignments through faith. It shows the sacrifice and dedication that is involved in releasing the anointing that is in us through faith. It also shows that these pioneers were not and are not complete without us. They ran the first leg of the race. However, we are the *finishers*. We are the ones that are to obtain and bring home the crown for them and us. We do that when we accomplish the *Purpose* God has for us. We do that when we release the anointing God has put in us.

CREATED ON *PURPOSE*

Now let's look back at Ephesians 2:10. *Purpose* is an Essential Key to the *release* of the anointing within you.

> For we are his workmanship, created in Christ Jesus unto good works, which God hath before ordained that we should walk in them.

God has already preordained you and me to walk in a specific purpose and assignment. It is to serve the overall purpose of His will. We were specially *handcrafted* by God, to fulfill a precise role in His kingdom. As we commit to fulfill what God has placed in us, by releasing the anointing within us, we will enrich His kingdom and we will be *enriched* in the process. Ephesians 2:10 says, "For we are his workmanship, created in Christ Jesus unto good works, which God hath before ordained that we should walk in them." Let's analyze that scripture further in order to see clearly how the release of the anointing within you is inextricably connected with your *Purpose*. Let's define the word "workmanship" from *Strong's Exhaustive Concordance of the Bible* and from *Webster's Dictionary*:

WORKMANSHIP

4161–Poiema

1. a product
2. a fabric
3. thing that is made
4. workmanship

WORKMANSHIP

1. the art or skill of a workman
2. the quality or mode of execution, as of a thing made
3. the product or result of labor and skill; work executed
4. the degree of art or skill exhibited in the finished product
5. the piece of work so produced

We are His *workmanship*, created in Christ Jesus unto good works, which God hath before ordained that we should walk in them. We are God's *product*. We are His *fabric* or *fabrication*. We are intricately knitted together for a specific purpose. We are not here without a purpose. God has a specific purpose for us. The *Strong's Concordance* says that "workmanship" means "product." Every product produced by a manufacturer is made with a preordained *Purpose*. God invested much labor and skill and forethought into designing and forging you and me. A product requires work for it to be produced. God worked on you before you were conceived in your mother's womb. He has continued to work on you from birth until now, and it's for a *Purpose*. Let's define the word *product*. It is one definition of *workmanship*. We are getting a clearer picture of *Purpose*, which is an Essential Key to the *release* of the anointing within you. *Webster's* defines product as:

1. a thing produced by labor, such as the product of his thought

2. a person or thing produced by or resulting from a process, as a spiritual, natural, social, or historical one; result (Ex: "He is a product of his times.")

3. the totality of goods or services that a company makes available

PURPOSE–THE 2ND ESSENTIAL KEY

We are God's specialty in the earth. We are His exclusive, premium product line. We represent His highest output. We are to have dominion over all other product lines.

In Psalms 139:13–18, David expresses his amazement at the revelation of himself as God's handiwork:

> *For thou hast possessed my reins: thou hast covered me in my mother's womb. I will praise thee; for I am fearfully and wonderfully made: marvellous are thy works; and that my soul knoweth right well. My substance was not hid from thee, when I was made in secret, and curiously wrought in the lowest parts of the earth. Thine eyes did see my substance, yet being unperfect; and in thy book all my members were written, which in continuance were fashioned, when as yet there was none of them. How precious also are thy thoughts unto me, O God! how great is the sum of them! If I should count them, they are more in number than the sand: when I awake, I am still with thee.*

David realized that he was the precious handiwork or *workmanship* of God. This was a key to his tremendous life of productivity, accomplishment, and worship unto God.

In another place, David expresses his acknowledgment and wonder at the premium God has placed on us, mankind, as His highest presentation of workmanship. Psalms 8:3–9 gives us a clear description of our place of honor as God's workmanship. This scripture also gives us further revelation of our *Purpose*:

> *When I consider thy heavens, the work of thy fingers, the moon and the stars, which thou hast ordained; What is man, that thou art mindful of him? and the son of man, that thou visitest him? For thou hast made him a little lower than the angels, and hast crowned him with glory and honour. Thou madest him to have dominion over the works of thy hands; thou hast put all things under his feet: All sheep and oxen, yea, and the beasts of the field; The fowl of the air, and the fish of the sea, and whatsoever passeth through the paths of the seas. O Lord our Lord, how excellent is thy name in all the earth!*

When verse 6 says, "Thou hast made him a little lower than the angels, and hast crowned him with glory and honour," the word "angels" actually is the Hebrew word "Elohim." It is a name for God Himself. Therefore, the scripture is actually saying "God has made man a little lower than Elohim (or God Himself), and hast crowned him with glory and honour." We are made in the image and likeness of God Himself. We are made in a higher order than the angels. God has given us dominion and authority even over the angels. They are subject to us. God's holy angels are ministering spirits, sent to minister for them who are the heirs of salvation (Hebrews 1:14). Evil spirits or fallen angels are subject to us as well, according to the words of Jesus. In Luke 10:17–20 Jesus lets us know that because we are redeemed back to our place of dominion and authority in Him, all evil spirits are underneath our feet. This is what He says to His disciples:

> And the seventy returned again with joy, saying, Lord, even the devils are subject unto us through thy name. And he said unto them, I beheld Satan as lightning fall from heaven. Behold, I give unto you power to tread on serpents and scorpions, and over all the power of the enemy: and nothing shall by any means hurt you. Notwithstanding in this rejoice not, that the spirits are subject unto you; but rather rejoice, because your names are written in heaven.

Therefore, this scripture clearly declares to us that "the spirits are subject" unto us. We are in a higher position in Christ. We are made in the image and likeness of God.

According to Psalms 8:6–8, God lets us know His overarching *Purpose* for mankind. This is what it says again:

Thou madest him *to have dominion* over the works of thy hands; thou hast put all things under his feet: All sheep and oxen, yea, and the beasts of the field; The fowl of the air, and the fish of the sea, and whatsoever passeth through the paths of the seas.

WE HAVE AN INDIVIDUAL *PURPOSE*

Now we have to realize our *individual* and specific *Purpose*. This is an Essential Key to the *release* of the anointing within us. Ecclesiastes 3:9–13 explains the mystery of *individual Purpose*. It begins:

> What profit hath he that worketh in that wherein he laboureth? I have seen the travail, which God hath given to the sons of men to be exercised in it.
>
> –Ecclesiastes 3:9-10

"Exercised" speaks of disciplining the flesh. This is necessary for us to release the anointing and wealth that God has put inside of us. *Without discipline, there is no release. Without release of the anointing, there is no wealth.*

PURPOSE—THE 2ND ESSENTIAL KEY

> *He hath made every thing beautiful in his time: also he hath set the world in their heart, so that no man can find out the work that God maketh from the beginning to the end.*
>
> *—Ecclesiastes 3:11*

He set the *world* or your *Purpose* and the purpose of all men and women in the heart. We have to endeavor to release what God has put in the heart so that it can become a physical reality in our lives. In doing so, we will discover the wealth God has for each of us.

> *I know that there is no good in them, but for a man to rejoice, and to do good in his life.*
>
> *—Ecclesiastes 3:12*

What God has placed within you is your *specific Purpose*. It is your place of *joy*! God is saying, "There is nothing better for you to do in life than to find and exercise yourself unto your *Purpose*." In doing so, you will release your wealth.

> *And also that every man should eat and drink, and enjoy the good of all his labour, it is the gift of God.*
>
> *—Ecclesiastes 3:13*

The *Purpose* that God has put in your heart is the source of your wealth and the source of your true joy in life. God is a good God. He truly and only desires for you and me to be blessed in life. He put your individual *Purpose* inside of you so that you could have a rewarding life. The more you fulfill your *individual Purpose*, the more God's *overarching Purpose* will be fulfilled. 3 John 2 says, "Beloved, I wish above all things that thou mayest prosper and be in health, even as thy soul prospereth." Also, 2 Peter 3:9 says the following concerning the Lord's purpose:

> *The Lord is not slack concerning his promise, as some men count slackness; but is longsuffering to us-ward, not willing that any should perish, but that all should come to repentance.*

It is not God's will that any of His creations be destroyed and perish without knowing His good will and purpose for their lives. God wants all to be saved. That is why He sent Jesus to give His life. Jesus made the sacrifice of His life so that all can be saved. It's God's will that all come to repentance. It's His will that all come back to the highest place from which mankind fell. When Adam disobeyed God in the garden and ate from the Tree of the Knowledge of Good and Evil, which God told him not to do, he fell from the high place of God's best. He fell from the high place of God's grace and favor. With Adam and Eve's fall, all of mankind fell with him, along with all creation. It is God's will that all of mankind return to God's perfect will for us. As each of us in the Body of Christ exercise ourselves unto the *specific* gift, talent, and calling which God has given us, we will be able to enjoy the "high-life" He intended for each of us. We will be able to enjoy the *good life* as examples of God's will, and spread the Gospel of God's love for all mankind.

God has put something *special* in all of us, by which we are to prosper and succeed. It is the gift of God. Ecclesiastes 5:18–20 says,

> *Behold that which I have seen: it is good and comely for one to eat and to drink, and to enjoy the good of all his labour that he taketh under the sun all the days of his life, which God giveth him: for it is his portion. Every man also to whom God hath given riches and wealth, and hath given him power to eat thereof, and to take his portion, and to rejoice in his labour; this is the gift of God. For he shall not much remember the days of his life; because God answereth him in the joy of his heart.*

Therefore, God has put something in each of us by which we are to succeed. God's favor and ability is *inclusive*. It is not *exclusive*. He includes everyone in the bounty of blessings which He has so lavishly spread upon the earth. It is our individual jobs to discover what God has put in us, in order that we may partake of our portion.

God desires to bring all people into the place of blessing which He planned for mankind. However, it is according to our choices as to whether we will receive Him, and whether we will receive the bounty of blessings He has in store for us. Romans 9:21–26 lets us know that God has riches prepared for all people. Yet, our choices make the difference as to whether we receive them.

> *Hath not the potter power over the clay, of the same lump to make one vessel unto honour, and another unto dishonour? What if God, willing to shew his wrath, and to make his power known, endured with much longsuffering the vessels of wrath fitted to destruction: And that he might make known the riches of his glory on the vessels of mercy, which he had afore prepared unto glory, Even us, whom he hath called, not of the Jews only, but also of the Gentiles? As he saith also in*

PURPOSE–THE 2ND ESSENTIAL KEY

> *Osee, I will call them my people, which were not my people; and her beloved, which was not beloved. And it shall come to pass, that in the place where it was said unto them, Ye are not my people; there shall they be called the children of the living God.*

Chapter 2 of 3 John lets us know that God wishes above all other things that we "prosper, be in health, even as our souls prosper." There is enough wealth and prosperity to be had for everyone on earth. We were born with a full supply. There is a full supply of natural resources in the earth to use to bring the supernatural supply into fruition. God desires for all of us to be prosperous, and be in good health, even as our soul (mind, will, emotions, personality) prospers and matures. *Why would God wish this for just a few? He wishes this for all.* John 10:10 says this:

> *The thief cometh not, but for to steal, and to kill, and to destroy: I am come that they might have life, and that they might have it more abundantly.*

Jesus specifically came in order to stop the devil from stealing, killing, and destroying all of our potential. Jesus came to destroy the works of the devil in order that we might be free to enjoy the wealth that He has invested within us and within the earth. This is what 1 John 3:8 says:

> *He that committeth sin is of the devil; for the devil sinneth from the beginning. For this purpose the Son of God was manifested, that he might destroy the works of the devil.*

God sent Jesus into the world to destroy the works of the devil and to prevent the devil from continuing to destroy our potential. When Jesus was manifested, He released the anointing for us during His death, burial, and resurrection. Through that anointing we have victory over Satan. We have been empowered to prosper and be in health, even as our souls prosper. As we become more aware of God's purpose for the anointing, we will prosper and live in greater victory. Ephesians 1:15–23 describes what Jesus accomplished for us like this:

> *Wherefore I also, after I heard of your faith in the Lord Jesus, and love unto all the saints, Cease not to give thanks for you, making mention of you in my prayers; That the God of our Lord Jesus Christ, the Father of glory, may give unto you the spirit of wisdom and revelation in the knowledge of him: The eyes of your understanding being enlightened; that ye may know what is the hope of his calling, and what the riches of the glory of his inheritance in the saints, And what is the exceeding greatness of his power to us-ward who believe, according*

> to the working of his mighty power, Which he wrought in Christ, when he raised him from the dead, and set him at his own right hand in the heavenly places, Far above all principality, and power, and might, and dominion, and every name that is named, not only in this world, but also in that which is to come: And hath put all things under his feet, and gave him to be the head over all things to the church, Which is his body, the fulness of him that filleth all in all.

We have been empowered to prosper and reign with Him by the anointing.

Romans 12:1-2 lets us know what we need to do in order to fulfill Gods purpose for the anointing. *Purpose* is an Essential Key to the *release* of the anointing within you. It says,

> I beseech you therefore, brethren, by the mercies of God, that ye present your bodies a living sacrifice, holy, acceptable unto God, which is your reasonable service. And be not conformed to this world: but be ye transformed by the renewing of your mind, that ye may prove what is that good, and acceptable, and perfect, will of God.

It is God's "good, acceptable, and perfect will" for us to "prosper and be in health, even as our souls prosper" (3 John 2). He wants you and me to release the wealth that He has invested in us in order that we may reign in the earth through Him. He also wants us to enjoy the life He has provided for us. We must be transformed in our thinking from the world's way of thinking and believing. In order for us to have what God, our Father, originally desired for us, we must rid our minds from "lack thinking." The world thinks in terms of *limits and scarcity.* God thinks in terms of *abundance.* There is an abundance of resources within you and me. The earth contains an abundance of resources. All the multitudes of good things that have been invented have come from the inside of someone. All the innovations that have been worked out of humanity, is because someone *dug deeper* and extracted the wealth they contained. Discovering our *Purpose*, and God's original *Purpose* for us is an Essential Key to the *release* of the anointing within you because **your wealth is in your anointing.**

CHAPTER EIGHT

III. *PASSION*: THE 3ᴿᴰ ESSENTIAL KEY TO THE *RELEASE* OF THE ANOINTING WITHIN YOU

THE FOUR COMPONENTS OF *PASSION:*

1. The *Joy of Pursuit*
2. The *Fight for Focus*
3. *Overcoming* the *Frustration of Perseverance*
4. The *Fight to Finish*

THE 1ST COMPONENT OF *PASSION*: THE *JOY OF PURSUIT!*

It takes an alert mind to be *inspired*. To be ignited by a dream, goal, vision, or possibility is the first step toward any worthwhile accomplishment. When the widow came to Elisha the prophet, she was open-minded for a supernatural answer. She expected something of him. She expected a miracle. She readily accepted his illogical instruction without question. She knew she was in a desperate situation. She needed an accelerated answer. She needed a miracle. She was willing to take whatever the prophet instructed at face value. She knew his reputation as a man of God. She knew he spoke for God and his words came to pass. Therefore, she had joy, excitement, and enthusiasm in response to the illogical instruction. She believed results would come. Let's look at the story once again in 2 Kings 4:1–7 as we look at the first component of *Passion*, the *Joy of Pursuit!*

> *Now there cried a certain woman of the wives of the sons of the prophets unto Elisha, saying, Thy servant my husband is dead; and thou knowest that thy servant did fear the Lord: and the creditor is come to take unto him my two sons to be bondmen. And Elisha said unto her, What shall I do for thee? tell me, what hast thou in the house? And she said, Thine handmaid hath not any thing in the house, save a pot of oil. Then he said, Go, borrow thee vessels abroad of all thy neighbours, even empty vessels; borrow not a few. And when thou art come in, thou shalt shut the door upon thee and upon thy sons, and shalt pour out into all those vessels, and thou shalt set aside that which is full. So she went from him, and shut the door upon her and upon her sons, who brought the vessels to her; and she poured out. And it came to pass, when the vessels were full, that she said unto her son, Bring me yet a vessel. And he said unto her, There is not a vessel more. And the oil stayed. Then she came and told the man of God. And he said, Go, sell the oil, and pay thy debt, and live thou and thy children of the rest.*

So we see, Elisha gave the woman an *illogical* instruction. He gave her a *Master Plan*—a plan from the *Master*. He told her to "Go! Borrow the empty pots, fill them from her one pot of oil and then go sell the pots of oil." In looking at *Passion* we are looking at the *Joy of Pursuit!* Look at verse 7 again:

> *Then she came and told the man of God. And he said, Go, sell the oil, and pay thy debt, and live thou and thy children of the rest.*

PASSION—THE 3RD ESSENTIAL KEY

The woman of God had gotten the plan. She had fulfilled the first portion of the plan. Yet, in order for her to get the *profit* out of the plan, she had to have *Passion*! She had to have *Passion* in order to get the *fruit* from her labor. After borrowing the pots and filling them, she had to *sell* them. She had finished the *production* phase of the miracle. Now it was time for the *sales* and *promotions* phase. She had to get the *money* out of her miracle. The only way to do that was through her *Passion and the Joy of Pursuit*!

The man of God said, "Go, sell the oil, and pay thy debt, and live thou and thy children of the rest." Let's look at that word "go." This is the optimal word. This is the *definition* of *Passion*. You have to "go!" Without action there is no satisfaction. Without action there are no results. Without action there is no fulfillment of the promise. "Go" is assurance of your miracle harvest. It is the *insurance* that the wealth contained in your anointing or pot of oil or "pot-ential" will pay off. Throughout the duration of your pursuit to obtain the wealth of your life, "go" is the prevailing force. Without "go," you forfeit your promise. Your wealth won't *come* without *"go!"* So let's define the word "go." We're looking at *Passion*, the third Essential Key to the *release* of the anointing within you. We are focusing on the first component of *Passion*—the *Joy of Pursuit*—as we explore the message **your wealth is in your anointing**.

WEALTH WON'T *COME*, WITHOUT *GO*!

Strong's Exhaustive Concordance of the Bible defines "go" like this:

GO

3212–yalak

1. to walk or follow after
2. get hence [or get "busy"]
3. cause to go
4. make one's way
5. grow, [which means, to come into being or be produced naturally; spring up; to thrive, to increase in size and develop toward maturity; to increase in size, quantity, or degree; to cultivate] [Therefore, we see it was God's will for the woman to take what she had produced miraculously with the pot of oil and then go to the *next level*. Elisha gave her the first miracle instruction, to *produce*. But now he wanted her to grow to the next level of financial maturity. He wanted her to *pursue* the profit from her miracle production.]

YOUR WEALTH IS IN YOUR ANOINTING

6. lead forth

7. march—to walk with regular, steady steps as in a military formation; to walk in a grave, stately way; to advance or progress steadily[Elisha advised the woman to go forth as a *soldier unto war*, along with her sons. This was a *serious* matter. She had to be brave, grave, and confident in advancing to obtain the financial wealth, which her oil was worth. This was the source of her financial deliverance, and the salvation of her sons from slavery. She had to be *deadly* serious in the execution of the sales portion of her miracle in order for the whole plan to come together. She had to "fight the good fight of faith" (1Timothy 6:12). It was a "good fight" because success was guaranteed if she would pursue unto the finish. Success is guaranteed to us, if we will fight to the finish to obtain the wealth God has put inside of us.]

8. prosper—to succeed, thrive, or grow, etc. vigorously

[Elisha gave the woman the *command* of God to prosper. He gave her the command "to succeed, thrive, grow, etc. vigorously." He spoke the *Blessing* over her. This is the same *Blessing* God has spoken over us in Genesis 1:28 and in Deuteronomy 28:8. This is what it says:

> *And God blessed them, and God said unto them, Be fruitful, and multiply, and replenish the earth, and subdue it: and have dominion over the fish of the sea, and over the fowl of the air, and over every living thing that moveth upon the earth.*
>
> *–Genesis 1:28*

> *The Lord shall command the blessing upon thee in thy storehouses, and in all that thou settest thine hand unto; and he shall bless thee in the land which the Lord thy God giveth thee.*
>
> *–Deuteronomy 28:8*

Elisha was speaking the *Blessing* over the woman to succeed. He was releasing her to prosper in her "oil business." He was releasing the *wealth* within her anointing. All she had to do was obey. The woman had experienced *miracle multiplication*. She had the wealth in the pots of oil. Yet, it was still only "*pot-ential*" wealth. The wealth was still in the pots. However, when Elisha told the woman to "go," he was releasing her power to *get* the wealth, which her oil contained. Deuteronomy 8:18 says,

PASSION–THE 3RD ESSENTIAL KEY

But thou shalt remember the Lord thy God: for it is he that giveth thee power to get wealth, that he may establish his covenant which he sware unto thy fathers, as it is this day.

The woman had the *potential* wealth. And God gave her the power or ability to *obtain* it. Yet, she still had to *get* it. "Go" and "get" are synonymous terms in this regard. The prophet Elisha was telling the woman to "go" and "get" the wealth that was locked up in those pots of oil!]

    9. pursue—to follow, in order to overtake, capture, etc.; *chase*. To follow or go on with a specified course of action, etc. To strive for; seek after [To pursue success]. To have as one's occupation, profession, or study; devote oneself to.

[I preached a message at our church, Faith Country Holiness Church in Gallatin, Tennessee, entitled "Pursue! Overtake! And Recover All!" It was from 1 Samuel 30. King David and his men left their wives, children, and property unguarded at Ziklag as they went off to war. While they were gone, another group of people came into the camp and stole their wives and children and their property and burned the city. When David and his men returned and saw their families and property gone, they cried until they could not cry anymore, and talked of stoning David. King David went and encouraged himself in the Lord and prayed. He asked God: should he pursue the enemy, and would he overtake them? God told David, "Pursue: for thou shalt surely overtake them, and without fail recover all" (1 Samuel 30:8). And he did. Well, this is what God is telling you and me. We have to "pursue, overtake, and recover all" that the enemy has stolen from us. We have to "go!" "Go" means to pursue the area God has given you. That is the only way you will overtake, and recover all the blessings He has for you.]

    10. to cause to *run*

    11. to spread forth

    12. to take a journey

    13. to cause to walk

So, we see that "go" involves *action*! We have to take action in order to obtain what God has for us. It requires *Passion* for: the *Joy of Pursuit*! **Your wealth is in your anointing.**

THE 2ND COMPONENT OF *PASSION*: THE *FIGHT FOR FOCUS*
YOU NEED A *VISION*

Now let's look at the second component of *Passion*, the *Fight for Focus*. As we saw in the first section of this book, *Focus* is the first Essential Key to the *release* of the anointing within you. Without *Focus*, you can't see *long* enough or *clearly* enough to know what you have. You have to have a clear picture of what you have on the inside to work with, before you can realize the *wealth* that you contain. Proverbs 29:18 says, "Where there is no vision, the people perish: but he that keepeth the law, happy is he."

Focus pertains to having a clear vision. If you don't have a clear vision of where you are going, you won't be *motivated* to get there. If you can't see clearly the reward at the end of the race, you won't pursue. If you don't see the potential prize for fighting, you will *forfeit* the fight. Therefore, it's necessary to have a clear focus for where you are going and *why*. We examined *Purpose* as the second Essential Key to the *release* of the anointing within you. *Purpose* is the *why*. *Focus* helps you see the *how*. *Passion* fuels the vision. However, you have to *Fight for your Focus*. There are many enemies to *Focus*. The main enemies can be summed up in three phrases: 1) the *flesh*, 2) the *world*, and 3) the *devil*. These will always be the enemies you will have to *fight* in regards to maintaining your *focus*.

Again, Proverbs 29:18 says, "Where there is no vision, the people perish: but he that keepeth the law, happy is he."

Vision *provokes Passion*. Through *Passion*, *Purpose* is obtained. *Passion* is the *ignition* for movement. Without movement nothing is accomplished. You must be focused on the purpose and have a clear vision of it long enough to allow your *Passion* to be provoked. You must let the purpose move you by clearly focusing on it. *Passion* is the third Essential Key to the *release* of the anointing within you. So, let's define the word "vision" used in Proverbs 29:18. *Strong's* defines it as:

PASSION—THE 3RD ESSENTIAL KEY

VISION

2377–chazown

    1. a sight (mentally)

    2. a dream

    3. a revelation

    5. an oracle (or a Word from God)

2372–chazah

    1. to gaze at

    2. mentally to perceive

    3. to contemplate with pleasure

    4. to have a vision of

    5. to behold

    6. to look at

    7. to prophesy or confess or predict

    8. provide

    9. see

Now we see that the first definition of "vision" as used in Proverbs 29:18 is to have "a sight (mentally)." In other words, you have to be able to *see* your outcome *mentally* in your mind before you see it on the outside. If you can't see it mentally in your mind, you won't *pursue* it. Without a mental vision of your desire, you won't pursue it with *Passion*. Once you get a vision of what God has to say about your life, you have to fight to keep a focus on it. Your three main enemies will always be 1) the flesh, 2) the world, and 3) the devil.

Proverbs 29:18 says "Where there is no vision, the people perish: but he that keepeth the law, happy is he." The word vision used here correlates with a word used in Proverbs 22:29. It says,

> Seest thou a man diligent in his business? he shall stand before kings; he shall not stand before mean men.

The word "seest" has to do with vision. Again, it says, "Seest thou a man diligent in his business? he shall stand before kings; he shall not stand before mean men." That word "seest" also has the meaning of "to prophesy" or "to see yourself." When it says "seest thou" a man diligent in his business . . ."

YOUR WEALTH IS IN YOUR ANOINTING

Well you are the "thou." See *yourself* as a man or woman diligent in your business and you will stand before kings. In other words, you will be *promoted* in life because of your diligence. You have to see yourself diligent *mentally* first. You have to see yourself diligent *internally*. It will then manifest on the outside. If you see yourself as a diligent worker in your business, whatever that business may be; if you see it *internally*, then you will *fulfill* it *externally*. So the Word says you will "stand before kings"; you will not stand before *average* men. Your diligence is the key to your promotion in life. You first have to have a vision of yourself as diligent *mentally*. The word "seest" and "vision" have the same connotation. In order to *see yourself* as diligent, and in order to have a vision of your outcome, you have to *focus* on it. You have to focus long enough and clearly enough and *doggedly* enough to get that picture *etched* in your mind. Because when you have it etched in your mind, then that's what you will *go after*! When you see it internally, you will have it externally.

THE WORD IS THE *SOURCE* OF VISION

Now let's look at the widow with the pot of oil. She came to Elisha the prophet. He gave her a vision. The vision was the Word. It was her desired outcome for financial deliverance. Again, Proverbs 29:18 says, "Where there is no vision, the people perish: but he that keepeth the law, happy is he." When it says the people "perish," it means the people just *give up*. They let their hands drop and they loose restraint of *Passion*. They have no clear picture of anything better for their lives to fight for. *You have to Fight for Focus*! We are looking at *Passion*, the third Essential Key to the *release* of the anointing within you. Also, we are looking at the second component of *Passion*, the *Fight for Focus*. You have to *Fight for your Focus*. "Where there is no vision, the people perish: but he the keepeth the law, happy is he." When it says "he that keepeth the law," the "law" is the law of God. It means "he that keepeth the *Word*." The "law" is the Word. When you keep the law, you *guard* it. You *preserve* it. You obey it. You watch over it. You *meditate* upon it. *Happy* is he that keeps the law of God. Why are you happy? Because you have a *clear picture* of what God has to say about your life. In other words, you have a *vision*. You catch a *vision* from meditating God's Word. You catch a vision of what God has said in His Word until you clearly see it. You are focused on what God said to you. You have to meditate it long enough until you have a clear focus of what God said to you. Again, let's look at the widow, who came

PASSION-THE 3RD ESSENTIAL KEY

to Elisha the prophet, in 2 Kings 4:1–7. We have to understand that even though we read this story and it all happened in 7 verses, we have to know that it was not an *overnight* success. She had to *gather* all the pots, *fill* all the pots, and *sell* all the pots. She had to *passionately* carry it out to its fulfillment.

> Now there cried a certain woman of the wives of the sons of the prophets unto Elisha, saying, Thy servant my husband is dead; and thou knowest that thy servant did fear the Lord: and the creditor is come to take unto him my two sons to be bondmen. And Elisha said unto her, What shall I do for thee? tell me, what hast thou in the house? And she said, Thine handmaid hath not any thing in the house, save a pot of oil. Then he said, Go, borrow thee vessels abroad of all thy neighbors, even empty vessels; borrow not a few. And when thou art come in, thou shalt shut the door upon thee and upon thy sons, and shalt pour out into all those vessels, and thou shalt set aside that which is full. So she went from him, and shut the door upon her and upon her sons, who brought the vessels to her; and she poured out. And it came to pass, when the vessels were full, that she said unto her son, Bring me yet a vessel. And he said unto her, There is not a vessel more. And the oil stayed. Then she came and told the man of God. And he said, Go, sell the oil, and pay thy debt, and live thou and thy children of the rest.

So we see, Elisha gave the widow a *Word from God*. He gave her a *vision*. He gave her a *revelation* of the supernatural! He gave her an *oracle* from God. Again, Proverbs 29:18 says, "Where there is no vision, the people perish: but he that keepeth the law, happy is he." Elisha gave the woman of God a vision of *full vessels*! He gave her a vision of *many vessels* when he spoke the Word to her. She received a vision of *many* vessels *full* from her *one* pot of oil. She caught that vision *internally* and she *acted* upon it. She had to keep the vision in front of her. She had to keep the revelation and divine instruction from the man of God in front of her. She had to keep meditating on the oracle from God. One of the definitions of the word vision is *oracle* or Word of God. She had to keep the oracle or Word of God in her mind in order to carry it out. Today you are receiving an *oracle* from God. This word is your *impetus* for action on that which God has placed in your heart. **Your wealth is in your anointing.**

The widow had to keep the Word of God in front of her. She had to keep the oracle or divine vision in front of her. She had to keep it in front of her in order for the oil to *multiply*. She had to *believe*! She had to have

YOUR WEALTH IS IN YOUR ANOINTING

faith to believe that the oil was going to multiply when she *gathered* those pots. She had to have enough faith to go out and gather the pots. Her faith was based on the Word of God. She received the Word as a revelation. She received it as a divine oracle of God. An oracle is an *utterance* of God or the Word from God's *lips*. The widow received the Word from Elisha, the man of God, as being the Word from God's lips. She had to *focus* on that Word long enough for her to *passionately* pursue it. It didn't happen overnight. But she did work with *Passion* because she was in a desperate situation. One of the reasons *our* blessing, change, and promise hasn't happened as fast as we say we want it, is because we are not as *desperate* as this widow was. When you get desperate enough, you will *act* on the wisdom that you know. Many of us have sat in church for years and years. We have heard good preaching. We have read good books. We have *good sense*! Yet, we haven't been *passionate* enough to *pursue* every word we have received. Our *action* hasn't been equal to the level of our *revelation*. The widow *fully* acted upon the amount of revelation she received. She was *diligent*. Diligence is *swift, insistence upon completion of an assigned task in an excellent manner*. The widow had to believe that once she borrowed the pots and she and her sons filled them, it would bring deliverance. She had to keep that vision in front of her. In verse 7, she came to the man of God. She had finished the first part of the instruction or vision. She maintained her *focus* until that point. In 2 Kings 4:7, we read:

> Then she came and told the man of God. And he said, Go, sell the oil, and pay thy debt, and live thou and thy children of the rest.

The widow had to have a clear focus in her mind. She had to believe that the oil would *sell*! She was going back to many of the same neighbors she had borrowed the *empty* pots from. Now she would be selling them their *own* pots back *filled with oil*! She had to have a clear focus that they would *buy* the oil. She had to have focus of her outcome that she was going to make enough money to pay her debt. She had to see in her mind that this plan and her efforts would deliver her sons from slavery. She had to keep her *future* before her. She had to *Fight for Focus*!

THREE ENEMIES TO *FOCUS*: THE *FLESH*, THE *WORLD*, AND THE *DEVIL*

ENEMY NUMBER ONE: THE *FLESH*

One of the main ways to *Fight for Focus* is to *meditate* the Word of God. The widow had to meditate the Word which Elisha the prophet spoke to her. She had to see it clearly through *focus*. Let's look at Psalms 1:1–3 as we get another witness regarding the *fight for focus*. We will see the *blessing* that will come as a result of *winning* the fight. Again, the main enemies to *Focus* are 1) the flesh, 2) the world and 3) the devil. But let's look at Psalms 1:1–3, and we will see a person who *wins* the fight. They do it through gaining a mental picture of a divine oracle from God. They have a clear picture on the inside and they pursue it with *Passion*. The Bible says this person will succeed and prosper.

> *Blessed is the man that walketh not in the counsel of the ungodly, nor standeth in the way of sinners, nor sitteth in the seat of the scornful. But his delight is in the law of the Lord; and in his law doth he meditate day and night. And he shall be like a tree planted by the rivers of water, that bringeth forth his fruit in his season; his leaf also shall not wither; and whatsoever he doeth shall prosper.*
> –Psalms 1:1-3

So, we see, the flesh does not capture this blessed person. This person is not *captured by the world*, and this person is not *captured by the devil*, because they will not *entertain* the flesh. They will not entertain the flesh of the *ungodly*. When I say "flesh," I mean the *fallen nature* of man. All that is *evil* or *base*. Galatians 5:19–21 lets us know what is the nature of the flesh, while verses 22–23 inform us of the "fruit" of our born-again *spirit*. This is what it says:

> *Now the works of the flesh are manifest, which are these; Adultery, fornication, uncleanness, lasciviousness, Idolatry, witchcraft, hatred, variance, emulations, wrath, strife, seditions, heresies, Envyings, murders, drunkenness, revellings, and such like: of the which I tell you before, as I have also told you in time past, that they which do such things shall not inherit the kingdom of God. But the fruit of the Spirit is love, joy, peace, longsuffering, gentleness, goodness, faith, meekness, temperance: against such there is no law. And they that are Christ's have crucified the flesh with the affections and lust.*

YOUR WEALTH IS IN YOUR ANOINTING

So again going back to Psalms 1:1–3 we see that this person does not allow their flesh to become *entrapped*. They also do not give *room* to the devil. They avoid his traps. In other words, this person is not receiving the images and counsel of the ungodly into their minds. *If you receive the images and counsel of the world, it will break your godly focus.* Again, Psalms 1:1–3 says,

> *Blessed is the man that walketh not in the counsel of the ungodly, nor standeth in the way of sinners, nor sitteth in the seat of the scornful. But his delight is in the law of the Lord; and in his law doth he meditate day and night. And he shall be like a tree planted by the rivers of water, that bringeth forth his fruit in his season; his leaf also shall not wither; and whatsoever he doeth shall prosper.*

It says "his *delight* is in the law of the Lord." When you *delight* in something it means you take *joy* in it! The Word of God became this *blessed* person's *focus*. Again, Proverbs 29:18 says, "Where there is no vision, the people perish: but he that keepeth the law, happy is he." Therefore, much of *Passion* has to do with *happiness*. When you are passionate about pursuing the vision, which God has for your life, you are *happy*! You have a joyful expectation that the promise will be *fulfilled*. Even when circumstances look different on the outside compared to what you see on the inside, you are still *happy*. If you truly have a clear focused vision inside, you can stay happy. You can *press forward* in spite of circumstances. You can press past what people say or do. You can press past your own contrary feelings. You can press past the lies of Satan telling you that you won't make it. No matter what the world says through television. No matter what the news report says. You can happily pursue what God has for you if you have a *vision*. Proverbs 29:18 says, "Where there is no vision, the people perish: but he that keepeth the law, happy is he." One way you stay happy is by meditating the law of God. You must meditate it until you *catch a vision*! Psalms 1:1–3 says,

> *Blessed is the man that walketh not in the counsel of the ungodly, nor standeth in the way of sinners, nor sitteth in the seat of the scornful. But his delight is in the law of the Lord; and in his law doth he meditate day and night. And he shall be like a tree planted by the rivers of water, that bringeth forth his fruit in his season; his leaf also shall not wither; and whatsoever he doeth shall prosper.*

It says this person's delight is in the law of the Lord. When you delight in something, it means you are happy. You are *thrilled*!

We looked earlier at the first component of *Passion*, the *Joy of Pursuit*! When you catch a vision and can passionately pursue it, you have joy. Psalms 1:2 says, "But his delight is in the law of the Lord; and in his law doth he meditate day and night." Proverbs 29:18 says, "Where there is no vision, the people perish: but he that keepeth the law, happy is he." Again, Psalms 1:2 says, "But his delight is in the law of the Lord; and in his law doth he meditate day and night." Therefore, the way to catch a vision of what God says is to "meditate" His Word "day and night."

The woman with the pot of oil had to meditate the vision, which the prophet spoke to her, in order for her to pursue it. In order for her to sell the oil, she had to gather the pots; she and her sons had to pour the oil into the pots; and she had to go out to sell the pots. To get out of debt, and have enough for her and her sons to live on for the rest of her life, the widow had to have a *vision*. She had to *Fight for Focus*. She had to have *Passion*! Psalms 1:3 says,

> And he shall be like a tree planted by the rivers of water, that bringeth forth his fruit in his season; his leaf also shall not wither; and whatsoever he doeth shall prosper.

"Whatsoever he doeth shall prosper!" So, when you *fight the good fight of faith*— which is the *Fight for Focus*—you will succeed! That's what it is. It is the *good fight of faith*. Why? You have *already won* the *fight* in Christ Jesus. **Your wealth is in your anointing**! Your victory is in your connection with the victorious Lamb of God. As He is seated in the heavens on the right hand side of God the Father, so are we in the earth. He sits crowned with full victory over the flesh, the world, the devil, death, hell, and the grave. You have that victory. Therefore, we have already defeated the three main enemies to our *Focus*. Those enemies are 1) the flesh, 2) the world, and 3) the devil. Concerning the flesh Galatians 2:20 and 5:24–25 says this:

> I am crucified with Christ: nevertheless I live; yet not I, but Christ liveth in me: and the life which I now live in the flesh I live by the faith of the Son of God, who loved me, and gave himself for me. And they that are Christ's have crucified the flesh with the affections and lusts. If we live in the Spirit, let us also walk in the Spirit.

The Apostle Paul also admonishes us with these words in Rom. 6:11–14:

> Likewise reckon ye also yourselves to be dead indeed unto sin, but alive unto God through Jesus Christ our Lord. Let not sin therefore reign in your mortal body, that ye should obey it in the lusts thereof. Neither yield ye your members as instruments of unrighteousness unto sin: but yield yourselves unto God, as those that are alive from the dead, and your members as instruments of righteousness unto God. For sin shall not have dominion over you: for ye are not under the law, but under grace.

So we see, as the "instruments of righteousness" of God, we are dead to sin. We are dead to the rule of the flesh over us. We don't have to be controlled by sin, habits, attitudes, hang-ups, or laziness. We have power to override these temptations to our *Focus*.

ENEMY NUMBER TWO: THE *WORLD*

In regard to the world, we have power over its influence. There is a *spirit* in the world that is trying to take over each of us. It is an ungodly, *antichrist* spirit. Many do not think about it. Many believers go along their merry-way, unconscious of it. We just go along unaware that there is a spirit in the world *fighting for your focus*. It is attempting to steal your *soul*. I say your soul, because your soul consists of your mind, will, and emotions. It consists of your personality, your likes and dislikes, and your disposition. The spirit that is in the world is attempting to *shape* you into its image. If you are born again, your spirit belongs to God. You are hid in Christ Jesus. However, your *soul* is vulnerable to impressions. Either you will diligently choose what you focus on, or the world will.

Regarding the spirit of the world, 1 John 2:15–18 has this to say:

> Love not the world, neither the things that are in the world. If any man love the world, the love of the Father is not in him. For all that is in the world, the lust of the flesh, and the lust of the eyes, and the pride of life, is not of the Father, but is of the world. And the world passeth away, and the lust thereof: but he that doeth the will of God abideth for ever. Little children, it is the last time: and as ye have heard that antichrist shall come, even now are there many antichrists; whereby we know that it is the last time.

If you look at all that the world has to offer on the television, the news, music, movies, commercials, etc., you will see "the lust of the flesh, and lust of the eyes, and the pride of life." This is not of the Father, but of the world. Each of these areas is part of the world's way to conform you and me into its image. It is the spirit of the world. God calls it an *antichrist* spirit, because it is *against* Christ. It is against the Spirit of God. It is against love. It is against decency. It is against righteousness. It is against your life. It is against freedom. It is against you and your ability to be who God made you to be. The antichrist spirit that is in the world *fights against your focus*. It distorts your vision of yourself. It fights against your vision of God. It fights against your vision of success in and through Christ. It attempts to dilute the power of the anointing in your life.

PASSION–THE 3RD ESSENTIAL KEY

So how do you *Fight for your Focus* in regard to the antichrist spirit? The antichrist spirit is an "anti-anointing" spirit. That is the spirit of the world. It is a spirit of man under the influence of *self* and Satan. It is mankind's rejection of the *presence* of God. It is mankind's independent spirit to succeed *without* God. That independent spirit to succeed without God is not really *independent*. Man not depending on God will be subject to the *other* spirit that is in the world. It is the spirit of Satan. Satan is the impetus of the antichrist spirit. The antichrist spirit is mankind trying to succeed or rule without God. It is mankind without the Anointed One and His Anointing—Christ Jesus.

OVERCOMING THE INFLUENCES OF THE WORLD

How do you and I overcome the influences of the world? Romans 12:1–3 tells us how:

> *I beseech you therefore, brethren, by the mercies of God, that ye present your bodies a living sacrifice, holy, acceptable unto God, which is your reasonable service. And be not conformed to this world: but be ye transformed by the renewing of your mind, that ye may prove what is that good, and acceptable, and perfect, will of God. For I say, through the grace given unto me, to every man that is among you, not to think of himself more highly than he ought to think; but to think soberly, according as God hath dealt to every man the measure of faith.*

In the *Fight for Focus*, first of all, we have to discipline our *bodies*. We have to give our bodies unto fulfilling God's plan for us. He wants us to prosper and succeed. He wants us to fulfill His perfect will for our lives. However, in order to do that, we have to be *disciplined*. We can't live any kind of way we want to live. We have to sacrifice our fleshly, natural will or desire, in order to obtain God's will. In fulfilling God's purpose and will for our lives, we will be happy and fulfilled. We have to sacrifice in our eating habits. We have to sacrifice in our money and spending habits. We have to sacrifice in the attitude we allow. We have to live a holy, sanctified life unto the Lord. We must live ever-conscious of and obedient to God. The Apostle Paul says it is "our reasonable service" in light of the mercy we have received from God. In other words, it just makes *sense*. "Reasonable" means it *makes sense*. It is the *logical* or *rational* response to God for setting us free from sin, death, and the world.

Verse 2 of Romans 12 tells us how to live this life free from the world's spirit. Again, it says,

YOUR WEALTH IS IN YOUR ANOINTING

> *And be not conformed to this world: but be ye transformed by the renewing of your mind, that ye may prove what is that good, and acceptable, and perfect, will of God.*

In other words, "do not allow the world to *press* you into its mold." Do not allow the pressure of the antichrist spirit to press you into its mold. The antichrist spirit of the world is an anti-anointing spirit. The spirit of the world opposes and attempts to live independent of God.

"Be not conformed to this world." The word *conformed* used in this verse has this meaning:

CONFORMED
4964–suschematizo
1. to fashion alike
2. to conform to the same pattern
3. fashion yourself according to
   –*Strong's Exhaustive Concordance of the Bible*

The Apostle Paul admonishes us not to be *fashioned* like the world. Do not conform ourselves to the same *pattern* of the world. Do not live our lives according to the fashion of the world. Do not conduct our marriages according to the fashion of the world. Don't listen to their advice. Don't take your counsel from the popular talk shows, magazines, movies, and sitcoms. Do not raise your children according to the fashion of a godless society. Raise your children with morality according to the Bible, not local or national politics. It may not be politically correct to despise and reject acceptance of what the Bible calls sin, such as homosexuality and lesbianism. However, God does not accept or approve that behavior as His natural plan for men and women. He calls it sin. Be not conformed to the world's thinking regarding sin and infidelity. God calls sex before marriage and adultery, sin. He does not accept it. He does not condone it. He will judge all sin. Be not conformed to the politicians view if they believe in killing innocent babies through abortion. It is *diabolical*. God hates murder. Be not conformed to the world.

How do we keep from being conformed? By being *transformed*. Read verse 2 of Romans 12 again:

> *And be not conformed to this world: but be ye transformed by the renewing of your mind, that he may prove, what is that good, and acceptable, and perfect, will of God.*

God tells us to be renewed in our minds. That is how we will be transformed into His perfect image. We will be able to fulfill His good, acceptable, and perfect will for us. The transformation comes by meditating His Word until you obtain a vision for what He is saying to you. You must *Fight for your Focus* passionately in order to fulfill God's plan for your life.

The woman with the pot of oil had to passionately *Fight for Focus* in order to obtain her financial deliverance. We have to *Fight for Focus* in order to obtain ours. If you do not passionately *Fight to maintain Focus*, you will never obtain what God has for you. Without *Focus*, you will not obtain the vision for your life. "Where there is no vision, the people perish: but he that keepeth the law, happy is he" (Proverbs 29:18).

ENEMY NUMBER THREE: THE *DEVIL*

As mentioned before, the third enemy in the *Fight for Focus* is the *devil*. The devil is always there, whispering, trying to put perceptions in your mind. The late actor and comedian Flip Wilson used to say, "The devil made me do it!" However, the devil can't *make* you do anything. He can *deceive* you. As I mentioned before, he didn't make Eve eat that fruit. He *deceived* her and presented to her the image that she was missing out on something, and she ate it. She didn't have the right *focus*. Adam had not made the focus of God's Word clear enough in her mind. Neither did he have it clear enough in his head of who he was. He didn't have it clear enough that he was made in the "image and likeness of God," and that they were already "the gods of the earth" (Psalms 82:6). The devil told them they would be *like God* if they ate the fruit. However, they were already *like God*. They were made in the image and likeness of God in the earth. And that's what the devil does; he creates *perceptions* in our minds.

The devil will make you feel like you are broke and barely making it, when in reality you are blessed. If you are blessed, but the devil has put a perception in your mind that you are barely getting along and that you are not blessed—even though you are blessed—you will forfeit the blessing of your blessed place because you will *act poor*. He will also make you feel like you are not doing anything or making any progress on your journey of faith. The devil tries to make you feel like you're losing, when in fact, you're winning as long as you keep fulfilling God's principles in His Word. We must continue to renew our minds to God's Word, in order to stay impervious to the lies of Satan.

THE 3ᴿᴰ COMPONENT OF *PASSION*:
OVERCOMING THE FRUSTRATION OF PERSEVERANCE

Now we are going to look at the third component of *Passion*, *Overcoming the Frustration of Perseverance*. A lot of times people wonder: "Why is it taking so long? God gave me a promise. There's a prophecy over my life. God's Word says this or that about my life. God says I'm the head and not tail. God says I'm above only and not beneath. I've sown my seed. I've prayed. I'm living a righteous life. Why is it taking so long?" And they're frustrated. Maybe they have an idea or concept, but it seems like it is not coming to pass. It seems like it's taking *so* long.

Well, a lot of times it's because God will not allow you to get into something you can't handle. If you can't handle it, God will not release it to you. If you can't handle a $100,000-a-year business, or a $1 million-a-year business, God won't put one in your hand. And literally, nothing is just *put in your hand*. If you are to obtain a $100,000-a-year business, you will have to put the *sweat* and *effort* into making it happen.

If you can't handle just paying your bills on time, and managing your own home and your own affairs, why would God trust you with a $100,000-a-year business. If you are not doing what's necessary to manage your current income, why would He entrust you with more? God blesses us in *increments*. He graduates us from *glory to glory, strength to strength*, and *faith to faith*. He blesses us with a certain amount and gives us an opportunity to grow that through wisdom and faithfulness. We are called to be *good stewards*. Matthew 25:14–30 tells the story of how God entrusts us with a certain amount according to our *abilities* and *inclinations*. He then grants us *time* and *grace* to increase what He has *invested* in us. It takes time to bring it to the place of increase. However, if we are *passionate* and if we have the right attitude we will be rewarded with more through our efforts. God's grace and favor will add His *super* to our *natural*. **Your wealth is in your anointing**. Now let's read Matthew 25:14–30:

> *For the kingdom of heaven is as a man travelling into a far country, who called his own servants, and delivered unto them his goods. And*

PASSION—THE 3RD ESSENTIAL KEY

> unto one he gave five talents, to another two, and to another one; to every man according to his several ability; and straightway took his journey. Then he that had received the five talents went and traded with the same, and made them other five talents. And likewise he that had received two, he also gained other two. But he that had received one went and digged in the earth, and hid his lord's money. After a long time the lord of those servants cometh, and reckoneth with them.

[Listen to when Jesus says, "After a long time…" We are talking about *Passion* and *Overcoming the Frustration of Perseverance*.]

> And so he that had received five talents came and brought other five talents, saying, Lord, thou deliveredst unto me five talents: behold, I have gained beside them five talents more. His lord said unto him, Well done, thou good and faithful servant: thou hast been faithful over a few things, I will make thee ruler over many things: enter thou into the joy of thy lord. He also that had received two talents came and said, Lord, thou deliveredst unto me two talents: behold, I have gained two other talents beside them. His lord said unto him, Well done, good and faithful servant; thou hast been faithful over a few things, I will make thee ruler over many things: enter thou into the joy of thy lord. Then he which had received the one talent came and said, Lord, I knew thee that thou art an hard man, reaping where thou hast not sown, and gathering where thou hast not strawed: And I was afraid, and went and hid thy talent in the earth: lo, there thou hast that is thine. His lord answered and said unto him, Thou wicked and slothful servant, thou knewest that I reap where I sowed not, and gather where I have not strawed: Thou oughtest therefore to have put my money to the exchangers, and then at my coming I should have received mine own with usury. Take therefore the talent from him, and give it unto him which hath ten talents. For unto every one that hath shall be given, and he shall have abundance: but from him that hath not shall be taken away even that which he hath. And cast ye the unprofitable servant into outer darkness: there shall be weeping and gnashing of teeth.

First of all, let's define a "talent." A talent is a denomination of money. A talent in this verse was worth $384,000. Therefore, the servant that received one talent had received $384,000. The servant that received two talents had received $768,000. And the servant that had received five talents had received $1,920,000. This is representative of the natural *gifts* and *talents* that God has *invested* in each of us. Each of our talents has *monetary* value. As we invest in, improve, and use our gifts and talents, their value increases. Our finances will also increase according to the use of our talents. As our finances increase, so will our level of influence and dominion in God's kingdom on the earth. The more responsible we are with what we already have, the more God will commit to us.

Each of the servants was entrusted with talents according to their *individual ability*. God expected them to use them and invest the talents in order to gain increase. God gave you and me talents to *use*, to gain increase and dominion in the earth. His original plan has been for you and me to have dominion. Genesis 1:26–28 tells us God's *original* plan:

> And God said, Let us make man in our image, after our likeness: and let them have dominion over the fish of the sea, and over the fowl of the air, and over the cattle, and over all the earth, and over every creeping thing that creepeth upon the earth. So God created man in his own image, in the image of God created he him; male and female created he them. And God blessed them, and God said unto them, Be fruitful, and multiply, and replenish the earth, and subdue it: and have dominion over the fish of the sea, and over the fowl of the air, and over every living that moveth upon the earth.

Therefore, "dominion" was God's original plan for us. He wants us to increase and multiply financially through the use of our gifts and talents. As we do, we will gain greater dominion and influence in the earth.

Here are some *solutions* to being *frustrated* while you *wait* for your wealthy place.

WHILE WE *WAIT*...

Notice that in Matthew 25:14–30, each of the servants were waiting for further increase and reward. However, the servant with "one talent" gave up without even *trying*. He didn't *use* what he had. The other two servants kept *using* what they had and "multiplied" it. (Genesis 1:28)

That which they multiplied wasn't their *final* reward. That wasn't their final harvest. Their final harvest was to share in the "dominion" and reigning joy of their lord. That's what we are to be focused on. It's not just in heaven. It starts on earth. However, the servants had to be "faithful over a little" before the lord released to them more. It took *time*. Waiting can be *frustrating*. However, if you *stay busy* on your assigned task, it will take the frustration out of waiting. Staying focused

PASSION—THE 3RD ESSENTIAL KEY

and busy and *passionate* about your assigned task, through using your gifts and talents, will take the *frustration* out of *perseverance*.

If you *trust* in the *character* of your Lord, and trust that He will *come through* on His Word, and if you trust that He will reward you for "diligently seeking to please Him" (Hebrews 11:6), you won't be frustrated and you won't *forfeit* your reward like the "unprofitable" servant did.

Let's look at Hebrews 11:6, Hebrews 10:35–36, and Isaiah 40:28–31:

> But without faith it is impossible to please him: for he that cometh to God must believe that he is, and that he is a rewarder of them that diligently seek him.
>
> —Hebrews 11:6

God is only "pleased" through our faith. We have to stay in faith and keep *advancing* toward the *hope* He has placed in our hearts. The unprofitable servant displeased his lord because he didn't even *try* to be profitable. He was in *unbelief*! We have to believe that *God is*, and that He is a *rewarder* of them that *diligently* seek Him. We have to keep advancing in faith. Keep our *vision* in front of us and know that God is *faithful*. If He did it for others, He will do it for you. He is "the same yesterday, today, and forever" (Hebrews 13:8). This is how we deal with *Overcoming the Frustration of Perseverance*. Keep our vision in front of us and keep passionately pursuing it in faith.

Hebrews 10:35–36 also tells us to stay in faith. God is a *rewarder*. This is what it says:

> Cast not away therefore your confidence, which hath great recompence of reward. For ye have need of patience, that, after ye have done the will of God, ye might receive the promise.

This passage is letting us know that we have to *stay in faith*. We have to have patience and persevere. We can't *cast away* or *abandon* our faith. We can't *abandon our dream*. We can't *abandon our vision*. We can't *abandon our hope*! Hebrews 11:1–2 says,

> Now faith is the substance of things hoped for, the evidence of things not seen. For by it the elders obtained a good report.

We have to stay in faith. We can't abandon our hope. Our hope is what gives our faith a *reason*. We must passionately pursue our *hope* in faith. We can't abandon our hope. If you abandon your hope, you abandon your faith. Only through faith is God pleased or satisfied with us. God wants to be *believed*. We must believe that He is faithful, and that He is a rewarder of those that diligently seek Him. Therefore, Hebrews 10:35–36 again tells us,

> Cast not away therefore your confidence, which hath great recompence of reward. For ye have need of patience, that, after ye have done the will of God, ye might receive the promise.

Our faith and confidence has a "great . . . reward" attached to it. God will *pay you back* for all the frustration and pain you have experienced attempting to obtain your promise. He has seen your *struggle*. He will reward you. However, we have to do the things that are *requisite* for the reward.

WE MUST *PLAY BY THE RULES*

God always *plays fair*. He always abides by His *rules*. He has certain *rules for success* in life. We have to play by those rules. If we stay in faith, and play by God's rules, we will get God's rewards. God is no *respecter of persons*. He is a *respecter of faith*. If it worked for someone else, it will work for you. Turn to 2 Timothy 2:5. This is what it says about our requirements for obtaining our reward:

> And if a man also strive for masteries, yet is he not crowned, except he strive lawfully.

In other words, we won't obtain our reward if we don't do what's necessary. We have to meet the requirements. We have to play by the rules. God wants us to obtain *mastery* in life. He wants us to wear the *crown* of dominion in the earth. That's what He said in the beginning, in Genesis 1:26–28. But what exactly is mastery? Let's define that word. In *Webster's New World Dictionary*, this is what it means:

1. mastership
2. ascendancy or victory; the upper-hand
3. expert skill or knowledge.

It is based on the word "master," which is defined like this:

1. a man who rules others or has control, authority, or power over something; specif., a) a man who is head of a household or institution b) an employer c) a victor

PASSION–THE 3RD ESSENTIAL KEY

2. a person very skilled in some work, profession, etc.; expert; specif., a) a highly skilled workman qualified to follow his trade independently

So you see mastery speaks of qualifications. It speaks of someone who has become *qualified to reign*. We say we want to *rule* and be in *authority*; however, many of us have not *qualified* ourselves to rule. We were born to *rule*. We were *born again* to *reign*. However, we must gain mastery over *ourselves* first. We must master our *time*. We must master our *emotions*. We must master our *tongue*. We must master our *wills* and put our will and body under subjection to Jesus. Jesus is the *Great Master*. We must submit ourselves to Him. As we do, we will be qualified to enter into greater *mastery* in life.

We also must focus on mastering the *dream* God has put in our hearts. We must master our *area*. This is the only way we will obtain the *crown* that was *predestined* for us. As we continually strive for the crowns of obedience, we will be relieved of the *Frustration of Perseverance*. We must be passionately focused on the crowns God has in front of us.

What is one of those crowns? Turn to Proverbs 14:23–24. It lets us know that there is great reward in our *labor*. There is *great reward* in our *perseverance*. The reward is a "crown" we all want and need. This is what it says:

> In all labour there is profit: but the talk of the lips tendeth only to penury. The crown of the wise is their riches: but the foolishness of fools is folly.

This is letting us know the only way to get the "crown" of "riches." It is through "labor." Those who *talk* and don't *do* are considered "foolish." That will lead only to poverty. "Penury" means poverty.

We must keep *applying* ourselves. This is how we deal with *Overcoming the Frustration of Perseverance*."

GOD WILL *STRENGTHEN* YOU WHILE YOU *WAIT*

Isaiah 40:28–30 gives us these encouraging words. It teaches us about perseverance and waiting on God:

> Hast thou not known? hast thou not heard, that the everlasting God, the Lord, the Creator of the ends of the earth, fainteth not, neither is weary? there is no searching of his understanding. He giveth power to

> the faint; and to them that have no might he increaseth strength. Even the youths shall faint and be weary, and the young men shall utterly fall: But they that wait upon the Lord shall renew their strength; they shall mount up with wings as eagles; they shall run, and not be weary; and they shall walk, and not faint.

So this is letting us know that God is our *strengthener*. He strengthens us as we patiently wait on Him. As we *persevere* in faith. As we continue to *push forward* toward the prize and the "crown." He strengthens us and renews our strength. However, one of the ways for obtaining that continual strength is through "waiting" on Him. What does that mean? "Waiting" on Him means to stay *actively involved* in accomplishing the goal He gave you. It means *serving* Him by obeying His assignment for you. It is *specific*. It is not just *anything* you want to do.

When a *waiter* or *server* at a restaurant comes to your table, you want them to carry out the *specific* assignment you asked of them. If you ask for cranberry juice with no ice, then, that's what you want. If you ask for your steak medium-well, then, that's what you want. Well, God has a specific assignment and instructions for you and me. That's what He wants. He wants us to be focused on fulfilling His plan for our lives. We must have *Passion* to pursue that *Purpose* even when it *takes time*. It *always* takes time. However, as we gain *mastery* over ourselves, our gifts, talents, ability, purpose, assignment, and skill, God will then bring us to the place of reward.

The widow with the pot of oil had to stay *passionate*. She had to fight through *Overcoming the Frustration of Perseverance* in order to obtain the *profit* from her *oil*. She had to obey the *specific instructions* given to her by the man of God, Elisha the prophet. As she did, she was able to obtain her *personal wealth*. She was able to redeem her sons from the threat of slavery. She and her children were able to have *more than enough* to live on for the rest of her life.

Let's continue examining how we can *overcome the frustration of perseverance*. It is an essential element of *Passion*, the third Essential Key to the *release* of the anointing within you.

USE WHAT YOU'VE GOT!

As you and I increase in knowledge, skill, and exercising faithfulness in what we already have, constantly adding to our knowledge, we will

PASSION–THE 3RD ESSENTIAL KEY

see the *waiting time* decrease. It is one thing to have faith, but we have to *add knowledge* to it. And as we do, God can *graduate* us to the next level. God doesn't want you to put your dependence on winning the lottery and then say, "Oh! I'm rich!" and then be poor again in less than two years later, back in poverty, owing more money than you did before you won the lottery. *That's* why it takes *time*. God is about *deliverance*. He is committed to you and your family's complete deliverance from poverty. Deliverance starts *internally*.

So, yes it is *frustrating*. The *waiting*. However, *we're not waiting on God*. God wants you to be rich *today*! He wanted you to be *born rich*! God wanted you to be rich when you were stepping out of high school. He wanted you to be going into your business. God wanted you to be going into college and preparing for your *wealthy place*. He wanted you to have the ability to be able to step into your business early on. He wanted you to get the training when you were a child on how to manage money and how to start a business. God wanted that for you.

However, the waiting and frustration of perseverance is not so much waiting on God, but God *waiting on you*. It's God *waiting on us*.

I've noticed that every new blessing, triumph, or accomplishment in my life wasn't because God *came down* from heaven to do it. *I did it.* I did something. In graduating college, I went to class. I *studied* for those tests. I *passed* the tests. I had favor on my efforts. He put His *super* on my natural. He gave me favor. He gave me *preferential* treatment or leniency where I needed it. I had favor with *God* and *man*. I had favor with the instructors. I had favor with my wife to cooperate with me in finishing my education and starting a business. However, I studied the Word. I prepared myself to be able to do the things I have been able to do. And I believe if each of us, who have been blessed in any kind of way, would testify, we could see the effort that went into obtaining a blessing. We know we had something to do with it.

I thank God for *miracles*. But even miracles have a *cause*. We're not called to *live by miracles*. We are called to *live by faith*. We are to live in *continual abundance*. That life is based on *eternal, universal principals*.

Perseverance can be frustrating in the passionate pursuit of *Purpose* because there is a *learning curve*. We also have to *fight the flesh*. We looked earlier at the *Fight for Focus* as a component of *Passion*. We looked at the *flesh* as being one of the *three main enemies* in the *Fight for Focus*. The

113

flesh, the *world*, and the *devil* are the three main enemies in our fight of faith. Therefore, you know, "If I'm going to have this, I will have to *work hard* for this"; yet, it's a fight. That fight can be frustrating. Yet, we must *persevere*.

STEPS TO OVERCOMING *FRUSTRATION*

Perseverance is a little different than *patience*. Perseverance is like a *wrestling match*! It's a wrestling match against the *resistance* in your situation. You're wrestling with the *flesh* in many cases. You're wrestling with your *mind* to *keep hope alive*. You're wrestling to stay passionate even when it seems you're not making the progress you would like to make. It's *Overcoming* the *Frustration of Perseverance*. However, if you fully understand the process, it will be easier.

You must obtain an *ordered* life. You must obtain a *plan* for your *Purpose*. This can take the frustration out of persevering. We've talked about *Focus* as being one of the Essential Keys to the *release* of the anointing within you. If you have a clear plan and *picture* in your mind, and realize and accept that it's going to take time, you can be relieved of frustration. If for instance, you know it's going to take *five years* to get where you want to be, you will be more *accepting* and less frustrated. You will also see that it will take a predetermined amount of *steps* during that five-year process. As you *commit* to that *series of steps* to get you to the final destination five-years from now, it will take frustration out of perseverance. You have had time to *evaluate* it. You have already *processed* it, because you now realize the time it takes and the *steps* are just a *part of the course*. You also know that there are others who have taken these same steps and have gotten the *outcome* you desire. You accept that if you take the same steps as others, having equal or superior intelligence and ability as others, you can have the same outcome or better in your own life.

It's just like a college student going to college for the first time. First, if the student is a studious person who is excited about learning, they are happy just to get into college. However, if they have a full understanding and proper advisement during their process and before starting classes, the advisor explains to them what is required. The advisor tells them, "It takes this particular set of classes. You need to join this particular club along the way. You should try to get an internship by this time in the process." Why? Because this is going to help the student in dealing with *Overcoming* the *Frustration of Perseverance* as their *passion* for school is *tested* because it's taking a *long time*. However, in reality, it's taking the *prescribed amount of time* it takes to get that particular degree. And if we are committed to being excellent and faithful at each step, we won't have to be frustrated.

We must have our *long-term* goal ahead of us. We must have a clear focus and picture of it. However, to take the frustration out of perseverance, we must let our energies be applied toward fulfilling the *next step*. Excel on the next step *in front of you*. Know what the required steps are, and *focus on each step*. This is how you will always be successful. This will take the frustration out of the steps. You can always look back on your successes and say:

I was successful on the last step. I can succeed on this step.

I was successful during the last class. I can succeed in this one.

I was successful on the last job. I can succeed in this one.

God blessed me with the last house. He will bless me with this one.

I was successful in finishing the last book I read. I can finish reading this one.

I was successful to go to that last seminar. I will be successful to go to the next one.

Therefore, you are doing what's necessary *step*, by *step*, by *step*. This takes the frustration out of perseverance. You are realizing that it's just a part of the course. You now can maintain your *Passion* in pursuing your *Purpose*.

REVIEW OF THE COMPONENTS OF *PASSION*

Let's review the components of *Passion* we've discussed so far. *Passion* is the third Essential Key to the *release* of the anointing within you. Remember that the first Essential Key is *Focus*. You must be focused enough to see clearly what you have. You must see what your life is about and what you really have.

The second Essential Key to the *release* of the anointing within you is *Purpose*. You have to focus long enough to actually see your *Purpose*. *Why am I here? What did God give me? What's my Purpose?*

YOUR WEALTH IS IN YOUR ANOINTING

Now we've been looking at the third Essential Key to the release of the anointing within you—*Passion*. *Passion* has four components. The first is the *Joy of Pursuit*! You have to have *joy* in pursuing a thing. You have to be excited! You have to be *enthusiastic*! This is an Essential Key to the *release* of the anointing within you. In order to get out of you what God put in you, you have to enthusiastically pursue what He gave you. It's not going to just come to you. You have to be *happy* about it! You have to get up in the morning with it on your mind. This is the *Joy of Pursuit*! You get up in the morning thinking about it. You stay up at night reading about it. The *Joy of Pursuit* is the first component of *Passion*.We also looked at the second component of *Passion*, which is the *Fight for Focus*.

Even when you gain your *Focus*, you have to *Fight for your Focus*. You have to *maintain your focus* from the distractions. There are three main enemies to your *Focus*. First of all, it is going to be the *flesh*. It will be either your flesh or somebody else's flesh. It will try to distract you from pursuing what God has for you. Your feelings, moods, appetite, or your "not feeling like it"; discouragement, doubt, or disappointment; all of these things in the flesh can war against your *Passion*. These can war against your *Focus*. Or, it can be somebody else's flesh through wrong interactions. Proverbs teaches us that your *associations will determine your location*. It says literally, "He that walks with wise men shall be wise; but a companion of fools shall be destroyed" (Proverbs 13:20).

You've heard the saying, "Birds of a feather, flock together." The entirety of that saying is "Birds of a feather, flock together, and the flock usually ends up in the same place." If they are all flying South, they will all end up on that coast somewhere. They will follow one another all the way to the Horn of Africa—all the way across the world—and then they will turn around and do it all over again and follow one another back home.

"Birds of a feather, flock together; and the flock usually ends up in the same place." You must ask yourself, "Where's my flock going?" Or, "Am I a part of a flock?" Or rather, *"Am I an eagle?"*

You don't see flocks of eagles. And they fly higher than the other birds. When those little birds start to peck on them because they're flying in a lower atmosphere, all the eagle has to do is go up higher, and they leave the little birds below, because they can't breath in that higher, purer atmosphere. You need to be flying in an atmosphere that little birds (*little critics!*) can't soar in. God has something greater for you.

PASSION–THE 3RD ESSENTIAL KEY

So again, the first enemy to your *Fight for Focus* is going to be the flesh. Number two, the *world*. It is specifically, the world's negative environment: hearing the bad news, and seeing the negative images of the world, listening to music with negative messages. This is the world's image. That's why Romans 12:1–2 tells us these words:

> I beseech you therefore, brethren, by the mercies of God, that ye present your bodies a living sacrifice, holy, acceptable unto God, which is your reasonable service. And be not conformed to this world: but be ye transformed by the renewing of your mind, that ye may prove what is that good, and acceptable, and perfect, will of God.

You have to hear what God says. You have to renew your mind. Because, as God says in Isaiah 55:8–9:

> For my thoughts are not your thoughts, neither are your ways my ways, saith the Lord. For as the heavens are higher than the earth, so are my ways higher than your ways, and my thoughts than your thoughts.

Therefore, in order for you and me to walk *above* this world, and the "world-think," and the world's way, and the world's limitations, we have to open our minds and expose ourselves to a higher level of thinking. That's God's Word. It comes when you open God's Word and begin to read it. "So then faith comes by hearing, and hearing by the Word of God" (Romans 10:17). Elevated thinking also comes when the Word is preached to you. Therefore, the world is an enemy in the *Fight for Focus*.

The third enemy in the *Fight for Focus* is the *devil* seeking to put his perceptions in your mind. He is a master deceiver. We have to continually renew our minds to God's truth in order to resist and counteract Satan's tactics.

You must renew your mind to a *wealth mindset*.

If you can't see it on the *inside*, you can't receive it on the *outside*.

You could go into a job interview, and they could like you. They could want to give you the job. They could need you on that job, but if you feel like you don't deserve the job, or that you can't do the job, or that *they don't want to give me the job*; you could sabotage your own opportunity by your *internal chatter*. It is the perception. That's how the devil steals from us. He steals from us through perceptions in the mind.

Things can be one way, but the devil will give you a perception that it's different. Someone could like you or love you, but the devil can put another perception in your mind. There are relationships that are never

YOUR WEALTH IS IN YOUR ANOINTING

pursued, friendships that are never pursued, and business relationships that are never pursued, because of people's perception.

People will stop talking to one another—including families, brothers and sisters, mothers and daughters, best friends—because of a word during a conversation, based on a perception; and it could be years and years before they will speak to one another again. And then, they get together after a longtime, maybe through something happening, such as a funeral or someone getting sick, and then the truth is revealed that it was only a wrong perception between the two people that divided them for so many years. Five, ten, or twenty years of those relationships can be wasted because of a perception. Therefore, we have to keep the Word of God at the center of our life, and *Fight for Focus*.

We've been looking at *Passion*, the third Essential Key to understanding that **your wealth is in your anointing**. Now, we are going to look at the most important component of *Passion*. This fourth and final component of *Passion* is what makes everything come together. That component is the *Fight to Finish*!

PASSION–THE 3RD ESSENTIAL KEY

THE 4TH COMPONENT OF *PASSION*: THE *FIGHT TO FINISH*

MY TESTIMONY AND *FIGHT TO FINISH*

You can't just start a thing and not *Fight to Finish it*. As I was pursuing my MBA from Tennessee State University, I couldn't just start it . . . I had to *Fight to Finish*! The process was like this: I finished kindergarten. I remember graduating from kindergarten. I had the little robe on and the little cap. My mother has a picture of me when I graduated kindergarten. *I was looking good too*! I had my little Afro and my little graduation cap on. I graduated kindergarten.

Then I went on to elementary school. I think I even failed a grade in elementary school, but I kept on going. I finished elementary school.

I went on a little further, and I got into junior high school: *Paul L. Dunbar Middle School* in Mobile, Alabama. I fought to finish through there, and I finished junior high school.

I started high school for my first two years at Murphy High School in Mobile, Alabama. Then, my mother decided to move, and we moved to Oak Ridge, Tennessee. And, I finished my last two years of high school at Oak Ridge High School. I graduated high school.

Some of the students I was around from Oak Ridge High School started talking about college. That stirred me up. I said to myself, "I want further success." So, I got into Roane State Community College. I graduated Roane State Community College.

I had to *Fight to Finish* every step of the way. That was the first time that anyone in my immediate family had gone to college. My oldest brother and I were in Roane State together. Then, my younger brother went to a junior college. Even my mother began to attend Roane State, and my aunt. It was starting to catch on! *Fighting to Finish*. I went up to Zanesville, Ohio for a couple of years, and got into Ohio University. I worked as far as I could go before my mother and grandmother and I decided to move back to Nashville.

YOUR WEALTH IS IN YOUR ANOINTING

I hadn't finished. I wanted to finish. I started it. I started my bachelor's degree. But, I got some delays. I had sickness hit my body. I had some situations happen. But I had to keep *fighting*!

When I got back to Nashville, I said to myself, "I'm not quite ready to get back into a four year university right now." So what I decided to do was take a class or two. I took a class or two at Volunteer State Community College in Gallatin, Tennessee.

It seemed like I went *down a level*. I went down to the associates level again. I was trying to go up to the bachelor's level, but I said, "Let me just keep going." "Let me keep fighting." So, I kept fighting. I kept doing *something*.

I wasn't actively in my career, but I said, "I will *volunteer*." I volunteered on Volunteer State's local radio station. I did news, weather, and sports. They didn't have to pay me. I wasn't getting a grade for it. I just went up there and was on time every morning. And I did it. They gave me an opportunity to do it, and I did it. *Fighting to Finish*.

Then, the opportunity came for me to get back into a four-year university at Tennessee State University, and I finished my bachelor's degree. God blessed me to fight through that. There were days that I didn't feel like going. There were times I felt like quitting. I felt like I needed to make me some real money right now! I said, "I don't need to be in school. I'm a grown man. I need some real money in my pocket!"

But, I had to *Fight to Finish*! God helped me to finish with *honors*. I graduated with honors with my bachelor's degree in Speech Communication and Theater, with a Mass Media emphasis.

God then allowed me to get back into school to go forward and finish my MBA in Finance and Supply Chain Management.

What I'm conveying to you in telling my story is that it's a *fight* no matter what. I had dreams, visions, and goals, but in every step you have to *fight for it*.

The widow with the "pot of oil" had to carry out the *total plan* in order to get the deliverance. Let's read 2 Kings 4:1–7:

> *Now there cried a certain woman of the wives of the sons of the prophets unto Elisha, saying, Thy servant my husband is dead; and thou knowest that thy servant did fear the Lord: and the creditor is come to take unto him my two sons to be bondmen. And Elisha said unto her,*

PASSION–THE 3RD ESSENTIAL KEY

What shall I do for thee? tell me, what hast thou in the house? And she said, Thine handmaid hath not any thing in the house, save a pot of oil. Then he said, Go, borrow thee vessels abroad of all thy neighbours, even empty vessels; borrow not a few. And when thou art come in, thou shalt shut the door upon thee and upon thy sons, and shalt pour out into all those vessels, and thou shalt set aside that which is full. So she went from him, and shut the door upon her and upon her sons, who brought the vessels to her; and she poured out. And it came to pass, when the vessels were full, that she said unto her son, Bring me yet a vessel. And he said unto her, There is not a vessel more. And the oil stayed. Then she came and told the man of God. And he said, Go, sell the oil, and pay thy debt, and live thou and thy children of the rest.

Notice in verse 7, the man of God told the widow, "Go, sell the oil, and pay thy debt, and live thou and thy children of the rest."

The woman of God had finished the first part of the instruction that the man of God gave her. However, in order for her to gain financial deliverance she had to *Fight to Finish*.

That's the way it is with us. God may have given you a dream. God may have given you an idea. God may have given you a talent. God may have given you some type of *advantage* in order to get out of your situation. However, the only way for you to gain the advantage or profit or wealth from what God gave you is you have to *fight!*

EXAMPLES OF FINISHERS

SOLOMON: *A FINISHER*

We looked at all of the distractions that can come when you start trying to get out of your financial situation. We looked at the second component of *Passion*, which was the *Fight for Focus*. We also looked at *Overcoming the Frustration of Perseverance*. In order to obtain your goal, there is a process. However, if you don't finish, all your efforts may be in vain. Let's look at some examples of *finishers* in the Bible. Turn to Ecclesiastes 9:10–12. King Solomon was a *finisher*. He knew the crucial necessity of finishing what he started. Let's heed his words of advice and example.

YOUR WEALTH IS IN YOUR ANOINTING

> *Whatsoever thy hand findeth to do, do it with thy might; for there is no work, nor device, nor knowledge, nor wisdom, in the grave, whither thou goest. I returned, and saw under the sun, that the race is not to the swift, nor the battle to the strong, neither yet bread to the wise, nor yet riches to men of understanding, nor yet favour to men of skill; but time and chance happeneth to them all. For man also knoweth not his time: as the fishes that are taken in an evil net, and as the birds that are caught in the snare; so are the sons of men snared in an evil time, when it falleth suddenly upon them.*

Solomon lets us know that *life is short*. He says "whatever your hand finds to do, do it with your might; because there is *no work, nor device, nor knowledge, nor wisdom, in the grave,* where you are going."

Solomon goes on to say that "the race in life does not go to the fast, or the battle in life does not go to the strong, or bread or provision to the wise, or riches to men of understanding, or favor to people of skill; but time and chance happens to them all." In other words, we all have a certain amount of *time*, and we all get a *chance* to take advantage of *opportunities* God gives us to gain wealth and significance in life.

However, Solomon also lets us know that we don't know when our life will end. We don't know when an opportunity may pass us by. Opportunities, ideas, talents, strength, favor, etc.—all have *expiration dates*.

However, people who seize their *thing* and get into their *thing*, get more strength. *The more you give into life; the more life gives into you.* That's why the prophet told the widow with the pot of oil to "borrow not a few." All she had was one pot of oil, but as her sons kept bringing the pots, the oil kept *pouring and pouring*. It only ceased from pouring when she had nothing else to pour into. *As long as you can find someone that needs what you have, and begin to pour what you have, you will have prosperity.* "What do you have in the house?" That's what the prophet asked the widow. He didn't ask "Do you have a *line of credit* at the bank that you can borrow from?" He didn't say "Why don't you go get a cash advance on your check to pay the debt?" No. He was trying to teach her how to get out of debt and poverty. He asked, "What do you have in the house?" She said she didn't have anything in the house "save a pot of oil." **Your wealth is in your anointing!** He told her to gather empty pots and begin to pour what she had into that which needed what she had. And as long as you keep pouring what you have into what needs what you have, what you have won't run out, and it will be the source of your wealth.

SEIZE THE DAY!

We have to *seize* the moment when we have it! We have to maximize the value of what God has given us in this moment. We have to *Fight to Finish!* Ecclesiastes 9:12 says,

> For man also knoweth not his time: as the fishes that are taken in an evil net, and as the birds that are caught in the snare; so are the sons of men snared in an evil time, when it falleth suddenly upon them.

In other words, we don't know how much time we have. We don't know when an opportunity may pass. We don't know when the economy may *shift*. We don't know when the industry may change. We don't know when our particular skill may become obsolete. We don't know if there may be a car accident that could change our whole life and plan. There are many things in life that we don't know. That's one reason we have to *Fight to Finish*. The woman with the pot of oil knew she only had a certain amount of time in order to carry out the instructions given by the man of God. It was *now or never*! It was now or her sons would be taken into slavery and she would lose her future and have to face poverty. Her sons were a part of her wealth. Her children were her future. When Elisha the prophet told her to "go, sell the oil, and pay your debt, and live you and your children on the rest," she *passionately* pursued that instruction all the way to the *finish line*! Let's look again at the words of King Solomon in Ecclesiastes 5:3:

> For a dream cometh through the multitude of business; and a fool's voice is known by multitude of words.

Solomon is telling us how to obtain our blessing. He is telling us how to capture our wealth. He is letting us know we have to *Fight to Finish!* He says that a dream or a vision or a plan or a goal will only come to pass through a *multitude of business*. In other words, we have to put forth *much activity*, and *Fight to Finish* what God has given us. That is the only way that we will obtain the wealth God has anointed us to have. **Your wealth is in your anointing.**

IT'S UP TO *YOU*

Solomon also lets us know, in order to finish what God has given us we must focus on it. No one else is going to do what God has given you. **"Your wealth is in your anointing."** Ecclesiastes 3:22 says,

YOUR WEALTH IS IN YOUR ANOINTING

> *Wherefore I perceive that there is nothing better, than that a man should rejoice in his own works; for that is his portion: for who shall bring him to see what shall be after him?*

In other words, Solomon is advising and greatly admonishing us to focus on what God has given us. He says, he has "perceived" it. He has *learned from observation and experience* based on the successes he's seen in his own life and in the lives of others, that there is nothing better that a man should do than rejoice in his own works, and *Fight to Finish* what God has given him, for this is his portion in life. He says, ". . . because who will bring him to see what is going to be after him." In other words, when you're dead, your dreams die with you if you have not taken time to *Fight to Finish* them. Your dreams die with you, if you have not taken time to develop them.

FINISH YOUR *DREAM*!

Let's look at a practical example from the life of Solomon in the *Fight to Finish!* In 1 Kings, God chose Solomon to build the temple of God. God put the vision and desire in the heart of King David, King Solomon's father. However, King Solomon was the one anointed to fulfill this dream. This was his destiny. This was one of his greatest assignments. Solomon asked God for wisdom to lead his people. He also asked for wisdom to fulfill what he was called to do. We too must ask for wisdom. The widow came to Elisha the prophet in her desperate situation, asking for wisdom. God gave her wisdom and the plan. And God put His *super* on her natural efforts. He put His *extra* on her ordinary diligence. She had to *Fight to Finish!*

King David inspired his son as he was growing up. He imparted to him the vision to build the temple. That was his assignment when he was to be king after King David his father. To build the temple was his assignment. Therefore, King David had reserved a portion of gold, silver, brass, iron, precious stones, etc. for Solomon to build the temple. He stored up a vast amount of resources for his son to finish his assignment from God. So, when King David was about to die, he turned the kingdom of Israel over to his son Solomon. When King David died, King Solomon *knew his assignment.*

King David helped his son Solomon *Focus* during his lifetime, so Solomon could *see* his *Purpose*, and could develop a *Passion* to *pursue it* joyfully! Therefore, during the first seven years of King Solomon's reign, he *fought to finish* the temple. Even before building his own house, his first assignment was to finish building the temple. In 1 Kings 6:38 we read:

> And in the eleventh year, in the month Bul, which is the eighth month, was the house finished throughout all the parts thereof, and according to all the fashion of it. So was he seven years in building it.

It only took King Solomon seven years to build the temple. However, look at 1 Kings 7:1:

> But Solomon was building his own house thirteen years, and he finished all his house.

King Solomon was a *finisher* because he was *focused* on his *purpose* first. His chief purpose was to finish the house of God. That was his assignment. God gave him that assignment. His father King David had imparted that assignment into him and inspired him to accomplish that assignment. And, that's what he *focused* on during the first seven years of his reign. He made sure that he *fought to finish*. There may be something that you have discovered that God has called you to do. Hopefully, by this time in reading this book, you are being stirred to discover and act on it. I'm giving examples of *finishers* in the Bible to let you know that **your wealth is in your anointing**. An Essential Key to *releasing* that anointing is that you have to *Fight to Finish!*" We learn more about King Solomon in 2 Chronicles 7:11:

> Thus Solomon finished the house of the Lord, and the king's house: and all that came into Solomon's heart to make in the house of the Lord, and in his own house, he prosperously effected.

King Solomon was a *finisher*. The scripture tells us to be "followers of them, who through faith and patience inherit the promises" (Hebrews 6:12). "These things were written for our examples" (1 Corinthians 10:11). Solomon "prosperously effected" or "successfully finished" all that came into his heart regarding God's house and his own house.

When King Solomon was given the assignment to build the temple, he made it his *number one thing*. He focused on building the Temple above everything else. He did not focus on anything else until he finished building the Temple. Solomon fought to finish the Temple in a short period of time. In 1 Kings 6:38 it tells us.

> And in the eleventh year, in the month Bul, which is the eighth month, was the house finished throughout all the parts thereof, and according to all the fashion of it. So was he seven years in building it.

YOUR WEALTH IS IN YOUR ANOINTING

King Solomon fervently fought to finish the Temple even before building himself a house. He knew that the key to his wealth and the success of his kingdom would be based on "seeking first the kingdom of God and his righteousness" (Matthew 6:33), and all these things would be added to him. Look again at 1 Kings 7:1:

> But Solomon was building his own house thirteen years, and he finished all his house.

So we see, it only took Solomon seven years of concentrated effort to finish building God's house. However, afterward he focused on building his own house. It took him almost twice as long, thirteen years, to finish building his own house. Once he had satisfied the requirements of fulfilling his destiny, his wealth was set to focus on the rest of his life. King Solomon realized that he had to *Fight to Finish!* The widow in 2 Kings 4:1–7 had to *Fight to Finish* to obtain the wealth that was contained in her pot of oil. Now, let's look further at examples of finishers in our message, ***your wealth is in your anointing***.

ZERUBBABEL: A *FINISHER*

Before we look at God's Word to Zerubbabel in Zechariah 4, let us first look at Ecclesiastes 5:19:

> Every man also to whom God hath given riches and wealth, and hath given him power to eat thereof, and to take his portion, and to rejoice in his labour; this is the gift of God.

God has given every man or woman also "riches and wealth" and has given him or her the ability to actually enjoy it and to possess it in his or her lifetime! Your *portion* is your inheritance. God says there is a portion that has been allotted for you. From before the foundation of the world, God allotted a portion for you.

Ephesians 2:10 says, "For we are his workmanship, created in Christ Jesus; unto good works; which God hath before ordained that we should walk in them." God has already "before ordained" that we walk in "good works." When we walk in them, we will get *paid*. You take possession when you *do* the works. Riches and wealth is attached to the inheritance. We should, therefore, labor to enter into *rest* (Hebrews 4:11).

Now let's look at Zechariah 4 as we look at *finishing* in regards to your specific *Purpose* in life. I'm still talking to you about *Passion* and the *Fight to Finish!*

PASSION–THE 3RD ESSENTIAL KEY

> *Then he answered and spake unto me, saying, This is the word of the Lord unto Zerubbabel, saying, Not by might, nor by power, but by my spirit, saith the Lord of hosts.*
>
> *–Zechariah 4:6*

The Holy Spirit is the *anointing*. The anointing is an expression of the Holy Spirit. The anointing is the *empowerment* to do beyond what your natural strength can do. The *wisdom* from God is a manifestation of the Holy Spirit. The supernatural insight and creativity is a manifestation of the Holy Spirit. The strength to do what would normally cause others to say, "You're doing too much!" The supernatural *Passion* to do what you're doing comes by the Holy Spirit.

The anointing will help you overcome obstacles that stand in your way. The widow with the "pot of oil" had only *one* pot of oil. The obstacle was that *mountain of debt* that stood in her way. But, the anointing began to *multiply*. She followed the instruction of the man of God. And the anointing began to multiply. And the anointing destroyed the *yoke* of poverty from her life! The anointing *lifted the heavy burden* off her sons from being taken into slavery. Zechariah 4:7 says:

> *Who art thou, O great mountain? Before Zerubbabel thou shalt become a plain: and he shall bring forth the headstone thereof with shoutings, crying, Grace, grace unto it.*

"Grace" is God's ability in you, to do what you don't have the ability to do. *Grace*! *Grace*! is the *Anointing*! The *Anointing*!

The *anointing* is a manifestation of the Grace of God. It is *God's ability in you to do what you don't have the ability to do*. The scripture says in Romans 5:20, "Where sin abounded, grace did much more abound." Ephesians 2:8 says "For by grace are ye saved through faith, and that not of yourselves: it is the gift of God."

The *anointing* comes by grace. It's God's *extra*. It's God's *more*! Beyond what you can *work up on* in your natural strength or your natural might. That's why He says it's "not by might, nor by power; but by my spirit, says the Lord of hosts" (Zechariah 4:6).

The widow didn't have the resources to buy more oil if she wanted to go into the *oil business*. However, that's what she did. She went into the *oil business*, selling pots of oil. She did not have the *material* for the containers. She had to go out and *borrow* them. The "grace" of God

YOUR WEALTH IS IN YOUR ANOINTING

touched the hearts of the neighbors to let her borrow the empty pots and vessels.

She did not have the resources for *mass production* of the oil. But, the grace and anointing caused multiplication of what she did have. *It multiplied miraculously!* God will give you miracle multiplication when you set your hand to carrying out what God has given to you to do.

It starts with a *vision*. You study the Word. You get the vision. Proverbs 29:18 says, "Where there is no vision, the people perish; but, he that keepeth the law, happy is he."

Why are you happy? Because you begin to see the *pieces come together*! God begins to give you a vision for the steps to take. And then He will put his *super* on your *natural*. He will put his *extra* on your *ordinary*.

God's grace releases the anointing. *Favor! Favor! Grace! Grace!* It's in the *anointing*. Zechariah 4:8–9 says,

> Moreover the word of the Lord came unto me, saying,
>
> The hands of Zerubbabel have laid the foundation of this house; his hands shall also finish it; and thou shalt know that the Lord of hosts hath sent me unto you.

It is the Anointed One in the midst of you, and that makes the difference. Jesus Christ is the *Anointed One*.

Your *wealth* is success at fulfilling whatever God has given you to do. Your *wealth* is success at fulfilling whatever God has placed in your life to accomplish. Your *wealth* is success at fulfilling the *assignment* God has placed on your life. Your *provision* is attached to that. Your *Purpose* is attached to that. And, your *significance* is attached to that.

There is a *grace* to finish. *Five* is the number of grace. On the fifth day, God finished. He had finished the "heavens and the earth." And on the sixth day, He created man, and gave him dominion over the earth. Everything was finished on the *fifth* day. All the creation was finished. The animals, the ocean life, the birds, etc., were finished on the fifth day. And the "evening and the morning was the fifth day" (Genesis 1:23). Then, on the sixth day He said, "Let us make man in Our image, after Our likeness" (Genesis 1:26). *Five* is the number of *Grace*. You have five fingers on your hands, representing *completion*. And, you have *power* in your hands. That's Grace. Grace is *power*.

God said the "hand" of Zerubbabel laid the foundation of the house, and his "hand" would also finish it.

God said the "hands" that He gave the anointing and power to lay the foundation of the house; would be the same "hands" that would "finish it."

God said, Zerubbabel started it and his hands shall "finish it." Jesus was a *finisher*. Solomon was a *finisher*. God is telling us, "There's a grace to finish! And it shall be finished!" There's an anointing released to finish.

In verse 9, God is encouraging Zerubbabel, that, though the house wasn't finished, he *would* finish. He had *laid the foundation*. His hands would finish it.

He would have to *Fight to Finish*! Yet, there is *grace to finish*!

> *For who hath despised the day of small things? For they shall rejoice, and shall see the plummet in the hand of Zerubbabel with those seven; they are the eyes of the Lord, which run to and fro through the whole earth.*
>
> *–Zechariah 4:10*

God knows about *small things*. In fact, even for God, everything started *small*.

He's a big thinker; but even the earth, in which we live, started off as a *thought*. It started off small in comparison to the reality of its creation.

Everything started small. *You* started small. But, the working of the Holy Spirit came into play when that seed and the egg came together and the *anointing* released *life*! You were conceived by the *anointing*!

GOD IS *LOOKING* FOR YOU TO FINISH!

God says, "You shall reign as a king in the assignment which He has given you. You shall finish it!" God's eyes have been running "to and fro through the whole earth" looking for someone that will believe Him. We must have *Passion*! We must have the *Fight to Finish!*

Even when what you are doing seems to be *small*: don't you *despise* it and don't let anyone else *despise* it.

You can ignore what *onlookers* may say because God's eyes have been running to and fro throughout the earth, looking for someone to shew Himself strong (2 Chronicles 16:9).

YOUR WEALTH IS IN YOUR ANOINTING

The anointing went *traveling* in the Old Testament when Samuel came to Jesse's house. God had told him that He had a king in Jesse's house. God was looking for "a man after His own heart" (1 Samuel 13:14). God was telling Samuel, "I've chosen Me a king. He's down at Jesse's house. Go call Jesse and his sons to the sacrifice." Samuel went with the horn of oil to the sacrifice and he called Jesse and his sons to the sacrifice. He knew that God had told him to *anoint* a king.

God told Samuel He was going to anoint a king. And they went to the sacrifice, and Jesse began to present his sons before Samuel. And he presented the oldest son, and Samuel said, "Surely, the Lord's anointed is before [me]" (1 Samuel 16:6).

Samuel's *eyes* were looking; however, in Zechariah 4:10, it didn't speak about *man's eyes* "running to and fro through the earth." It was talking about *God's eyes* looking. Because, God's eyes sees where the *anointing* should be released.

Samuel looked and said, "Surely, the Lord's anointed is before me!"

But, God said, "I have rejected him. This is not him" He said, "Man looks on the outward appearance, but the Lord looks on the heart" (see 1 Samuel 16:7).

I encourage you today as you are reading this book: what God has put in your heart, He *sees* it. Your uprightness in heart before Him; God sees it. That promise that God has put in your heart; God sees it. The giving of your tithes and offering and being faithful in giving; God sees it. Your faithfulness in seeking God and walking before Him; God sees it. Your prayer time and worshipping Him and honoring Him; God sees it. He sees you walking in forgiveness and love toward other people. His "eyes" have been "running to and fro" looking for someone to "show Himself strong" in your life!

Continuing with the story, Jesse called his next son up.

Samuel said, "Surely, this is the Lord's anointed." He was strong. He was tall. He was big. He looked like a king in Samuel's eyes—natural eyes.

Natural eyes may see a "small thing" and "despise" a small thing. They may look at your dream or goal or what you are doing, and they may "despise" it because they perceive you and your dream as a "small thing."

They may look at your career or your schooling, and they may "despise" a "small thing." Natural eyes.

PASSION–THE 3RD ESSENTIAL KEY

But, the "eyes" of God are looking; and He sees differently, because He looks on the heart.

Well, the next son stood up. God said, "I've rejected him." Seven sons. These sons stood up before Samuel to be anointed; and the anointing *would not flow*. The anointing to be king would not flow on any of them. Zechariah 4:10 says,

> *For who hath despised the day of small things? For they shall rejoice, and shall see the plummet in the hand of Zerubbabel with those seven; they are the eyes of the Lord, which run to and fro through the whole earth.*

The "plummet" represents *kingship*. It is reigning. The anointing would not flow for any of Jesse's other sons for *kingship*.

So, Samuel asked, "Do you have any more sons?" Jesse said, "I have another son. He's out there in the field."

They didn't even call David for the sacrifice and anointing as a *possibility*! Someone may say, "What you're doing doesn't even seem like a possibility." They may say, "It doesn't even seem possible that you could succeed at this particular career"; "It doesn't seem like you could possibly overcome in this school"; "You don't look like college material."

I read an autobiography by General Colin Powell. He tells a story about when he was in the military. He was a grown man at this time. He had children. However, he started hearing about some of his fellow soldiers going back to graduate school while in the military. The government would pay for them to go to graduate school.

He said, "Maybe I'll take advantage of this opportunity." So, he put in his application.

He wanted to get an MBA. However, he didn't have a lot of the math. He didn't have a background in statistics. So the guy that was evaluating his application said, "Well, just based on what you have taken, and what you have already done; it doesn't' look like you are prepared for succeeding in an MBA program." In other words, he told him he "wasn't college material" for an MBA program. He said, "Especially, in a two year time period that is normally required."

In other words, he was "despising" what seemed to be a "small thing" in his eyes, because he was evaluating him based on his natural *eyes*.

YOUR WEALTH IS IN YOUR ANOINTING

This was like when Jesse presented David. They didn't think he was *king material*. So, they didn't present him at first. They left him out in the field. But, God called for David because, the "eyes" of the Lord had been "running to and fro" throughout the earth and they saw him. God's "eyes" saw him singing psalms and playing the harp in the field and worshipping God. He saw how he worshipped God. He saw how he loved God when nobody else was looking. Nobody else's eyes were looking David's way. Nobody else's eyes may be looking at what you're doing in your business, or how you're serving your customers or working on your business or whatever you are doing. Nobody else's eyes may be seeing it. But, God's eyes are seeing it.

When Samuel called David, God said, "This is him! Anoint him!" And the anointing fell upon David. It flowed all the way down upon his garments. "And the Spirit of the Lord came upon David from that day forward" (1 Samuel 16:13).

That same Spirit was with David from that day onward, and helped him kill Goliath. It helped him overcome many trials, situations, circumstances, and oppositions, and the mountains that stood before him.

And he did become king.

I'm talking to you about having *Passion* to *fight to finish!* The anointing helped David finish. God has been looking for you. You can finish that which God has given you through the anointing. There is an anointing for finishing. There's grace for finishing. Even when what you're doing seems like a "small thing", the Bible says to despise not "the day of small things." David seemed like a "small thing."

General Colin Powell became a world leader. *That MBA has served him well.* He became a political leader. He became the 16th National Security Advisor under President Ronald Reagan. He became the 12th Chairman of the Joint Chiefs of Staff under George H.W. Bush. He became the 65th United States Secretary of State under President George W. Bush. He became a very well known American that has served our nation well.

The point is that General Powell didn't give up. He had to *Fight to Finish*. He said to himself, "This MBA will be a good *finishing school* for me." Therefore, he graduated with his MBA from George Washington University, in spite of the initial doubtful comments.

He was a well-seasoned soldier. He was a well-seasoned fighter. But, the MBA program was a further *finishing school* for him—for *refining*

PASSION—THE 3RD ESSENTIAL KEY

him for higher positions, not just as a soldier. He was a general. But, the MBA program helped to prepare him for further service and advancement.

Furthermore, the anointing upon David positioned him for *kingship*. It positioned him for reigning. So, God has been looking for you. Look at 2 Chronicles 16:9:

> *For the eyes of the Lord run to and fro throughout the whole earth, to shew himself strong in the behalf of them whose heart is perfect toward him...*
>
> *—2 Chronicles 16:9a.*

Notice, the connection between Zechariah 4:10 and 2 Chronicles 16:9. The connection is that God's "eyes" have been "running to and fro" throughout the earth to "shew Himself strong on the behalf" of someone whose heart is perfect toward him.

My main point is that whatever God has given you to start, you must *Fight to Finish* it. Just like the widow with the pot of oil had to *Fight to Finish* the instruction that the prophet gave her in order for her to gain the financial deliverance that the Word of God promised. You too have to *Fight to Finish* what God gave you. When you finish, you will *reign* in it. Your wealth is there.

God said in Zechariah 4, that the "hands" of Zerubbabel laid the foundation of the house and his hands will also finish it.

God is letting you know that not only did you lay the foundation of your business, not only did you lay the foundation of your career, not only did you lay the foundation of your family, but you will finish it! You started raising your children; they will finish school. You started your marriage; you will finish strong! You started that career; you will finish at the top! You started school; you will graduate!

> *The hands of Zerubbabel have laid the foundation of this house; his hands shall also finish it; and thou shalt know that the Lord of hosts hath sent me unto you. For who hath despised the day of small things? For they shall rejoice, and shall see the plummet in the hand of Zerubbabel with those seven; they are the eyes of the Lord, which run to and fro through the whole earth.*
>
> *—Zechariah 4:9-10*

When the Word went forth to Zerubbabel, the dream still looked *small*. There was a "foundation" laid—a certain amount of work had been done on the foundation, but it was not finished.

YOUR WEALTH IS IN YOUR ANOINTING

Some of you reading this book have laid the foundation of certain things. You started doing the work to lay the foundation of your faith in certain areas. You've been speaking the Word and confessing the Word. You've been singing and worshipping. You've been calling on the name of Jesus for your family. You've been building on it. God says, "You're going to finish!"

> *For the eyes of the Lord run to and fro throughout the whole earth, to shew himself strong in the behalf of them whose heart is perfect toward him...*
>
> *–2 Chronicles 16:9a.*

God's "eyes" have been looking for you. He's been looking for someone who has the *Passion to finish*. I'm encouraging you to *stay in the fight!* Don't give up! Don't "despise the day of small things." *Fight to Finish* what God has given you. God said, "It's not by might, nor by power, but by my Spirit says the Lord of hosts" (Zechariah 4:6). When God says the eyes of the Lord are running to and fro throughout the earth to show Himself strong, I really believe that He is talking about the angels of the Lord and the Holy Spirit.

The angels are *reporting* on us. They see your faithfulness. "The angels of the Lord are encamped around about them that fear Him" (Psalms 34:7). And, they keep them in all their ways. And the good work, which God has begun in you, He will perform it until the day of Jesus Christ. He will complete it (see Philippians 1:6). He will finish!

JESUS CHRIST: A *FINISHER*

In this section of the message, we have been looking at the Essential Keys to the *release* of the anointing within you. We've been evaluating the third key to the release of the anointing within you, which is *Passion*. We've been looking at the fourth component of *Passion*, the *fight to finish*. We are currently looking at some examples of passionate finishers of their purposes. We've evaluated King Solomon and Zerubbabel. Now, we are going to look at our Lord Jesus Christ.

Let's turn our attention to Matthew 16. We will now examine the life of our Lord and Savior Jesus Christ as the "author and finisher of our faith" (Hebrews 12:2). He is our Example.

PASSION–THE 3RD ESSENTIAL KEY

Even from a child, once He caught a vision of Who He was, Jesus had a desire, drive, and determination to *Fight to Finish*.

Jesus's earthly parents, Mary and Joseph, took Him to the temple from an early age, and He discovered Himself through the teachings of the scriptures. This is the same way that we discover ourselves—through meditating God's Word.

The scripture lets us know in Proverbs 29:18, "Where there is no vision, the people perish; but, he that keepeth the law, happy is he." The word, "perish" means "to lose restraint" or "to become naked and vulnerable." In other words, there are no boundaries. There is no goal. For example, if people have no weight goals, they will just eat anything anytime. If people have no fitness goals, they don't exercise. They don't walk because they don't have any fitness goals. They don't have any time schedules or time management goals. They just *hang out*! "Wherever I am, I am." If they don't have any monetary goals or budgeting goals, they just spend, spend, spend! As soon as they get money in, they spend it. Why? They have no boundaries.

So, where there is no vision or when you can't see a clear focus of a goal, the "people perish or lose restraint."

For example, think about a basketball team. If there were no goals on each end of the court, they would just be running up and down the court or just standing there. What's the purpose? Why am I going to run up and down the court? Why am I sprinting? The reason basketball players sprint up and down the court is because there's a goal on this end and there's a goal on the other end. And whoever gets down here and gets the ball in the goal the most, they win! So, that's the *vision*. So, where there is no vision, the people perish. They lose restraint. But "he that keepeth the law," or the *purpose*, or the *goal*, "happy is he." It brings joy! *Passionate* is he!

Jesus discovered his *Purpose* as a child. Even as a 12-year-old child, he went up to the temple and was sitting with the teachers and lawyers and scribes, trying to hear them and ask them questions, because he discovered himself. And as he grew on, and was baptized by John the Baptist, he was passionately pursuing, and *fighting to finish* what he came to earth to do. Jesus knew what he was here for.

THE FIGHT TO FINISH WHEN MISUNDERSTOOD

Now let's look at Jesus's *Fight to Finish* when those who surrounded Him didn't understand Him or His true mission. Jesus had to *Fight to Finish* at each stage to accomplish what He came to do.

YOUR WEALTH IS IN YOUR ANOINTING

> *When Jesus came into the coasts of Caesarea Philippi, he asked his disciples, saying, Whom do men say that I the Son of man am? And they said, Some say that thou art John the Baptist: some, Elias; and others, Jeremias, or one of the prophets.*
>
> *—Matthew 16:13-14*

> *So, Jesus was asking them, "What are people saying about me? Who do they think I am? What do they think I'm here to do?" In other words, "Do those on the outside know Who I am, and why I'm here?" "What are people saying about me?" Now, verse 15: He saith unto them, But whom say ye that I am?*
>
> *—Matthew 16:15*

Now, He's asking those that are *close* to Him, "Do you know Who I am? And, what I'm about?"

> *And Simon Peter answered and said, Thou art the Christ, the Son of the living God.*
>
> *—Matthew 16:16*

Peter got a revelation of Who Jesus is, and why He came. He called Him "the Christ," the "Anointed One." That's what "Christ" means—"the Anointed One and His Anointing." The anointing that "destroys the yoke and lifts the burden" of sin off our lives. (Isaiah 10:27) He was saying, "You're the One that was anointed to do what no one else could do... to deliver us from sin. You are the *Messiah*. You are the *Deliverer*. You are the One that came to deliver us from sin, sickness, poverty, lack, depression, oppression, and bondage. You came to deliver us. *Thou are the Christ, the Son of the Living God!*"

> *And Jesus answered and said unto him, Blessed art thou, Simon Bar-jona: for flesh and blood hath not revealed it unto thee, but my Father which is in heaven. And I say also unto thee, That thou art Peter, and upon this rock I will build my church; and the gates of hell shall not prevail against it. And I will give unto thee the keys of the kingdom of heaven: and whatsoever thou shall bind on earth shall be bound in heaven: and whatsoever thou shalt loose on earth shall be loosed in heaven. Then charged he his disciples that they should tell no man that he was Jesus the Christ. From that time forth began Jesus to shew unto his disciples, how that he must go unto Jerusalem, and suffer many things of the elders and chief priests and scribes, and be killed, and be raised again the third day.*
>
> *—Matthew 16:17-21*

PASSION–THE 3RD ESSENTIAL KEY

Though Peter got a revelation of Who Jesus is, he only saw a *part* of it. He saw Who Jesus was, but he didn't' understand *why* He was and is. Peter didn't understand what the process was going to be. He saw a part of it. But, he didn't see the *way*. Peter saw *who* He was. He knew Jesus was the "Christ, the Son of the Living God." He saw that Jesus was the glorious Messiah, but he didn't see the *way* that Jesus was going to bring this deliverance.

> *Then Peter took him, and began to rebuke him, saying, Be it far from thee, Lord: this shall not be unto thee.*
>
> *–Matthew 16:22*

Peter understood *who* Jesus was; but he didn't understand Jesus's *mission*.

In this section of the message, I'm connecting the widow with the pot of oil, which we said represents the *anointing*, with Jesus, the *Anointed One*. She had to *Fight to Finish* in order to release the wealth that was contained in her anointing oil, in order to obtain the deliverance from her desperate financial situation.

Jesus, being the *Anointed One*, also had to *Fight to Finish* the mission for which He came, in order to bring deliverance to us from the bondage of sin. He had to *Fight to Finish* to release the anointing to deliver us. So, we see He was *Fighting to Finish* when those that were around Him didn't understand Who He was or His true mission.

> *But he turned, and said unto Peter, Get thee behind me, Satan: thou art an offence unto me: for thou savourest not the things that be of God, but those that be of men.*
>
> *–Matthew 16:23*

In other words, Jesus was saying to Peter, "You may have caught a revelation of who I am, as the *Christ*, but *your ways are not God's ways* (Isaiah 55:8-9), and you are an offense unto me, because I'm here to do the will of God."

> *Then said Jesus unto his disciples, If any man will come after me, let him deny himself, and take up his cross, and follow me. For whosoever will save his life shall lose it: and whosoever will lose his life for my sake shall find it. For what is a man profited, if he shall gain the whole world, and lose his own soul? Or what shall a man give in exchange for his soul? For the Son of man shall come in the glory of his Father with his angels; and then he shall reward every man according to his*

> works. Verily I say unto you, There be some standing here, which shall not taste of death, till they see the Son of man coming in his kingdom.
>
> –Matthew 16:24-28

THE *PASSION* OF THE CHRIST

We're examining Jesus in His *Fight to Finish*. We're examining *Passion* and the *Fight to Finish*. Jesus's redemptive work on the cross is called the *Passion of the Christ*. Many saw the Mel Gibson movie of that same title. Jesus was fighting to finish the redemptive work for our deliverance. It was His *Passion* to see us delivered from sin, poverty, sickness, disease, oppression, and depression. He was fighting for our release. He was *anointed* for it. **Your wealth is in your anointing.** Jesus was *anointed* to deliver us from sin.

Let's look at Luke 22:14–34. We're going to look at Jesus's *Fight to Finish* even when being betrayed by those He loved. He was fighting to finish when those closest to Him denied that they even knew Him. He was fighting to finish. Why are we looking at Jesus? Jesus is our number one *example*. Whatever God has called you to do regarding your purpose, ministry, business, family, marriage, etc.; you have to *Fight to Finish* in order to receive the blessing, benefit, promise, or reward God has for you. You have to *Fight to Finish*!

> And when the hour was come, he sat down, and the twelve apostles with him. And he said unto them, With desire I have desired to eat this Passover with you before I suffer: For I say unto you, I will not any more eat thereof, until it be fulfilled in the kingdom of God. And he took the cup, and gave thanks, and said, Take this, and divide it among yourselves: For I say unto you, I will not drink of the fruit of the vine, until the kingdom of God shall come. And he took bread, and gave thanks, and brake it, and gave unto them, saying, This is my body which is given for you: this do in remembrance of me. Likewise also the cup after supper, saying, This cup is the new testament in my blood, which is shed for you. But, behold, the hand of him that betrayeth me is with me on table.
>
> –Luke 22:14-21

Jesus was fulfilling what God called Him to do, but He knew that "the hand of him" that was going to betray him was on the table. But, He was still *fighting to finish* it. He was committed unto the end.

PASSION–THE 3RD ESSENTIAL KEY

> *And truly the Son of man goeth, as it was determined: but woe unto that man by whom he is betrayed! And they began to enquire among themselves, which of them it was that should do this thing.*
>
> *–Luke 22:22-23*

So, Jesus was talking about Judas who was about to betray him. Jesus was *fighting to finish* even when He was betrayed by those that He loved. Judas was about to betray Him, but He was fighting to finish when betrayed by someone that He loved.

Now, we are going to see Him *fighting to finish* when those that are close to Him *deny* that they even know Him. Now, let's go down to Luke 22:31.

> *And the Lord said, Simon, Simon, behold, Satan hath desired to have you, that he may sift you as wheat: But I have prayed for thee, that thy faith fail not: and when thou art converted, strengthen thy brethren. And he said unto him, Lord, I am ready to go with thee, both into prison, and to death. And he said, I tell thee, Peter, the cock shall not crow this day, before that thou shalt thrice deny that thou knowest me.*
>
> *–Luke 22:31-34*

So, we see, Jesus was letting Peter know that he was going to deny that he even knew Jesus. But, Jesus was still *fighting to finish*.

We are looking at Jesus as an example. He is our *Great Example*. He is our *Model*. Let's look at John 19:26–30. Jesus was fighting to finish what God's Word had said concerning Him. He was constantly *fighting to finish*. We saw that from a child he went into the temple as a twelve year old. He wanted to be in the temple to hear what God's Word said about Him. He said to His parents, "How is it that you sought me? Knewest thou not that I must be about my Father's business?" (Luke 2:49). He was fighting to finish. When He went to be baptized by John the Baptist, John said, "How is it that you are coming to be baptized by me? I'm the one that need to be baptized by you!" Jesus said, "Suffer it to be so now. For it becometh us to fulfill all righteousness" (Matthew 3:15). Jesus was *fighting to finish* what God's Word had said concerning Him. He was fighting to fulfill what the prophecies had spoken concerning Him. He was fighting to finish what God had given Him to do. He was obeying the Father.

Here in John 19:26–28, we see that Jesus is fighting to finish what God's Word says concerning Him:

> *When Jesus therefore saw his mother, and the disciple standing by, whom he loved, he saith unto his mother, Woman, behold thy son! Then saith he to the disciple, Behold thy mother! And from that hour that disciple took her unto his own home. After this, Jesus knowing that all things were now accomplished, that the scripture might be fulfilled, saith, I thirst.*

He was *fighting to finish*! His whole ministry, His whole mission was to *finish* what God had sent Him here to do.

I'm talking to you about *Passion* and the *fight to finish* as an Essential Key to the *release* of the anointing within you. **Your wealth is in your anointing.** The reason you are *anointed* is because you are *in* the Anointed One, the Lord Jesus Christ. 1 Corinthians 5:17 says, "If any man be in Christ, he is a new creature, old things are passed away, behold, all things have become new." You are "in Christ." "Christ" means "the Anointed One and His Anointing." It is the *anointing* upon the *Anointed One* that empowers us. We can do all things through Christ, which strengthens us. We can do all things through the *anointing* upon the *Anointed One*. We can succeed in our businesses. We can succeed in our homes. We can succeed in our families. We can succeed in our marriages. We can succeed with raising our children. We can succeed in every area, because of the *anointing* upon the *Anointed One*. He destroyed the yoke of sin. He destroyed the yoke of failure. He destroyed the yoke of disease. He destroyed the yoke of defeat through the *Anointing*. And, He was *fighting to finish* to *release* this anointing upon us. If He had not finished His work on the cross, we would not be free, and we would still be bound. Jesus was *fighting to finish* His redemptive work to set us free. And, "whom the Son sets free, is free indeed" (John 8:36). Amen. Hallelujah!

Look at verse 28 of John 19:

> *After this, Jesus knowing that all things were now accomplished, that the scripture might be fulfilled, saith, I thirst.*

In other words, He had *finished* all things! "All things were now *accomplished*, that the scripture might be fulfilled."

FULFILLING THE *VISION* OF THE SCRIPTURE

Jesus was *fulfilling the scripture*. Proverbs 29:18 says, "Where there is no vision, the people perish; but, he that keepeth the law, happy is he." The

PASSION–THE 3RD ESSENTIAL KEY

thing that kept Jesus *passionate*, and gave Him *joy*, was the *law of God*. It was the *outcome* of God's Word concerning Himself that kept Him passionate. He *kept* the law. He *discovered* Himself in the scripture. Jesus discovered Who He was from meditating the Word. He read the scriptures in the Old Testament and discovered Who He was. That's why He went to the temple. That's why He wanted to hear the teachers and doctors of the law. He discovered Himself. He discovered the "vision" for Himself. This is what kept Him *passionately pursuing*. Therefore, here in verse 28 of John 19, it says, "After this, Jesus knowing that all things were now accomplished, that the scripture might be fulfilled, saith, I thirst."

The scripture says, "Jesus knowing . . ." How did He know? He had read. He had studied. He discovered Himself in the scripture. He spent time with the Father in the Word, and in prayer, and got a revelation of His *destiny*. He obtained the "vision" for His life.

It's the same with us. Through meditating God's Word, spending time in prayer, hearing from God, letting Him minister to your spirit, getting a revelation of *who you are*, and discovering your *why*, you will discover your *Purpose*.

> Now there was set a vessel full of vinegar: and they filled a sponge with vinegar, and put it upon hyssop, and put it to his mouth.
>
> –John 19:29

He was fulfilling what was written of Him in the Psalms. This was written of Him in the Psalms. Psalms 69:20–21 says,

> Reproach hath broken my heart; and I am full of heaviness: and I looked for some to take pity, but there was none; and for comforters, but I found none. They gave me also gall for my meat; and in my thirst they gave me vinegar to drink.

Jesus fulfilled this scripture in John 19:29–30. He declared, "It is finished" after He had fulfilled the Word of God written concerning Him. He fulfilled the "vision" for His life. He had *Passion* and the *fight to finish!*

> When Jesus therefore had received the vinegar, he said, it is finished: and he bowed his head, and gave up the ghost.
>
> –John 19:30

After he had fulfilled what was already written, He said, "It is finished." Jesus was a *finisher*. King Solomon was a *finisher*. Zerubbabel was a *finisher*. Jesus was a *finisher*. "And he bowed his head and gave up the ghost."

He was a *finisher*. He fulfilled the scripture. He finished the redemptive work.

UNFINISHED BUSINESS

Now, let's look at John 20:1-20. Jesus's *redemptive work* is finished. However, He didn't finish *every* part of what He came to do.

> The first day of the week cometh Mary Magdalene early, when it was yet dark, unto the sepulchre, and seeth the stone taken away from the sepulchre. Then she runneth, and cometh to Simon Peter, and to the other disciple, whom Jesus loved, and saith unto them, They have taken away the Lord out of the sepulchre, and we know not where they have laid him. Peter therefore went forth, and that other disciple, and came to the sepulchre. So they ran both together: and the other disciple did outrun Peter, and came first to the sepulchre. And he stooping down, and looking in, saw the linen clothes lying; yet went he not in. Then cometh Simon Peter following him, and went into the sepulchre, and seeth the linen clothes lie, and the napkin, that was about his head, not lying with the linen clothes, but wrapped together in a place by itself.
>
> –John 20:1-7

What did Jesus say? He said *He would rise again*. Not only would He die; but, He would *rise again*. That's why we're *saved*, because He *rose again*! Amen. We're talking about Jesus. He was *Fighting to Finish*!

> And the napkin, that was about his head, not lying with the linen clothes, but wrapped together in a place by itself. Then went in also that other disciple, which came first to the sepulchre, and he saw, and believed.
>
> –John 20:7-8

What did he believe? He believed what Jesus had said concerning Himself. That He would die for our sins, and after three days, He would rise again.

> For as yet they knew not the scripture, that he must rise again from the dead. Then the disciples went away again unto their own home. But Mary stood without at the sepulchre weeping: and as she wept, she stooped down, and looked into the sepulchre, And seeth two angels in

PASSION–THE 3RD ESSENTIAL KEY

> *white sitting, the one at the head, and the other at the feet, where the body of Jesus had lain. And they say unto her, Woman, why weepest thou? She saith unto them, Because they have taken away my Lord, and I know not where they have laid him. And when she had thus said, she turned herself back, and saw Jesus standing, and knew not that it was Jesus. Jesus saith unto her, Woman, why weepest thou? Whom seekest thou? She, supposing him to be the gardener, saith unto him, Sir, if thou have borne him hence, tell me where thou hast laid him, and I will take him away. Jesus saith unto her, Mary. She turned herself, and saith unto him, Rabboni; which is to say, Master. Jesus saith unto her, Touch me not; for I am not yet ascended to my Father: but go to my brethren, and say unto them, I ascend unto my Father, and your Father; and to my God, and your God.*
>
> *–John 20:9-17*

Jesus had restored the fellowship between us and the Father. He said, "My Father and your Father; My God and your God." He is telling us, "I have *finished* this redemptive work. I have risen from the dead to restore you into *fellowship* with your Father and My Father. My God and your God."

> *Mary Magdalene came and told the disciples that she had seen the Lord, and that he had spoken these things unto her. Then the same day at evening, being the first day of the week, when the doors were shut where the disciples were assembled for fear of the Jews, came Jesus and stood in the midst, and saith unto them, Peace be unto you. And when he had so said, he shewed unto them his hands and his side. Then were the disciples glad, when they saw the Lord.*
>
> *–John 20:18-20*

Jesus fulfilled the scripture. He went to the cross. He died on the cross, and He rose again.

MORE *UNFINISHED* BUSINESS

Now, let's look at Acts 1. Jesus was a *finisher*! And, whatever God has called you to do you must finish as well, in order to obtain your wealth, benefit, blessing, and promise in life. Your *fulfillment* is in your *anointing*. It's in the *release* of the anointing within you. You have to *Fight to Finish* whatever God has given you. Jesus fought to finish. This is an Essential Key to the release of whatever God has put on the inside of you.

YOUR WEALTH IS IN YOUR ANOINTING

> *The former treatise have I made, O Theophilus, of all that Jesus began both to do and teach, Until the day in which he was taken up, after that he through the Holy Ghost had given commandments unto the apostles whom he had chosen:*
>
> –Acts 1:1-2

Jesus was *fighting to finish* until the day that He was taken up.

> *To whom also he shewed himself alive after his passion by many infallible proofs, being seen of them forty days, and speaking of things pertaining to the kingdom of God.*
>
> –Acts 1:3

What are we talking about? *Passion* and the *Fight to Finish*! Verse 3 says "... to whom also he shewed himself alive after his *passion* by many infallible proofs..." Jesus *passionately* fought to finish what God sent Him to accomplish in the earth for us.

> *And, being assembled together with them, commanded them that they should not depart from Jerusalem, but wait for the promise of the Father, which, saith he, ye have heard of me.*
>
> –Acts 1:4

Now, Jesus was *fighting to finish* the mission of *restoring* His Church to a place of *power!* By sending the Holy Ghost! By sending the Holy Spirit, Jesus was *fighting to finish* the mission of restoring His Church to a place of power! He had gone to the cross. He had risen from the dead. But that wasn't all. He came to restore us to a *place of power*, by sending the Holy Ghost. This lets us know that He wasn't *finished* yet just by going to the Cross, or just with Him dying, or just with Him being raised from the dead, and you believing and receiving salvation by accepting that He rose from the dead and paid for your sins. No. He wanted you to be restored to a place of *power*. He was telling his disciples, "I want you to wait in Jerusalem until you are restored unto a place of power, because I want my Church to be a powerful church!" God wants us to be a powerful people! He wants us to be an influence in the earth. He wants you to be *change agents!* He wants you to *straighten things out!* He wants you to "be fruitful, multiply, replenish the earth, subdue it, and have dominion" (Genesis 1:28). He wants you and me to be restored to a place of power! Hallelujah!

PASSION–THE 3RD ESSENTIAL KEY

> *And, being assembled together with them, commanded them that they should not depart from Jerusalem, but wait for the promise of the Father, which, saith he, ye have heard of me.*
>
> *–Acts 1:4*

So, He had been telling them, it wasn't for Him to go back to Heaven, without giving them power! He wasn't going to leave them without restoring them back to power. Jesus had been talking to them about the Holy Ghost. John the Baptist had announced regarding Jesus when he introduced Jesus on the scene, "I have baptized you with water, unto repentance; but there cometh One mightier than I, after me, the latchet of whose shoes I am not worthy to unloose; He shall baptize you with the Holy Ghost, and with fire" (Matthew 3:11). So, we see that it was a part of Jesus's mission to *baptize us with the Holy Ghost and with fire!* To restore us back to power. Jesus was *fighting to finish* that!

> *For John truly baptized with water; but ye shall be baptized with the Holy Ghost not many days hence.*
>
> *–Acts 1:5*

Jesus wanted to restore His Church to a place of power! God in us, the hope of glory! *Christ in us, the hope of glory*! (see Colossians 1:27) *The Anointed One and His Anointing in us, the hope of glory!* **Your wealth is in your anointing!** Christ is the Anointed One and it is His Anointing. Christ in you, the hope of glory, is the hope of God getting the *glory* out of your life.

> *When they therefore were come together, they asked of him, saying, Lord, wilt thou at this time restore again the kingdom to Israel?*
>
> *–Acts 1:6*

They wanted a *physical* manifestation of power being restored to their lives. They wanted restoration of a physical kingdom. But, Jesus let them know that the way to get a physical manifestation of the kingdom, is through the *spiritual* manifestation of the kingdom.

Jesus said, "The kingdom of God is within you" (Luke 17:20–21). The kingdom of God is *within* you. The Apostle Paul lets us know in Romans 14:17–18 what the *kingdom* is:

> *For the kingdom of God is not meat and drink; but righteousness, and peace, and joy in the Holy Ghost. For he that in these things serveth Christ is acceptable to God, and approved of men.*

YOUR WEALTH IS IN YOUR ANOINTING

In other words, God's way of doing and being right and God's way of living, is the restoration of the kingdom of God in the earth. It is *God's order* in the earth. Something has to happen *in you*. Like the song says, "Something on the inside, working on the outside; Oh, what a change in my life!"

> When they therefore were come together, they asked of him, saying, Lord, wilt thou at this time restore again the kingdom to Israel? And he said unto them, It is not for you to know the times or the seasons, which the Father hath put in his own power. But ye shall receive power, after that the Holy Ghost is come upon you: and ye shall be witnesses unto me both in Jerusalem, and in all Judea, and in Samaria, and unto the uttermost part of the earth.
>
> –Acts 1:6-8

He tells them that they're going to receive power, authority, rulership, etc. Jesus is saying, "Through you receiving the baptism of the Holy Ghost, and through God in you, which is Christ in you the 'hope of glory', you're going to restore My kingdom in Jerusalem, in Judea, in Samaria, and unto the utmost parts of the earth. I want to put something in you that spreads My influence throughout the earth." **Your wealth is in your anointing!**

I'm talking to you about the Essential Keys to the *release* of the anointing within you. Jesus was *fighting to finish* so He could put something *in you* that would restore His *Kingdom* and His *Presence*, His *Reign* and His *Authority*, and His *Rulership* and His *Influence* in the earth. Wherever you go, you're called to be a *carrier* of the influence of God. Hallelujah! Hallelujah! Hallelujah!

THE *FINISHED* WORK OF THE *SPIRIT!*

Look at verse 14 of Acts 1:

> These all continued with one accord in prayer and supplication, with the women, and Mary the mother of Jesus, and with his brethren.

So, after Jesus told them that they would receive power after the Holy Ghost came upon them, they began to seek God for the Holy Ghost, and *wait* on the Holy Ghost. Now, look at Acts 2:1-4.

> And when the day of Pentecost was fully come, they were all with one accord in one place. And suddenly there came a sound from heaven

> *as of a rushing mighty wind, and it filled all the house where they were sitting. And there appeared unto them cloven tongues like as of fire, and it sat upon each of them. And they were all filled with the Holy Ghost, and began to speak with other tongues, as the Spirit gave them utterance.*

[Or, rather, "as the Spirit gave them what to say".]

> *And they were all filled with the Holy Ghost, and began to speak with other tongues, as the Spirit gave them utterance.*
>
> –Acts 2:4

They had already been *converted* by the Holy Ghost when they believed on and received Jesus as Lord and Savior. They had been *born again* by believing that Jesus Christ is the Son of God and that God raised Him from the dead, and by faith they received *salvation*. That was a work of the grace of God, through faith, by the Holy Spirit. But, *this* was a *second event*. This was a *separate* event, where they were *filled* to capacity. In fact, they were filled to *overflow!*

"Something on the inside, working on the outside; Oh, what a change in my life!!!"

They were all *filled* with the Holy Ghost, and the *initial evidence* given in scripture, of being filled to *overflow*, was "they *began to speak with other tongues as the Spirit gave them utterance*" (Acts 2:4) or gave them what to say. *They* began to speak. This bubbling on the inside, or this being filled to capacity by the Spirit, began to *bubble up* out of their mouths, and they began to speak. They began to *express* those *inexpressible* things that were coming up out of their belly, as the Spirit continually gave them what to say. *Hallelujah! Hallelujah!*

Now, look at verse 21 of Acts 2:

> *And it shall come to pass, that whosoever shall call on the name of Lord shall be saved.*

THE AUTHOR AND FINISHER OF OUR FAITH

Now, look at Hebrews 12:1–4. We're looking at Jesus because Jesus was a *finisher* and Jesus is our Example.

> *Wherefore seeing we also are compassed about with so great a cloud of witnesses, let us lay aside every weight and the sin which*

YOUR WEALTH IS IN YOUR ANOINTING

> *doth so easily beset us, and let us run with patience the race that is set before us,*
>
> –Hebrews 12:1

The "great cloud of witnesses" refers to all those that lived by faith before us. Hebrews chapter 11 is often called the Faith Hall of Fame. It talks about Enoch, Noah, Abraham, Sarah, Jacob, Isaac, Moses, and all those that *lived by faith*. And, these all died in faith. It talks about Samson, David, Samuel, and how they lived by faith and died in faith. They were *finishers* by faith. What am I telling you? You have to *Fight to Finish* by faith as well.

We know that the widow with the pot of oil is also in the Faith Hall of Fame. She was able to get her sons out of debt and potential slavery. And, she and her sons were able to live on the benefits of that miracle for the rest of their lives. My message is **your wealth is In your anointing**.

We've been looking at Jesus as a *finisher*.

> *Wherefore seeing we also are compassed about with so great a cloud of witnesses, let us lay aside every weight, and the sin which doth so easily beset us, and let us run with patience the race that is set before us. Looking unto Jesus, the author and finisher of our faith; who for the joy that was set before him, endured the cross, despising the shame, and is set down at the right hand of the throne of God.*
>
> –Hebrews 12:1-2

In this message, we are "looking unto Jesus." We have to take time to *look*. He's the "author and the finisher of our faith." Jesus had the joy "set before him" of you and me being made free. Proverbs 29:18 says "Where there is no vision, the people perish; but, he that keepeth the law, happy is he."

Jesus "endured the cross" because of the "joy that was set before Him." Jesus is the "author and finisher of our faith." We've been looking at *Jesus* as our chief example of a *finisher*. "Looking unto Jesus, the Author and the Finisher of our faith." And, that's why were saved today. Praise God!

PASSION—THE 3RD ESSENTIAL KEY

APOSTLE PAUL: A *FINISHER*

Now, I want to continue to explore our message, **your wealth is in your anointing.** *Wealth* is not *just* money. Wealth is your *health*. It is your *happiness*. It is your *peace*. It is a successful, happy *family* life. It is a happy *marriage*. It is healthy *children*. It is having the finances to have an abundant life to meet all your needs, and to be able to take care of you, your family, and to be able to help *others*. Wealth is being able to leave an inheritance for your children, and your children's children. Everything that the Bible describes as the will of God for your life is *wealth*. This is what God desires for you and me. And, He has anointed you for a purpose. He has anointed you to accomplish a certain thing in life that is meant to bring about the *Purpose* for your life—the satisfaction, the fulfillment, and also the *provision* for your life. There is *something* that God has put on the *inside* of you, that He has put His anointing upon. It is your *Purpose* for you to accomplish and fulfill. In that, you will find the sustaining of your life, the sustenance for your life, and the fulfillment in your life in your *Purpose*. God has anointed that.

So, we've been looking at the Essential Keys to the *release* of the anointing within you. We looked at the first Essential Key, which was *Focus*; and the second Essential Key, which was *Purpose*; and now we are looking at the third Essential Key, which is *Passion*. *Passion* has four components. We looked at the first component of *Passion*, which is the *joy of pursuit*. We then looked at the second component of *Passion*, which is the *Fight for Focus*. Once you have obtained your *Focus*, you have to *fight for it*, because there are distractions. Next, we looked at the third component of *Passion*, which is *Overcoming the Frustration of Perseverance*. In other words, whatever God has given you, usually has a *time* component to it. It usually has a time requirement. And, you can become *frustrated* in persevering through the time of accomplishing what God has for you, especially if you don't *accept* in your heart that everything requires certain *steps*. God didn't create the earth in one day. He took 6 days to create the earth, and He rested on the seventh day. So, He did it in *stages*. After every "evening and morning" God said that "it was good" and He stopped until the next day. He did so much each day to restore the earth back to the beauty that He desired for it. But, He had a *vision* for the finished product from the beginning. And, so you and I have to have a *vision*. We must have a vision of what we desire.

Now, we will continue looking at the 4th component of *Passion*, which is the *Fight to Finish*!

We've been looking at some *finishers* in the Bible.

The foundation for our message is found in 2 Kings 4:1–7. In this passage, we looked at the story of the widow with the "pot of oil." She came to Elisha after her husband died. Her husband was one of the prophets. Her sons were about to be taken into slavery to pay off her husband's debt. She was in a desperate situation. She didn't recognize what she had "in the house." The man of God helped her discover what she had in the house, and gave her a *supernatural plan* to find financial deliverance. Her one pot of oil was the key to her financial deliverance. The oil represents the *anointing*. She had one pot of oil. It was her *potential* deliverance. The pot represented *potential*. God had anointed her potential, which she had in the house to bring her financial deliverance for her and her family for the rest of their lives.

You have certain gifts and talents, which God has put on the inside of you. There are certain keys within your ideas, ability to think, talk, and your personality, which God has given you that will bring your deliverance and provision. God has given you a specific purpose, capacity, or focus toward things. It may be how you deal with people, or understanding numbers, music, writing, computers, and negotiation, or something else. There are certain things, which God has put on the inside of you, which are *potential*. Now that you're born again, God has placed His *anointing* on those things. He's put *Himself* and His *oil* upon it. And, now your *wealth* is there. He has given it to you to succeed and prosper in life.

I'm trying to build in your heart the *Focus* to see what God has given you. Proverbs 29:18 says "Where there is no vision, the people perish; but, he that keepeth the law, happy is he." If there is no *sight*, the people perish. The word "perish" means "to lose restraint." They give up and lose restraint, because there is no goal. There is no *reason*. There's no *focus*. There's no desirable *outcome* to *pursue*.

The first *finisher* we looked at was King Solomon. We explored how he fought to finish the building of the temple. He made it his main concern, even before building his own house. King Solomon fought to finish the

PASSION—THE 3RD ESSENTIAL KEY

building of the temple in *seven years*. It is estimated by some that the value of the temple, in today's money, was over *$500 billion*!

It took him *thirteen years* to build his own house. In a little more than half of the amount of time that it took him to build his own house, King Solomon *fought to finish* the building of God's house. In other words, King Solomon was *passionate* about finishing what God had given him to do because it was a part of his essential *Purpose*. His father, King David, had implanted this purpose in King Solomon's heart from an early age. God put the vision in his father King David. But, God told David that he didn't want him to build it. He was going let his son, Solomon, build it. So, David began to put back gold, silver, and precious stones, during his time as king, for the building of the temple. And, he began to impart the vision into his son, so that he could have a clear vision and focus. So, when it was time for King Solomon to reign, he knew what he was going to do. He was going to build the temple. Matthew 6:33 says, "But, seek ye first the kingdom of God, and his righteousness, and all these things shall be added unto you." King Solomon sought first to finish his responsibility to build the kingdom of God.

We also looked at our Lord Jesus Christ. The Lord Jesus, He is the *Author* and the *Finisher* of our faith. We wouldn't be saved if Jesus didn't *finish*. If He only had began to do the work, but didn't finish we wouldn't be saved. If He stopped in the Garden of Gethsemane, we would not be saved. Jesus *fought to finish* His redemptive work on earth, in order for us to be saved. He fought through persecution, temptation, betrayal, pain and suffering, doubt, fear, feelings of being lonely and forsaken, and much more in order to finish the redemptive work. *Passion* compelled Jesus to finish his redemptive work for us. Jesus was a *finisher*.

Why are we looking at *finishers*? The widow with the pot of oil had received miracle multiplication of the oil. Her potential had produced miracle multiplication. But, she had to *Fight to Finish*! She had to *go and sell the oil* in order to pay her debt, and live with her children on the rest. She had to fight to get the oil *out of the house* and *into the marketplace*! That's a *fight*! It's one thing to be able to do a thing or produce a thing; but it's another thing to *market it*, and get what you need *from it*!

Now, we're going to look at our final example of a *finisher*—the Apostle Paul.

As we look at the Apostle Paul, we must start in Acts 6:8. The Apostle Paul's story rests upon the beginnings of the Church. This background information is very important in understanding the Apostle Paul as a *finisher*, because it helps us to understand his *personality* and what was behind his *drive*. The Apostle Paul was anointed to finish a great work for the Lord Jesus Christ. *Your wealth* is in you finishing everything that God called you to do. And, everything that comes *to you* will come *through you* doing what God called you to do. In other words, "But, seek ye first the kingdom of God, and His righteousness, and all these things will be added unto you" (Matthew 6:33). Doing God's will and doing what God has called you to do, and whatever He has anointed you for, is the key to your *true* wealth. If you give yourself fully unto that thing and make it your number one goal, God can add to you all that you desire and need in life. He can add to you all that is requisite for your provision, protection, family, legacy, children, etc. God can provide for you everything you need as you put Him *number one*. The Apostle Paul was anointed to do a great thing for the Lord. He started off wrong, but he was committed and passionate for what he believed. The Apostle Paul had this *fighting attitude!* He had this *Passion*, whether *right* or *wrong*. And God said he could *use* him. God can use anybody that's passionate, because He can turn you around. A lot of people are *asleep!* They're *sleepwalking* through life. They're the *walking dead*. Nothing moves them to passionately pursue *anything*. They're sitting around. They're not *moving* in life. They're not *trying* to go forward. They're just taking what life *hands* them. They haven't *seen* anything. Again, the first Essential Key to the release of the anointing within you is Focus. Proverbs 29:18 says, "Where there is no vision, the people perish; but he that keepeth the law, happy is he." *Passionate* is he! *Motivated* is he! *Enthusiastic* is he! that keepeth the law. When you get a *vision* of what God has called you to do, you realize, "I've got something! God has something for me! God has chosen me for something! I can do a thing!" It stirs you up! And, if you begin to passionately pursue that thing, it adds *gas to your engine*! Amen!

THE STONING OF STEPHEN

Now, we have to lay some background beginning at Acts 6:8, because this introduces us to the Apostle Paul. We will start by looking at Stephen. In the early Church, the *stoning* of Stephen precedes our introduction to the Apostle Paul.

> *And Stephen, full of faith and power, did great wonders and miracles among the people. Then there arose certain of the synagogue, which*

> is called the synagogue of the Libertines, and Cyrenians, and Alexandrian's, and of them of Cilicia and of Asia, disputing with Stephen. And they were not able to resist the wisdom and the spirit by which he spake. Then they suborned men, which said, we have heard him speak blasphemous words against Moses, and against God. And they stirred up the people, and the elders, and the scribes, and came upon him, and caught him, and brought him to the Council, and set up false witnesses, which said, this man ceases not to speak blasphemous words against this holy place, and the law: For we have heard him say, that this Jesus of Nazareth shall destroy this place, and shall change the customs which Moses delivered us. And all that set in the Council, looking steadfastly on him, saw his face as it had been the face of an angel.
>
> –Acts 6:8-15

The Apostle Paul, who was called Saul at this time, is in this crowd as they are accusing and examining Stephen.

> Then said the high priest, Are these things so? And he said, Men and brethren, and fathers, hearken; The God of glory appeared unto our father Abraham, when he was in Mesopotamia, before he dwelt in Charran, and said unto him, Get thee out of thy country, and from thy kindred, and come into the land which I shall show thee. Then came he out of the land of the Chaldeans, and dwelt in Charran: and from thence, when his father was dead, he removed him into this land, wherein ye now dwell. And he gave him none inheritance in it, no, not so much as to set his foot on: yet he promised that he would give it to him for a possession, and to his seed after him, when as yet he had no child.
>
> –Acts 7:1-5

I'm presenting this passage to show that this sermon and *revelation* of the Lord Jesus Christ *stirred up* this man called Saul before he was the Apostle Paul. This is what stirred him to wrath.

> And God spake on this wise, That his seed should sojourn in a strange land; and that they should bring them into bondage, and entreat them evil 400 years. And the nation to whom they shall be in bondage I will judge, said God: and after that shall they come forth, and serve me in this place. And he gave him the covenant of circumcision: and so Abraham begat Isaac, and circumcised him the eighth day; and Isaac begat Jacob; and Jacob begat the twelve patriarchs.
>
> –Acts 7:6-8

YOUR WEALTH IS IN YOUR ANOINTING

So, Stephen began, from scripture, to lay the establishment of the Church from the Old Testament, because he is talking to the priests, scribes, and the elders; and he is going to reveal to them Jesus. But first, he is laying the foundation that Jesus is built upon the rock of the Old Testament.

> *And the patriarchs, moved with envy, sold Joseph into Egypt: but God was with him, And delivered him out of all his afflictions, and gave him favor and wisdom in the sight of Pharaoh king of Egypt; and he made him governor over Egypt, and all his house. Now there came a dearth over all the land of Egypt and Chanaan, and great affliction: and our fathers found no sustenance. But when Jacob heard that there was corn in Egypt, he sent out our father's first. And at the second time Joseph was made known to his brethren; and Joseph's kindred was made known unto Pharaoh. Then sent Joseph, and called his father Jacob to him, and all his kindred, threescore and fifteen souls. So Jacob went down into Egypt, and died, he, and our fathers And were carried over into Sychem, and laid in the sepulcher that Abraham bought for a sum of money of the sons of Emmor the father Sychem. But when the time of the promise drew nigh, which God had sworn to Abraham, the people grew and multiplied in Egypt, Till another king arose, which knew not Joseph. The same dealt subtly with our kindred, and evil entreated our fathers, so that they cast out their young children, to the end they might not live. In which time Moses was born, and was exceeding fair, and nourished up in his father's house three months: And when he was cast out, Pharaoh's daughter took him up, and nourished him for her own son. And Moses was learned in all the wisdom of the Egyptians, and was mighty in words and deeds. And when he was full forty years old, it came into his heart to visit his brethren the children of Israel. And seeing one of them suffer wrong, he defended him, and avenged him that was oppressed, and smote the Egyptian: For he supposed his brethren would have understood how that God by his hand would deliver them: but they understood not.*
>
> *–Acts 7:9-25*

Stephen is relating to them about Moses, because Moses represented an Old Testament *deliverer* like Jesus. He was the deliverer of the people. Just like Moses brought the children of Israel out of Egyptian bondage, Jesus in the New Testament, brought us out the bondage of sin. So, Stephen is preaching the sermon to connect Jesus to the Old Testament in order to reveal to these priests, scribes, and Pharisees, who Jesus is. Saul, who would later become the Apostle Paul, was in this crowd hearing this message; and this is what stirred him to wrath. Look at verse 35:

PASSION–THE 3RD ESSENTIAL KEY

> *This Moses whom they refused, saying, Who made thee a ruler and a judge? the same did God send to be a ruler and a deliverer by the hand of the angel which appeared to him in the bush.*

The children of Israel originally rejected Moses in the Old Testament. They did not want him. They said, "Who made you a ruler and a judge over us?" Yet, it says here in verse 35:

> *This Moses whom they refused, saying, Who made thee a ruler and a judge? the same did God send to be a ruler and a deliverer by the hand of the angel which appeared to him in the bush.*

In other words, the one that they rejected is the one that God *chose*. Therefore, Stephen was relaying the story of Moses to them in the Old Testament, and saying, "Just like the one that you rejected in the Old Testament was the one that God chose to bring deliverance to the children of Israel; the One that you're rejecting *now*, the Lord Jesus, is the One that God chose to bring His people out of sin." Hallelujah!

And so, Saul was hearing this revelation of Jesus.

> *He brought them out, after that he had showed wonders and signs in the land of Egypt, and in the Red Sea, and in the wilderness forty years. This is that Moses, which said unto the children of Israel, a prophet shall the Lord your God raise up unto you of your brethren, like unto me; him shall ye hear.*
> –Acts 7:36-37

So, he's revealing unto them Jesus. This is what Stephen was revealing and this is what Saul was hearing. Now, let's look at verse 52:

> *Which of the prophets have not your fathers persecuted? And they have slain them which shewed before of the coming of the Just One; of whom ye have been now the betrayers and murderers:*

So again, Stephen is preaching the Word, and revealing to them Jesus, according to scripture. Stephen is telling the scribes and Pharisees, "You betrayed Jesus and murdered Him. But, He was the Chosen One by God!"

> *Who have received the law by the disposition of angels, and have not kept it. When they heard these things, they were cut to the heart, and they gnashed on him with their teeth. But he, being full of the Holy Ghost, looked up steadfastly into heaven, and saw the glory of God, and Jesus standing on the right hand of God,*
> –Acts 7:53-55

YOUR WEALTH IS IN YOUR ANOINTING

Stephen had preached this message, and revealed Jesus so well, and so succinctly, that Jesus *stood up!* Jesus stood and said "Amen!" Jesus stood up in Heaven and said "Amen!" Now, we know when Jesus went back to Heaven, He sat on the right hand side of God the Father, until He makes His enemies His footstool (Matthew 22:44). But Stephen had preached so *strong*, and revealed the Word so *clearly*, that Jesus *stood up!* And said, "Amen!"

> And said, Behold, I see the heavens opened, and the Son of man standing on the right hand of God. Then they cried out with a loud voice, and stopped their ears, and ran upon him with one accord,
>
> —Acts 7:56-57

They didn't want to hear this revelation, so they "stopped their ears."

> And cast him out of the city, and stoned him: and the witnesses laid down their clothes at a young man's feet, whose name was Saul.
>
> —Acts 7:58

The *Passion* of Saul, who would later be named the Apostle Paul, was first revealed as a *persecutor* of the Church. He started as a *persecutor* of the Church.

> And they stoned Stephen, calling upon God, and saying, Lord Jesus, receive my spirit. And he kneeled down, and cried with a loud voice, Lord, lay not this sin to their charge. And when he had said this, he fell asleep.
>
> —Acts 7:59-60

This is where we get the first revelation of the Apostle Paul. He was Saul then. And he was passionate about the law of God. He was a "Pharisee, the son of Pharisees" (Acts 23:6). He was passionate about the law of God, but he didn't have the revelation of Jesus Christ at this time. And when Stephen preached it, Saul was the overseer of Stephen's murder. So we notice that this is the introduction to the Apostle Paul. He *passionately resisted* the Church when his name was called Saul. The Apostle Paul, who was called Saul, was fighting to finish *destroying* the Church.

PASSIONATELY *FIGHTING* THE CHURCH

Let's look at Acts 8:1-4. We will see that the Apostle Paul was passionately fighting the Church of the Lord Jesus Christ. Saul thought he

PASSION–THE 3RD ESSENTIAL KEY

was working for God as he was fighting against the Church. Saul, who became the Apostle Paul, had *Passion*, even as a young man, because the scripture says, "the witnesses laid down their clothes at a young man's feet, whose name was Saul" (Acts 7:58). He was passionate at this time. He was *fighting to finish* destroying the Church. Let's look further at his *Passion*:

> And Saul was consenting unto his death. And at that time there was a great persecution against the church which was at Jerusalem; and they were all scattered abroad throughout the regions of Judaea and Samaria, except the apostles.
>
> –Acts 8:1

Saul was fighting against the Church, because he thought he was standing up for God.

> And devout men carried Stephen to his burial, and made great lamentation over him. As for Saul, he made havoc of the church, entering into every house, and haling men and women committed them to prison.
>
> –Acts 8:2-3

He was passionately fighting against the Church. He was passionate in what he believed.

> Therefore they that were scattered abroad went every where preaching the word.
>
> -Acts 8:4

DOING RIGHT, EVEN WHILE *DOING WRONG*

Notice verse 4 shows that though the Apostle Paul was passionately resisting the Church, his resistance actually caused the Church to *grow* and *spread abroad*. God was using him, even as he was opposing His Church. It was God's original plan and command to the early Church to spread the Gospel around the world. However, they were trying to settle only in Jerusalem at first. God used Saul to *stir them up*, through persecution, and get them moving out of Jerusalem. God told the apostles in Mark 16:15–20 these words:

> And he said unto them, Go ye into all the world, and preach the gospel to every creature. He that believeth and is baptized shall be saved; but

> he that believeth not shall be damned. And these signs shall follow them that believe; In my name shall they cast out devils; they shall speak with new tongues. They shall take up serpents; and if they drink any deadly thing, it shall not hurt them; they shall lay hands on the sick, and they shall recover. So then after the Lord had spoken unto them, he was received up into heaven, and sat on the right hand of God. And they went forth, and preached every where, the Lord working with them, and confirming the word with signs following. Amen.

Jesus did not tell the apostles to stay in Jerusalem. He said, "Go ye into all the world, and preach the gospel." The Apostle Paul, while still called Saul, was responsible for causing the early Church to *spread abroad* due to his persecution of them. Look at verses 3–4 again:

> As for Saul, he made havoc of the church, entering into every house, and haling men and women committed them to prison. Therefore they that were scattered abroad went every where preaching the word.

We notice, in verse 4, that though the Apostle Paul was passionately resisting the Church, his resistance actually caused the Church to grow and spread abroad. I'm talking to you about *Passion*, the *Fight to Finish*!

CAPTURED BY THE LORD

Now let's look at Acts 9:1–31. We will see where the Lord Jesus Christ captures the Apostle Paul for his own service.

We are looking at the Apostle Paul as an example of a *finisher*. He was *passionate* in the beginning of his life. The reason I'm writing about this, is because God put something in you before your were conceived in your mother's womb. He put something in you to *finish*! He put something in you to *complete*. He put a *Purpose* on the inside of you. You had a *Purpose* before you were born. You have to *Focus* to discover that *Purpose*. And then you have to *passionately* pursue it.

You see, the Apostle Paul was passionate before he received Jesus as Lord and Savior, because it was a part of his personality. He was passionately *"doing him!"* And, God says, now that you are born-again, there are some things He's *anointed* that He has put in you. Thus, **your wealth is in your anointing.** The anointing on what God put in you is the source of your wealth. Your wealth is in the anointing on your *Purpose*. It's that *potential*, it's that *gifting*, it's that *talent* that God put in you. And, now that you're born again, you are "in Christ" (2 Corinthians 5:17). "Christ"

PASSION—THE 3RD ESSENTIAL KEY

means the "Anointed One and His *Anointing*." "Therefore, if any man be in Christ he is a new creature; old things are passed away, behold, all things have become new" (2 Corinthians 5:17). "Old things," including, *sin*, *weakness*, *defeat*—these are the things that came as a result of being born in sin. Those things are "passed away, behold, all things have become new." In other words, you are *fresh* and *new* like God planned from the beginning. Now you can fulfill what God planned for you from the beginning. The natural *gifting, talents, skills, drive, personality, capability, imagination,* and *intellect* that God gave you from the beginning, which He has placed His anointing and *new life* upon, empowers you *supernaturally* to be *successful*! It's for you to be *supernaturally prosperous*! He's put His *super* on your *natural*! He's put His *extra* on your *ordinary*! It is so that you can get a *supernatural* result! It's so you can get an *extraordinary* harvest!

"If any man be in Christ, he is a new creature. Old things are passed away; behold, all things are become new" (2 Corinthians 5:17). *Christ* in you . . . the *Anointed One* in you . . . the *Anointed One* and His *Anointing* in you . . . the hope of glory! It's about God getting *the glory* out of your life. Ephesians 2:10 says,

> *For we are his workmanship, created in Christ Jesus unto good works, which God hath before ordained that we should walk in them.*

In other words, we're God's *craftsmanship*. We're God's *product*. He *manufactured* us. He skillfully crafted us. We're His "workmanship," created in Christ Jesus, the Anointed One and His Anointing, unto—or for the *purpose of*—good works, which He has before-ordained that we should walk in. He already planned it. He ordained that we should walk in specific good works, before the foundation of the world.

We are the Father's workmanship. We are His skillful craftsmanship. We are His *precision tools* for a *specific* purpose. There are "good works" that God has already ordained that we should "walk in them." Now, in Acts 9, we will see how Jesus captures the *Passion* of the Apostle Paul to use him for His service. Jesus will turn that *Passion* that the Apostle Paul had for fighting *against* the Church, and use it to *build* the Church unlike any other apostle. We're examining *Passion* and the *Fight to Finish*. The Apostle Paul was a *finisher* and he was passionate to do what God gave him to do.

YOUR WEALTH IS IN YOUR ANOINTING

> *And Saul, yet breathing out threatenings and slaughter against the disciples of the Lord, went unto the high priest,*
>
> *–Acts 9:1*

In other words, the words were still in his mouth, and he was still passionately persecuting the Church. And desired of him letters to Damascus to the synagogues, that if he found any of this way, whether they were men or women, he might bring them bound unto Jerusalem.

> *And as he journeyed, he came near Damascus: and suddenly there shined round about him a light from heaven: And he fell to the earth, and heard a voice saying unto him, Saul, Saul, why persecutest thou me? And he said, Who art thou, Lord? And the Lord said, I am Jesus whom thou persecutest: it is hard for thee to kick against the pricks.*
>
> *–Acts 9:3-5*

Saul was like a horse kicking against the pricks. If they kick against the pricks, it hurts their hooves. Jesus was saying, "It's hard for you to kick against the pricks, because you are hurting yourself by trying to hurt Me, by hurting My Church. Why? I've called you. So, if you are coming against Me, you're hurting yourself. Because, I've called you to serve Me. You're trying to hurt Me, but you're hurting yourself, because I've chosen you."

> *And he trembling and astonished said, Lord, what wilt thou have me to do? And the Lord said unto him, Arise, and go into the city, and it shall be told thee what thou must do.*
>
> *–Acts 9:6*

You see, the Apostle Paul was *passionate*. He was just on the *wrong* side at this time. But, he *instantly* said, "Who art thou Lord?" He submitted himself to the voice of the Lord. He recognized the authority of the Lord. He was just confused on how to serve Him in regards to what he needed to be doing. Yet, once Saul heard the voice of God, and Jesus revealed Himself to him, he submitted. He was *willing* and *passionate*. In other words, he said, "Lord, if I'm going at it the wrong way, show me the right way. And, the same passion that I'm pursuing this way, I will apply it the other way."

> *And the men which journeyed with him stood speechless, hearing a voice, but seeing no man. And Saul arose from the earth; and when his*

PASSION—THE 3RD ESSENTIAL KEY

> *eyes were opened, he saw no man: but they led him by the hand, and brought him into Damascus.*
>
> *–Acts 9:7-8*

This is Apostle Paul's conversion from Saul to the *Apostle* Paul.

> *And he was three days without sight, and neither did eat nor drink. And there was a certain disciple at Damascus, named Ananias; and to him said the Lord in a vision, Ananias. And he said, Behold, I am here, Lord. And the Lord said unto him, Arise, and go into the street which is called Straight, and enquire in the house of Judas for one called Saul, of Tarsus: for, behold, he prayeth, And hath seen in a vision a man named Ananias coming in, and putting his hand on him, that he might receive his sight. Then Ananias answered, Lord, I have heard by many of this man, how much evil he hath done to thy saints at Jerusalem: And here he hath authority from the chief priests to bind all that call on thy name. But the Lord said unto him, Go thy way: for he is a chosen vessel unto me, to bear my name before the Gentiles, and kings, and the children of Israel: For I will shew him how great things he must suffer for my name's sake.*
>
> *- Acts 9:9-16*

The Apostle Paul was chosen from before the foundation of the world. He was fighting *against* the Church, but God said, "It's hard for you to kick against the pricks because as you try to hurt me and My Church, you're hurting yourself; because I have chosen you to serve the Church. I've chosen you to build the Church. I've chosen you to be a part of the Church."

> *And Ananias went his way, and entered into the house; and putting his hands on him said, Brother Saul, the Lord, even Jesus, that appeared unto thee in the way as thou camest, hath sent me, that thou mightest receive thy sight, and be filled with the Holy Ghost. And immediately there fell from his eyes as it had been scales: and he received sight forthwith, and arose, and was baptized. And when he had received meat, he was strengthened. Then was Saul certain days with the disciples which were at Damascus. And straightway he preached Christ in the synagogues, that he is the Son of God.*
>
> *–Acts 9:17-20*

Passionately! *Immediately*! He didn't have to go to Bible School. He didn't have to have someone *coach* him into it. He was *against* the

Church; but when he got a revelation of Jesus, he was *for* it. And, he was *passionate*. He was going to *Fight to Finish* what God called him to do!

> But all that heard him were amazed, and said; Is not this he that destroyed them which called on this name in Jerusalem, and came hither for that intent, that he might bring them bound unto the chief priests?
>
> –Acts 9:21

It was such a quick turnaround, and such a *passionate, immediate, full-force* turnaround, that the people were *amazed*! They said, "In *one step*, he was coming to persecute us; and then in an *immediate turnaround*, he's preaching the Gospel!" It was *amazing*! But, Paul was saying, "I just want to be right!"

He was *passionate*. And, when Jesus straightened him out, he was just as passionate *for* Him as he was *against* Him.

> But Saul increased the more in strength, and confounded the Jews which dwelt at Damascus, proving that this is very Christ. And after that many days were fulfilled, the Jews took counsel to kill him:
>
> –Acts 9:22-23

The Jews said, "He's *over-the-top!*" They wanted to kill him now! He was so against the Church, and now he's *for* them? And, he's *100%*!

> But their laying await was known of Saul. And they watched the gates day and night to kill him. Then the disciples took him by night, and let him down by the wall in a basket. And when Saul was come to Jerusalem, he assayed to join himself to the disciples: but they were all afraid of him, and believed not that he was a disciple.
>
> –Acts 9:24-26

The Apostle Paul had been so passionate in persecuting the Church, that the Church was now afraid of him!

> But Barnabas took him, and brought him to the apostles, and declared unto them how he had seen the Lord in the way, and that he had spoken to him, and how he had preached boldly at Damascus in the name of Jesus. And he was with them coming in and going out at Jerusalem. And he spake boldly in the name of the Lord Jesus, and disputed against the Grecians: but they went about to slay him. Which when the brethren knew, they brought him down to Caesarea, and sent him forth to Tarsus. Then had the churches rest throughout all Judaea and

> *Galilee and Samaria, and were edified; and walking in the fear of the Lord, and in the comfort of the Holy Ghost, were multiplied.*
>
> *–Acts 9:27-31*

The Apostle Paul's *Passion* brought *multiplication*. The Apostle Paul was anointed to *build* the Church. And when he passionately started to preach the Gospel, and turned from Saul *the persecutor* to Paul *the Apostle*, it brought *multiplication*! That was his "*wealth.*" His wealth was the multiplication of the Church. The building of the Church was his *Passion*. That was his *Purpose*. **Your wealth is in your anointing.**

The passages which we just read lay the foundation for the life and Passion with which the Apostle Paul helped to build the Church. *Passion* is the third Essential Key to the *release* of the anointing within you. He was anointed to carry out a specific calling.

You too are anointed to carry out a specific calling in life. God has given you *gifts* and a *calling* to bring wealth to your life. **Your wealth is in your anointing.** You and I must passionately pursue what God has given us to do in life. We must focus long enough to clearly see our *Purpose*, and then we must passionately pursue it. No matter what the opposition, we must *Fight to Finish*!

ANALYSIS OF THE APOSTLE PAUL'S LIFE

Now let's continue to examine the life of the Apostle Paul as a *finisher*.

Let's look at Galatians 1:11. We're going to look at the Apostle Paul as he details his own passionate *Fight to Finish* as we continue with our message that **your wealth is in your anointing**.

> *But I certify you, brethren, that the gospel which was preached of me is not after man. For I neither received it of man, neither was I taught it, but by the revelation of Jesus Christ. For ye have heard of my conversation in time past in the Jews' religion, how that beyond measure I persecuted the church of God, and wasted it:*
>
> *–Galatians 1:11-13*

Notice some of the words that the Apostle Paul uses. He says "beyond measure." He was saying, "I *passionately* persecuted the Church." He said that "*beyond measure* I persecuted the Church." In other words, "beyond what was reasonable." In other words, it's like when some people do certain things, and people say, "You're just doing *too much*! You just work

YOUR WEALTH IS IN YOUR ANOINTING

too much! You're just *too focused* on that!" The Apostle Paul said he was *obsessive* at achieving his goal.

But, we understand from the Apostle Paul, after his conversion, that he was just that obsessive concerning *building* the Church. And that's why we *remember* the Apostle Paul today. The Apostle Paul wrote over *two-thirds* of the New Testament, which was more than any other of the apostles. It is because, "beyond measure," he was just that *passionate*! Look at verse 13:

> For ye have heard of my conversation in time past in the Jews' religion, how that beyond measure I persecuted the church of God, and wasted it: And profited in the Jews' religion above many my equals in mine own nation, being more exceedingly zealous of the traditions of my fathers.
>
> –Galatians 1:13-14

Notice the Apostle Paul said "*beyond measure* . . . And profited *above many* my equals in my own nation . . . being *more exceedingly zealous* of the tradition of my fathers." Does that sound like *Passion* to you?

He is telling us, "I was *passionate*. I was *fighting to finish* my assignment in persecuting the Church." This was the Apostle Paul's *nature*. This was something that was *in* the Apostle Paul! He had a *Fight to Finish* whatever it was he was assigned to.

We're looking at the Apostle Paul as a *finisher*. We're looking at *Passion* as an Essential Key to the *release* of the anointing within you. It is essential for you to accomplish your *purpose*. It is essential for releasing the anointing within you. It is essential for releasing the *potential* God has put on the inside of you. The Apostle Paul said that the way he did it was "beyond measure." Look at verse 14 again:

> And profited in the Jews' religion above many my equals in mine own nation, being more exceedingly zealous of the traditions of my fathers.

In other words, "There were others that *graduated* with me, others that went to the same *class*, others that went to the same *school*, others that lived in the same *neighborhood* . . . but, I *profited* in the Jews' religion *above many* my equals." The Apostle Paul was saying, "I *graduated* with them, but I didn't *stay* with them." He said this is because of his "being *more exceedingly zealous* of the tradition of my fathers." Hallelujah!

The Apostle Paul said he "*profited* in the Jews' religion above many my equals." The Apostle Paul was *passionate* and *profitable* in what he

PASSION–THE 3RD ESSENTIAL KEY

did from the beginning, whether *right* or *wrong*. He was *passionate* and *profitable*.

You look at some people that are living outside of the law and doing crime, selling drugs, etc.; even those that are doing that who end up *on top* in their game, driving the big cars, making the big money, gained above average success because they *passionately* pursued their activity. They just need to learn how to do things God's way, and live according to God's principles, but if they take that same *Passion* and pursue *right* and *godly* businesses, lawful businesses, then "beyond measure" they could be *profitable* in the *right thing*.

The Apostle Paul was on the *wrong side* of God's law, yet, "beyond measure," "exceedingly zealous," "above many" his equals, he pursued what he was passionate about. He was *Fighting to Finish!* This is essential for releasing the anointing contained in that which God has anointed for you. The Apostle Paul said he was "exceedingly zealous." In other words, the Apostle Paul was *exceedingly passionate* to finish whatever his assignment was because of what he *believed*!

I encourage you, as I encourage myself, we must be passionate to finish what God has assigned us to do in life.

Why can we use the Apostle Paul as an example of a *finisher*, and as an example of accomplishment? The Apostle Paul's *attitude, work ethic*, and *pursuit* of what God assigned him, changed the whole face of *history*! His passionate pursuit of what God called him to do changed the whole face of *history*! He wrote over two-thirds of the New Testament! He wrote more than any other apostle of Jesus Christ. *He didn't even walk with Jesus!* He wasn't one the *twelve*. He was introduced to Jesus after Jesus left the earth. Yet, "beyond measure" the Apostle Paul worked "above others" his equal.

APOSTLE PAUL'S *PERSONAL* EVALUATION

Let's quickly look at 1 Corinthians 15:9–10:

> *For I am the least of the apostles, that am not meet to be called an apostle, because I persecuted the church of God.*
>
> *–1 Corinthians 15:9*

So, we see how the Apostle Paul felt about himself. He felt that he was the "least" of the apostles. He felt as if he wasn't even *suitable* to be an apostle because he had persecuted the Church. And maybe that was a part of the reason why he worked so hard. Maybe he said, "I know what I did. I still feel badly about what I did in persecuting the Church. Therefore, I'm going to work even harder to build up the Church. I'm going to love the Church and the Lord Jesus Christ, by building up the Church." That was a part of the Apostle Paul's *motivation*. And he worked "beyond measure" compared to those his "equal." *Before* he was converted, he worked "beyond measure" when he was persecuting the Church, above those his equal; and, *after* he was converted, he worked "beyond measure." So, the Apostle Paul was a *passionate pursuer*, and he was a *finisher*—he *fought to finish*! Look at verse 10:

> But by the grace of God I am what I am: and his grace which was bestowed upon me was not in vain; but I labored more abundantly than they all: yet not I, but the grace of God which was with me.
>
> –1 Corinthians 15:10

In verse 9, the Apostle Paul said, "for I am the least of the apostles, that am not meet to be called an apostle, because I persecuted the Church of God." Yet, in verse 10, he says, "But, by the grace of God, I am what I am, and His grace which was bestowed upon me, was not in vain . . ." He said God didn't *waste this grace* that he gave me. He continues, ". . . but I labored *more abundantly* . . ." Listen to the Apostle Paul: "Above many"; "beyond measure"; "exceedingly zealous." And here he says, ". . . I labored *more abundantly* than they all, yet, not I, but the grace of God, which was with me." The "grace of God" is the *anointing* of God. We're talking about **your wealth is in your anointing**. The others were anointed, but the Apostle Paul had an *extra-abundant Passion* to *release* his anointing! I'm talking to you about the Essential Keys to the *release* of the anointing within you. You must be willing to go "beyond measure" in order to release the potential that your anointing contains. Hallelujah!

The Apostle Paul was more passionate to *release* the anointing. He was *more successful*. And, he was *more productive*. He fought to finish what God gave him.

FIGHTING TO FINISH *IN MINISTRY*

Let's quickly look at Acts 20:16–28:

PASSION—THE 3RD ESSENTIAL KEY

> *For Paul had determined to sail by Ephesus, because he would not spend the time in Asia: for he hasted, if it were possible for him, to be at Jerusalem the day of Pentecost.*
>
> *–Acts 20:16*

Notice, the scripture says the Apostle Paul "hasted." This also speaks of his *Fight to Finish* what God gave him to do. He had this sense of *urgency* that was *driving* him. Some say of certain people, "You're *obsessed* with that!" Yet, I heard Dr. Mike Murdock say, "You will never be *successful* with anything, until it becomes an *obsession*!" It must become your *chief focus*. It must become your *chief aim* in life. Napoleon Hill, author of the book *Think and Grow Rich*, says you must have a "definite chief aim" in order to become wealthy and rich.

The Apostle Paul had a *definite chief aim* to fulfill the will of God for his life. That's where his *wealth* was—the fulfillment of the will of God for his life.

> *For Paul had determined to sail by Ephesus, because he would not spend the time in Asia: for he hasted, if it were possible for him, to be at Jerusalem the day of Pentecost.*
>
> *–Acts 20:16*

The Apostle Paul had a *strong sense of urgency*! He "hasted"!

> *And from Miletus he sent to Ephesus, and called the elders of the church. And when they were come to him, he said unto them, Ye know, from the first day that I came into Asia, after what manner I have been with you at all seasons, Serving the Lord with all humility of mind, and with many tears, and temptations, which befell me by the lying in wait of the Jews: And how I kept back nothing that was profitable unto you, but have shewed you, and have taught you publickly, and from house to house.*
>
> *–Acts 20:17-20*

The Apostle Paul was *profitable* unto the people. He was preaching the Word that was *profitable* to the people. He was *passionate* about doing the will of God.

> *Testifying both to the Jews, and also to the Greeks, repentance toward God, and faith toward our Lord Jesus Christ. And now, behold, I go bound in the spirit unto Jerusalem, not knowing the things that shall befall me there: Save that the Holy Ghost witnesseth in every city,*

> saying that bonds and afflictions abide me. But none of these things move me, neither count I my life dear unto myself, so that I might finish my course with joy, and the ministry, which I have received of the Lord Jesus, to testify the gospel of the grace of God.
>
> –Acts 20:21-24

The Apostle Paul was a *finisher*! He was *fighting to finish*! He knew *afflictions* and *persecutions* were waiting on him; but he was *fighting to finish* what God had called him to do. He was *fighting to finish his course with joy!* The Apostle Paul was saying, "I have a *leg in the race* and I'm going to finish what God called me to do!"

> And now, behold, I know that ye all, among whom I have gone preaching the kingdom of God, shall see my face no more. Wherefore I take you to record this day, that I am pure from the blood of all men.
>
> –Acts 20:25-26

The Apostle Paul was saying, "I have finished what God assigned me to do for you. I am *free* from the blood of all men."

> For I have not shunned to declare unto you all the counsel of God.
>
> –Acts 20:27

He said he had declared "*all* 'the counsel of God."

> Take heed therefore unto yourselves, and to all the flock, over the which the Holy Ghost hath made you overseers, to feed the church of God, which he hath purchased with his own blood. For I know this, that after my departing shall grievous wolves enter in among you, not sparing the flock. Also of your own selves shall men arise, speaking perverse things, to draw away disciples after them. Therefore watch, and remember, that by the space of three years I ceased not to warn every one night and day with tears. And now, brethren, I commend you to God, and to the word of his grace, which is able to build you up, and to give you an inheritance among all them which are sanctified. I have coveted no man's silver, or gold, or apparel. Yea, ye yourselves know, that these hands have ministered unto my necessities, and to them that were with me. I have shewed you all things, how that so laboring ye ought to support the weak, and to remember the words of the Lord Jesus, how he said, It is more blessed to give than to receive. And when he had thus spoken, he kneeled down, and prayed with them all. And they all wept sore, and fell on Paul's neck, and kissed him. Sorrowing most of all for the

PASSION–THE 3RD ESSENTIAL KEY

> words which he spake, that they should see his face no more. And they accompanied him unto the ship.
>
> –Acts 20:28-38

The Apostle Paul *fought to finish* his ministry to them. As he said in verse 24, "But none of these things move me, neither count I my life dear unto myself, so that I might finish my course with joy, and the ministry, which I have received of the Lord Jesus, to testify the gospel of the grace of God."

He was *passionate*. He was *fighting to finish*. So, the Apostle Paul was *profitable*, and he was *passionate*. He fought to finish what God gave him, and he taught those that followed him to be just as *passionate* and *profitable* in what they were anointed to do. Let's look at Acts 18. This scripture will show that the Apostle Paul was profitable and passionate. Starting at verse 1:

> After these things Paul departed from Athens, and came to Corinth; And found a certain Jew named Aquila, born in Pontus, lately come from Italy, with his wife Priscilla; (because that Claudius had commanded all Jews to depart from Rome:) and came unto them. And because he was of the same craft, he abode with them, and wrought: for by their occupation they were tentmakers.
>
> –Acts 18:1-3

The Apostle Paul was not only passionate in regards to preaching the Gospel; he was also passionately involved with a *craft*. He had his own craft. He was a skillful workman as a "tentmaker." He was a *craftsman*. So, he was a worker with his own hands. He was skillful at doing something beyond just preaching. He was a skillful craftsman in a chosen field as a "tentmaker." Verse 3 says,

> And because he was of the same craft, he abode with them, and wrought: for by their occupation they were tentmakers.
>
> –Acts 18:3

He was working his craft, as a tentmaker, but he was also preaching the Gospel.

> And he reasoned in the synagogue every Sabbath, and persuaded the Jews and the Greeks.
>
> –Acts 18:4

YOUR WEALTH IS IN YOUR ANOINTING

So, every Sabbath he was *reasoning* in the synagogue; but he was doing his craft during the week.

> And when Silas and Timotheus were come from Macedonia, Paul was pressed in the spirit, and testified to the Jews that Jesus was Christ.
>
> –Acts 18:5

He was "pressed in the spirit." The phrase "*pressed* in the spirit" indicates that he was *passionate* in the spirit! He felt a Passion and *compelling* inside of his spirit, inside of his *belly*, to preach the Gospel.

> And when they opposed themselves, and blasphemed, he shook his raiment, and said unto them, Your blood be upon your own heads; I am clean: from henceforth I will go unto the Gentiles. And he departed thence, and entered into a certain man's house, named Justus, one that worshipped God, whose house joined hard to the synagogue.
>
> –Acts 18:6-7

The Apostle Paul hooked up with other *passionate* people. Justus' house "joined hard" to the synagogue. They joined *passionately* to the synagogue. The Apostle Paul hooked up with other passionate people.

> And Crispus, the chief ruler of the synagogue, believed on the Lord with all his house; and many of the Corinthians hearing believed, and were baptized. Then spake the Lord to Paul in the night by a vision, Be not afraid, but speak, and hold not thy peace: For I am with thee, and no man shall set on thee to hurt thee: for I have much people in this city. And he continued there a year and six months, teaching the word of God among them. And when Gallio was the deputy of Achaia, the Jews made insurrection with one accord against Paul, and brought him to the judgment seat, Saying, This fellow persuadeth men to worship God contrary to the law.
>
> –Acts 18:8-13

So, they began to oppose Paul. But, the Apostle Paul was *passionate* in pursuing what God had given him. The Apostle Paul hooked up with other *profitable* and *passionate* people. He hooked up with Aquila and Priscilla, and Justus, other people that were passionate and profitable about their craft. You can't hook up with people who do not have *Passion*, and who are not pursuing something, and still remain successful. They will hinder you from *releasing* the anointing and potential which God has put in you. You must hook up with someone who is pursuing something *too*. Then, if you can go in the same direction, passionately pursuing what God has called you to do, you can *compliment* one another.

Therefore, the Apostle Paul hooked up with other *profitable, passionate* people. He *inspired* profit and *Passion* as he *fought to finish* what God had called him to do. He taught the Church to be *passionate* and *profitable*. He was fighting to finish what God had called him to do, and he was passionate and profitable. This is a key to the release of the wealth contained in your anointing. **Your wealth is in your anointing.**

THE *ADVICE* OF A *FINISHER*

Let's look at 1 Thessalonians 4:11-12. We're examining the Apostle Paul, as a *finisher*. He fought to finish what God called him to do. The Apostle Paul hooked up with other profitable and passionate people. He inspired profit and *Passion* as he fought to finish what God called him to do. He taught the Church to be passionate and profitable. And, this is a key to the release of the wealth contained in the Church. You were *anointed* to do a particular *thing*. Again, Ephesians 2:10 says, "For we are His workmanship, created in Christ Jesus unto good works, which God has before ordained that we should walk in them." We are the Father's "workmanship." We have been created for the *purpose* of "good works." You were created to be profitable. God created you and me to be profitable. God created you and me to do something to release *profit* in the earth. And, you have to be a *passionate finisher* in order to release the profit in the earth, which God anointed you for. Genesis 1:28 says, "He blessed them, and said unto them, Be fruitful, and multiply, and replenish the earth, and subdue it, and have dominion…" So, you were "blessed" to be profitable from the *beginning*. **Your wealth is in your anointing.**

> And that ye study to be quiet, and to do your own business, and to work with your own hands, as we commanded you;
>
> –1 Thessalonians 4:11

The word "study" means to be *emulous*. Or, it means to study other profitable people to be *emulous* or to *imitate* what they did. So, you read books of profitable people and you imitate what they did to become profitable. The Apostle Paul is encouraging the Church to "study" people that have become profitable, and that have already succeeded; so that you can learn *how* to succeed and be profitable. The Apostle Paul was encouraging the Church to be profitable and passionate. Why? Let's look at 1 Thessalonians 4:11–12 once again:

> *And that ye study to be quiet, and to do your own business, and to work with your own hands, as we commanded you;*
>
> *–1 Thessalonians 4:11*

The word "quiet" means to "have rest," or to "enter into a place of rest." It means to enter into a place of *peace* or *shalom*. "Shalom" means *peace, prosperity, happiness, joy, fulfillment, blessing, wholeness, wellness, soundness, security, strength, victory; a happy, healthy, holy, friendly relationship with God and man*. This is what "quiet" means. So, the Apostle Paul was telling the Church to "study to be quiet." He was telling them they had to *study* and *prepare* themselves in order to enter into *Shalom*. There has to be a *mind transformation*.

"And that you study to be quiet, and to do your own business . . ." In other words, "run your own businesses; start your own businesses." The Apostle Paul is encouraging them to be *profitable*.

"And to work with your own hands, as we commanded you . . ." The Apostle Paul commanded the early Church to "study to be quiet and to do your own businesses", and to "work with your own hands, as we commanded you." Why? Look at verse 12:

> *That ye may walk honestly toward them that are without, and that ye may have lack of nothing.*
>
> *–1 Thessalonians 4:12*

The word "honestly" means "honorably." It is so you can be *honored* in society. People that "are without" are those that are in the world, who do not know Jesus. "And that you may have lack of nothing." In other words, so that your needs will be *met*.

So, the Apostle Paul encouraged the Church to be *like him*. We just examined in Acts 18:3 that the Apostle Paul was a *craftsman*. This is what is says:

> *And because he was of the same craft, he abode with them, and wrought: for by their occupation they were tentmakers.*

He was a "tentmaker" as well as an apostle, preaching the Word. And, the Apostle Paul was profitable. The Apostle Paul taught the early

Church to start businesses and to be profitable. He wanted them to be *independently wealthy* and free from being *dependent* on the world for their provision. He knew that they would gain more *influence* and *respect* by being wealthy. He *fought to finish* what God called him to do!

Now, let's look once again at Galatians 1:11. This is where we started looking at the Apostle Paul. Again, the Apostle Paul taught the early Church to start businesses. He wanted them to be independently wealthy and free from being dependent on the world for their provision. He knew that they would gain more influence and respect by being wealthy. Therefore, Paul *fought to finish* what God called him to do.

The widow with the "pot of oil" that came to Elisha the prophet, with her two sons about to be taken into slavery because her husband died with debt, received a supernatural plan from the man of God to get supernatural multiplication from her potential. And that's where she gained her wealth. The pot was what God had anointed for her to get her wealth. She had to *Fight to Finish* what was required in order to "pay her debt" and "live her and her children on the rest." This is the same thing the Apostle Paul wanted for the Church, when he told them to "study to be quiet, and to do your own business, and to work with your own hands, as we commanded you. That ye may walk honestly toward them that are without; and that you may have lack of nothing."

CONTINUE THE APOSTLE PAUL'S *TESTIMONY*

In Galatians 1:11, the Apostle Paul recounts his conversion.

> *But I certify you, brethren, that the gospel which was preached of me is not after man. For I neither received it of man, neither was I taught it, but by the revelation of Jesus Christ. For ye have heard of my conversation in time past in the Jews' religion, how that beyond measure I persecuted the church of God, and wasted it:*
>
> *–Galatians 1:11-13*

Again, the Apostle Paul was *passionate* from the beginning.

> *And profited in the Jews' religion above many my equals in mine own nation, being more exceedingly zealous of the traditions of my fathers.*
>
> *–Galatians 1:14*

YOUR WEALTH IS IN YOUR ANOINTING

We see that the Apostle Paul was profitable, even before he became an apostle.

> *But when it pleased God, who separated me from my mother's womb, and called me by his grace,*
>
> *–Galatians 1:15*

So we see that the Apostle Paul discovered his *Purpose*! At the *Damascus road*, he had a vision of the Lord Jesus. Proverbs 29:18 says, "Where there is no vision, the people perish; but he that keepeth the law, happy is he." You and I need to have a "Damascus Road Experience" of catching the vision God has for our lives! *Focus* is the first Essential Key to the *release* of the anointing within you. You have to become *focused* long enough to see what God called you to do. *Purpose* is the second Essential Key to the *release* of the anointing within you. You have to discover your *Purpose* and *pursue* it. *Passion* is the third Essential Key to the *release* of the anointing within you. You have to *passionately* pursue what God called you to do. Therefore, Galatians 1:15 says,

> *But when it pleased God, who separated me from my mother's womb, and called me by his grace,*

In other words, the Apostle Paul was saying, "This was my *purpose* for being born!"

> *To reveal his Son in me, that I might preach him among the heathen; immediately I conferred not with flesh and blood:*
>
> *–Galatians 1:16*

"Immediately" refers to *Passion*!

> *Neither went I up to Jerusalem to them which were apostles before me; but I went into Arabia, and returned again unto Damascus. Then after three years I went up to Jerusalem to see Peter, and abode with him fifteen days. But other of the apostles saw I none, save James the Lord's brother. Now the things which I write unto you, behold, before God, I lie not. Afterwards I came into the regions of Syria and Cilicia; And was unknown by face unto the churches of Judaea which were in Christ: But they had heard only, That he which persecuted us in times past now preacheth the faith which once he destroyed. And they glorified God in me.*
>
> *–Galatians 1:17-24*

PASSION–THE 3RD ESSENTIAL KEY

FATHER TO *SON* ADVICE: *FINISH*!

The Apostle Paul was *fighting to finish* what God called him to do.

> The Apostle Paul charged his son, in the Lord, Timothy to Fight to Finish what God called him to do. Let's look at 1Timothy 6, starting at verse 11: But thou, O man of God, flee these things; and follow after righteousness, godliness, faith, love, patience, meekness. Fight the good fight of faith, lay hold on eternal life, whereunto thou art also called, and hast professed a good profession before many witnesses.
>
> *–1 Timothy 6:11-12*

The Apostle Paul was telling Timothy, "You have to *Fight to Finish* what God called you to do! You have to fight with *Passion*." We saw that the Apostle Paul was *passionate* from the beginning, and he was teaching his son Timothy in the Lord, how to finish his race. Paul told Timothy to "lay hold" on eternal life. He was saying to him "put forth diligent, passionate effort for eternal life, which is the God quality of life, which God has given you." The Apostle Paul was letting Timothy know that it is the will of God for us to be blessed, and he wanted him to *Fight to Finish*!

In the end, the Apostle Paul tells Timothy, and each of us, to *Fight to Finish*! Let's look at 2 Timothy 4:1–8:

> I charge thee therefore before God, and the Lord Jesus Christ, who shall judge the quick and the dead at his appearing and his kingdom;
>
> *–2 Timothy 4:1*

The Apostle Paul is also charging you and me with the same charge:

> Preach the word; be instant in season, out of season; reprove, rebuke, exhort with all long suffering and doctrine.
>
> *–2 Timothy 4:2*

The Apostle Paul was showing Timothy *how* he accomplished what God told him to do:

> Preach the word; be instant in season, out of season; reprove, rebuke, exhort with all long suffering and doctrine.
>
> *–2 Timothy 4:2*

He told Timothy to be "instant!" In other words, "Be ready! Be immediate! In season, out of season." Whether they come, or whether they

YOUR WEALTH IS IN YOUR ANOINTING

don't come, "be instant; in season, out of season." When you are needed, "be instant, in season, out of season." When it seems like the right time; when it doesn't seem like the right time, "be instant; in season, out of season; reprove, rebuke, exhort with all long suffering and doctrine."

> *For the time will come when they will not endure sound doctrine; but after their own lusts shall they heap to themselves teachers, having itching ears; And they shall turn away their ears from the truth, and shall be turned unto fables. But watch thou in all things, endure afflictions, do the work of an evangelist, make full proof of thy ministry.*
>
> *–2 Timothy 4:3-5*

One last time, the Apostle Paul is teaching Timothy, his son in the Lord, how to *finish his race*. He said, "But watch thou in all things . . ." In other words, "Be alert."

> *But watch thou in all things, endure afflictions, do the work of an evangelist, make full proof of thy ministry. For I am now ready to be offered, and the time of my departure is at hand.*
>
> *–2 Timothy 4:5-6*

These were the Apostle Paul's *parting words* to his son, Timothy:

> *I have fought a good fight, I have finished my course, I have kept the faith: Henceforth there is laid up for me a crown of righteousness, which the Lord, the righteous judge, shall give me at that day: and not to me only, but unto all them also that love his appearing.*
>
> *–2 Timothy 4:7-8*

"Unto all them also . . ." who *Fight to Finish*! "Unto all them also . . ." who are *passionate* about fulfilling what God has called them to do!" The Apostle Paul realized that he "fought a good fight," he "finished his course." Not only did the Apostle Paul receive earthly rewards from being *passionate* and pursuing what God called him to do through passion and diligence, but also, most importantly, he would receive eternal, heavenly rewards! He would receive the eternal *crown of life*. We too must *Fight to Finish* what God called us to do in order to receive wealth in this life and in the life to come. **Your wealth is in your anointing!**

We've been examining the Essential Keys to the *release* of the anointing within you. We've been examining *Passion* as the third Essential Key to the *release* of the anointing within you. We've been looking at the

PASSION—THE 3RD ESSENTIAL KEY

fourth component of *Passion*, the *Fight to Finish*. We've looked at some examples of passionate *finishers*. We examined *King Solomon* as a *finisher*. We examined *Zerubbabel* as a *finisher*. We examined our *Lord Jesus Christ* as the *Author* and *Finisher* of our faith. And, we just explored the life of the *Apostle Paul* as a *finisher*. He "fought a good fight" and "finished his course" and received the *crown of life*. We too, must finish what God has called us to do.

PART THREE
ANOINTED TO LEAVE A LEGACY

Praise ye the Lord. Blessed is the man that feareth the Lord, that delighteth greatly in his commandments. His seed shall be mighty upon earth: the generation of the upright shall be blessed. Wealth and riches shall be in his house: and his righteousness endureth for ever.

–Psalms 112:1-3

CHAPTER NINE
FAITHFULNESS: AN ESSENTIAL KEY TO *MAINTAINING* WEALTH

The final key that we will look at in this book is the key that is necessary for you and me to *maintain* the wealth that God has given us through the anointing. The key is *Faithfulness.* We must be faithful to all of God's principles in order for wealth, happiness, fulfillment, accomplishment, etc., to be *sustained* or maintained *beyond* us.

Let's examine 2 Kings 4:1–7 once again in order to review the foundation of the entire message in this book.

This book is not just an *inspirational* message or *motivational* message. Rather, the purpose of this book is for complete financial and life *deliverance.* My hope is that you as the reader have gained clear, extensive instruction, revelation and *deliverance* from the truths presented. God's Word teaches us how to *come out* of poverty. My goal as a pastor and author in this book is to illustrate the heart of God for the prosperity and blessing for each of our lives. It's teaching how to come out of lack. It's not just a *prosperity message*, in the sense of saying, "God's going to bless you!" But, it's a message on how to come out of the *cycle*. The goal is to break the *generational* cycle of poverty. Only through *applying* the truth of God's Word can we be set free. This is a book and message that if heeded, can set the *mind* free. This revelation is the *Gospel* or *good news* to the poor. The good news to the poor is that *we don't have to be poor anymore*. And the continuation of the good news is to show God's people the specifics on how to change their situation. It's the *anointing* that destroys the "yoke" of poverty and "lifts the heavy burden" from our lives (Isaiah 10:27).

In 2 Kings 4:1–7, the widow with the "pot of oil" discovered the *anointing* that she had in her house. *Discovery* is the key. You and I have been

YOUR WEALTH IS IN YOUR ANOINTING

anointed for something. God has *anointed* something *in* you. He has anointed something He called you to do. Your *purpose*, your *gifts*, your *talents* . . . have been anointed, and your *wealth* is there. The fulfillment for your life is there. Wealth is not just money; but it does *include* money. Wealth is *total fulfillment*. Wealth is fulfilling your "Why?" It is fulfilling your *Purpose*. It is fulfilling your *reason* for being. The more you fulfill your *Why?* in the earth, the more successful and fulfilled you will be. And, money is *included* in that success. Money is an *essential* part of that success. King Solomon says in Ecclesiastes 10:19, "A feast is made for laughter, and wine maketh merry: but money answereth all things."

We can't act like money is *not* important. Solomon says, ". . . money answereth all things." We need "things" in life. We need shoes, food, clothing, houses, cars, education, etc. We need to go to the doctor. We need to send our children to school. We all need "things," Job 1:21 says, "Naked came I out of my mother's womb, and naked shall I return thither." However, in the *meantime* we need some "things." Let's read 2 Kings 4:1 again:

> Now there cried a certain woman of the wives of the sons of the prophets unto Elisha, saying, Thy servant my husband is dead; and thou knowest that thy servant did fear the Lord: and the creditor is come to take unto him my two sons to be bondmen.

So, we see, the widow was in a desperate situation. Her husband had died, leaving the family with debt, and her two sons were about to be taken into slavery to pay off the debt to the creditor. In Proverbs, the Bible lets us know that "the borrower is slave to the lender" (Proverbs 22:7). That sounds like the "yoke," doesn't it? Jesus said He's come to "preach the gospel to the poor" to "destroy the yoke and lift the heavy burden" (Luke 4:18–19). The *anointing* destroys the yoke and lifts the heavy burden (Isaiah 10:27). The *Blessing* of Deuteronomy 28:12 says that, "you will be the *lender* and not the borrower. The *curse* says that others will *lend* to you and you will borrow. The *Blessing* is that you will "lend unto many" and *borrow* from none. However, society has been set up to advantage some people that are in power and to *keep* them in power. They push the propaganda of *debt*. The propaganda is that in order to be *honorable* in society, you must have *good credit*. You do want to have a *good name*. The Bible talks about having a "good name is rather to be chosen than great riches, and loving favour rather than silver and gold"

FAITHFULNESS–AN ESSENTIAL KEY TO MAINTAINING WEALTH

(Proverbs 22:1). This is a *good reputation*. However, when the world system typically says *good credit*, they are referring to a person's ability *borrow and borrow and borrow*! In other words, the more ability you have to borrow, the better *credit* you have because you can continue to *pay back someone* and *pay back* someone and *pay back someone*. Contrarily, what the Bible calls *good credit* is the ability to be the *lender* and *not the borrower* according to Deuteronomy 28:12. That's *good credit*! When you can be in the position to be the *lender* and *not the borrower*: that's *good credit*! That's *good credit* working on *your behalf*! You're the *lender* and *not the borrower*. I'm emphasizing this point to show that the widow and her husband were not in the place of *Blessing* that God wanted them to be in before the husband died. When he died, she was left with *debt*. Elisha the prophet wanted the widow to get into the place of *Blessing*. The *Blessing* was contained in her *anointing*.

DESCRIPTION OF THE *BLESSING*

Look quickly at Psalms 112. I'm going to describe this *Blessing* that the Word of God promises. This is the condition we should be living in. This is what God desires for all of His children. The widow was not experiencing the *Blessing* at this time, because her *anointing* was *hid* in the *pantry* of the house. Her anointing was still in the *pot*! It was still "pot-ential." It was *unused*, *latent* ability. It could be used. It had the potential to create wealth. But it was in the pantry, in the pot. It was still in *"pot-ential"* form. The anointing was in potential form. It was in the pantry. *Unreleased potential fails to benefit you*. We examined the Essential Keys to the *release* of the anointing within you. The keys are *Focus*, *Purpose*, and *Passion*. We examined the various components of each.

We looked at 2 Kings 4:1 and saw that the widow was in debt as a result of her husband dying and leaving her and her sons in debt. We know that was *not* the place God wanted her to be. That was not the *blessed* condition. The husband died and left his wife and children with debt, though they had a "pot of oil" that had the potential to bring wealth. They had the *potential* in the pantry all the time, but it was not *released*. Often, we also go most of our lives with our potential undiscovered and unreleased. Thus, we suffer lack, distress, and much less than God's best for us. God, our Heavenly Father, wishes "above all things that we prosper, and be in health, even as our souls prosper" (3 John 2). However, we

YOUR WEALTH IS IN YOUR ANOINTING

must take time to discover what He has given us to release His anointing in our lives. God has given each of us gifts, talents, and potential for wealth and prosperity. Yet, we must look within and discover those tools for change, and allow Christ's anointing to flow through those specific areas of our lives. We will then discover and release our wealth. The husband of the widow, though a prophet and man of God, failed to completely release or utilize the potential wealth in his anointing. The Bible gives us clear descriptions of the characteristics of the man or woman that is truly manifesting the *Blessing* of God. Now, I want to examine the condition of the *blessed* person. Let's look at Psalms 112.

> *Praise ye the Lord. Blessed is the man that feareth the Lord, that delighteth greatly in his commandments. His seed shall be mighty upon earth: the generation of the upright shall be blessed.*
>
> *–Psalms 112:1-2*

In other words, "his children shall be mighty upon the earth . . ." This should have been the condition of her children. This should have been the condition of her husband. Hosea 4:6 says, "My people are destroyed for lack of knowledge . . ." God says, "My people."

The *Blessing* is "His seed shall be mighty upon earth." That's the *Blessing*. The Bible says, "...the generation of the upright shall be blessed." It did not say, "We shall go into bondage." It didn't say, "We will be passing down debt, from the parents to the children." That's not the condition of *Blessing*. Proverbs says, "A good man leaves an inheritance to his children's children, and the wealth of the wicked is laid up for the righteous" (Proverbs 13:22). Not *debt*, and *bills*, because you didn't *release* your *pot-ential*. God doesn't want your children going into debt, due to you failing to release your potential and your anointing. He doesn't want your children to live in poverty, because you didn't *discover your Purpose*! God wants you to *focus*! God wants you to discover your *Purpose*. He wants you to *passionately pursue* it. So, that you can create the wealth that God has invested in your *pot-ential*. It's your "pot of oil." It's your *anointing*, for you and your family. Look at Psalms 112 again:

> *His seed shall be mighty upon earth: the generation of the upright shall be blessed. Wealth and riches shall be in his house: and his righteousness endureth forever.*
>
> *–Psalms 112:2-3*

FAITHFULNESS–AN ESSENTIAL KEY TO MAINTAINING WEALTH

Now, "wealth and riches" *was* in her "house," and in her husband's house when he was *alive*. It was in "pot-ential" form. It was the "pot of oil." The potential was there, in the *pantry*. It was "in the house," but it was *unreleased*. The *solution* to the debt was in the house, but it was *unreleased*.

> Wealth and riches shall be in his house: and his righteousness endureth forever.
>
> –Psalms 112:3

The *influence* of your *godly life shall endure forever*. You can be *rich and* you can be *righteous*. Maybe her husband was just focusing on being *righteous*, and he wasn't focusing on being *rich*. This is how many saints of God have been taught. In other words, "Just give me Jesus, and you take this ole' world." No! I want *something* in this world!

Personally, *I've got Jesus!* I accepted Him as my Lord and Savior . . . but I want some of *these benefits* while in the world! I want some "wealth and riches" in my house! I'm going to live righteously. I'm going to do right. God can *trust* me with some *money*! I've got *good sense*! I've got *good morals*! I'm not going to turn into the *devil* because I've gotten some *money*! In many cases, it's been taught like that. People say things like, "Money will takeover you! People lose their soul over some money. What would it profit a man to gain the whole world and lose his soul?" My answer to that is "Give Jesus your soul, and gain everything He has for you!" Then, "when the righteous are in authority, the people [will] rejoice" (Proverbs 29:2).

We would have less *negative* things going on in the world, if we take our *position*. God gave *us* the *world*. "The earth is the Lord's and the fullness thereof; the world and they that dwell therein" (Psalms 24:1). "We are His people and the sheep of His pasture" (Psalms 100:3). He's already told you that He gave you the *world*. Psalms 115:16 says, "The heaven, even the heavens are the Lord's; but the earth has He given to the children of men." He's already given it to you. But, we have to *take it*, and not leave it in the hands of the *wicked*!

> Wealth and riches shall be in his house: and his righteousness endureth forever.
>
> –Psalms 112:3

YOUR WEALTH IS IN YOUR ANOINTING

So, you can have "wealth and riches" and you can be *righteous*. That's liberating to know. You can have "wealth and riches" and you can be *righteous*. Your "righteousness" can *endure forever*. You can stay *holy and happy*! You can stay holy, happy, and *fat*! *Fat*! Fat with *wealth*! Fat with *plenty*. Holy, happy, and *fat*! The "oil" represents *richness, fatness,* and *plenty*. **Your wealth is in your anointing!**

> Unto the upright there ariseth light in the darkness: he is gracious, and full of compassion, and righteous.
>
> —Psalms 112:4

This is describing the *blessed* person's characteristics. This describes their heart.

> A good man sheweth favour, and lendeth: he will guide his affairs with discretion.
>
> —Psalms 112:5

This describes the *righteous man*. It says, "a good man sheweth favour, and lendeth: he will guide his affairs with discretion." It didn't say, "A good man is desperate, and goes to the check exchange and borrows." It didn't say, "A good man goes to the pawn shop and pawns his watch to try to pay his light bill." We all have gotten into tight situations. However, we should be constantly pushing forward to get to a better position. Make sure that the loan is pushing you forward if you have to borrow. Don't just habitually get into debt and stay in the same place.

The widow's husband was a *prophet*. He was a *righteous* man, but he got into a *desperate* situation. But, that wasn't God's *best* for him. This verse in Psalms 112:5 is a better description of what God's *best* looks like:

> A good man sheweth favour, and lendeth: he will guide his affairs with discretion.

You and I should be in the position to "show favor." We should be in the position to show favor to someone else. We should be able to help someone else pay their light bill or pay off their house. **Your wealth is in your anointing.** You are connected with the *Anointed One*.

> A good man sheweth favour, and lendeth: he will guide his affairs with discretion.
>
> —Psalms 112:5

FAITHFULNESS–AN ESSENTIAL KEY TO MAINTAINING WEALTH

As a "good man" or *righteous* person, God expects you to guide your business affairs "with discretion." He expects you and me to guide our affairs with *good judgment*. According to the *Blessing* of Deuteronomy 28:1–14, God wants you and me to be the "head and not the tail," "above only and not beneath," "the lender and not the borrower." That's the *Blessing*. Jesus said, "The Spirit of the Lord is upon Me, and He has anointed Me to preach the Gospel to the poor . . ." (Luke 4:18). This is the *Good News* to the poor. This is the position that God has given you as a Christian. You are in Christ, the Anointed One. And you have the *Blessing*. The curse of poverty is officially a thing of the past for you. "If any man be in Christ, he is a new creature; old things are passed away; behold, all things have become new" (2 Corinthians 5:17).

THERE'S A *BLESSING* IN THE *HOUSE*

Now let's look back at 2 Kings 4:1–2:

> Now there cried a certain woman of the wives of the sons of the prophets unto Elisha, saying, Thy servant my husband is dead; and thou knowest that thy servant did fear the Lord: and the creditor is come to take unto him my two sons to be bondmen. And Elisha said unto her, What shall I do for thee? Tell me, what hast thou in the house? And she said, Thine handmaid hath not anything in the house, save a pot of oil.

Why did Elisha ask the widow, "What hast thou in the house?" Because, Psalms 112:3 says, "Wealth and riches shall be in his house: and his righteousness endureth for ever." In other words, there's supposed to be something *in your house!* In other words, Elisha was saying to the widow, "I know your husband. He was a good man. He was a righteous man. He was one of the prophets. So, I know that there is something *in your house*! You're coming to me, child of God; but I know that there is something in your house. Your husband was a good man. Your husband feared the Lord. He may not have tapped into it while he was alive, but I know that there is something *in your house*. I was trying to teach him. I was trying to convince him and enlighten him. I was trying to help him while he was alive. He may not have fully caught what I was trying to teach him about prospering through the anointing. But, there is something *in your house* because I know that Psalms 112:3 says, 'Wealth and riches shall be in his house: and his righteousness endureth for ever.'" So, Elisha was saying to the widow that he knew that

YOUR WEALTH IS IN YOUR ANOINTING

there was something *in her house* because the scripture said of the righteous person, "wealth and riches shall be in his house." So Elisha says to the widow in verse 2,

> ... What shall I do for thee? Tell me, what hast thou in the house? And she said, Thine handmaid hath not anything in the house, save a pot of oil.

The widow said she didn't have anything in the house, "save a pot of oil." In other words, "I don't have anything in the house; except the *anointing!*" The oil in her *pot* represented the *anointing*. It was her *potential* deliverance!

> Then he said, Go, borrow thee vessels abroad of all thy neighbors, even empty vessels; borrow not a few.
>
> –2 Kings 4:3

The reason that Elisha told the widow to "borrow not a few" is because the anointing has the power to fulfill the first, *Original Blessing*, from Genesis 1:28, which is "And God Blessed them, and God said unto them, be fruitful, and multiply, replenish the earth, subdue it, and have dominion."

In the *anointing* is the power for the *Blessing* of Genesis 1:28 to be *released*. The anointing was given to "destroy the yoke, and lift the heavy burden" off of our lives so that the *Blessing* could be *released* and *manifest* in our lives. Isaiah 10:27 says,

> And it shall come to pass in that day, that his burden shall be taken away from off thy shoulder, and his yoke from off thy neck, and the yoke shall be destroyed because of the anointing.

The *anointing* was released to *destroy the yoke* of poverty, *constraints* and *restrictions*, and lack off of your life, so that the *Blessing*, which God declared in Genesis 1:28, could be released in our lives. The original plan of God was for mankind to be blessed and walk in the *Blessing*. God's original plan wasn't for Jesus to have to come to die on the cross to pay for our sins. He was anointed with the *Anointing* to come *undo* what the devil had done. The devil put us in bondage and the "yoke" of poverty through the introduction of *sin*. As a result, lack, depression, failure, defeat, and poverty came too. The *anointing* came to destroy the "yoke" of sin, sickness, bondage, lack, and poverty, so that we may regain the

FAITHFULNESS–AN ESSENTIAL KEY TO MAINTAINING WEALTH

Original Blessing. God had already given us the *power to prosper* in the beginning. Deuteronomy 8:18 says,

> But thou shalt remember the Lord thy God: for it is he that giveth thee power to get wealth, that he may establish his covenant which he sware unto thy fathers, as it is this day.

So, God had already given the "power to get wealth." It had already been given. But, He gave the anointing to destroy the yoke that was *preventing* the "power to get wealth" from *manifesting* in our lives. The *anointing*, which comes through the *preached* Word, was given to deliver us from a *poverty mindset*. God sent the anointing to deliver us from a *poverty mentality*. God sent the anointing to deliver us from a *failure mindset*. He sent the anointing to deliver us from a *limited perspective* of what we can *do* and what we can *have*. God sent the anointing to deliver us from feeling *bound* in life. He sent the anointing to deliver us from feeling like the *tail* and not the *head*! He wanted to deliver us from feeling like we are *beneath* and not *above*. He wanted to deliver us from feeling like we are the *borrower* and not the *lender*. That feeling and perspective is the result of the *curse*. The curse *switched* us from the original *role* and *position* that we were *created* in. The curse made us the *tail* and not the *head*, *beneath* and not *above*, the *borrower* and not the *lender*. But, the *Blessing* made you the *head* and not the *tail*, *above only* and not *beneath*, the *lender* and not the *borrower*. That's the *Blessing*! The *anointing* was released to *destroy the yoke* that had us bound, due to sin entering into the world. We were *born* into sin. John 10:10 says, "The thief cometh not but for to steal, and to kill, and to destroy; but I am come that they might have life, and that they might have it more abundantly." The "thief," Satan, was *stealing* your ability to *thrive, prosper,* and *succeed*. But Jesus said, "I Am come . . ." Who is He? He is the *Anointed One*, and it is His Anointing that destroys the yoke. Jesus declared Himself and why He came in Luke 4:18: "The Spirit of Lord is upon Me, because He has anointed Me to preach the Gospel to the poor . . ."

> Then he said, Go, borrow thee vessels abroad of all thy neighbours, even empty vessels; borrow not a few. And when thou art come in, thou shalt shut the door upon thee and upon thy sons, and shalt pour out into all those vessels, and thou shalt set aside that which is full. So she went from him, and shut the door upon her and upon her sons, who brought the vessels to her; and she poured out.
>
> *–2 Kings 4:3-5*

YOUR WEALTH IS IN YOUR ANOINTING

So, Elisha switched the widow from being the *tail* to being the *head*. She went from being in a desperate situation to having an *oil business*. She went from being *a beggar* to becoming *a manufacturer*. She went from having *potential* in the pot of oil, to becoming a *producer*. You have to take your potential from the state of being *potential* to *becoming a producer*. The difference between a *producer* and a *consumer* is that one is the *head* and the other is the *tail*. One is *above* and the other is *beneath*. One is *the provider* and the other is *in need*. One is the *borrower* and the other is the *lender*. You must become the *producer*. You must become the *problem-solver*. You must become the *head* and not the *tail*, *above only* and not *beneath*!

> *And it came to pass, when the vessels were full, that she said unto her son, Bring me yet a vessel. And he said unto her, There is not a vessel more. And the oil stayed.*
>
> *–2 Kings 4:6*

In other words, the widow had "more than enough." She had more oil, more *potential*, more *anointing* than her vessels could contain! "And the oil stayed." It just *rested* from issuing forth. It didn't say it *stopped* or *ceased*. It didn't say she didn't have *any more*. There just wasn't anything to pour into *at the time*. It says it "stayed." If you tell your dog to "stay," it's not the same as telling your dog to go back into the doghouse and take a nap. You just said, "Stay." You said, "Wait right here" until the next command. You said, "Stay." The fact that you said "stay" means there is something else that is going to come. Maybe you're going to give him a little biscuit, or you're going to tell him to *come on*. You were telling him to *wait* until the next command. You didn't say, "Go to bed." If you would have said that, the dog would have turned around and went to bed for the night and that would have been the end of the commands for the night. But, you said, "Stay" because something else was coming. So, the widow had *some more*. Something else was *coming*. How do I know? Look at verse 7:

> *Then she came and told the man of God. And he said, Go, sell the oil, and pay thy debt, and live thou and thy children of the rest.*
>
> *–2 Kings 4:7*

"The rest" means she had *something left over*. "The rest" means you have more than enough. *The rest of it* means you have *some more*.

FAITHFULNESS–AN ESSENTIAL KEY TO MAINTAINING WEALTH

The purpose of looking at what the widow had remaining, was to review the fact that she had *more than enough*, as a result of her obtaining her miracle.

YOU HAVE SOMETHING *LEFT*!

Now the remaining portion of this message is to explore the fact that the *Blessing* that God has for you should go on *beyond you*. This is not just a *bless me* message. It's not just to show you how God will pay your rent or light bill. No. It's a *deliverance* message. The purpose is to deliver you out of a poverty and lack mindset. It is so you can create a new condition for you, your children, and your children's children. It is so that you can *be a blessing*, and you can expand this *blessing* to someone else, by showing them that they don't have to be the *tail* anymore, but they can be the *head*.

Now, let's talk about *Faithfulness* as an Essential Key to *maintaining* wealth. Look again at 2 Kings 4:7:

> *Then she came and told the man of God. And he said, Go, sell the oil, and pay thy debt, and live thou and thy children of the rest.*

In other words, it is expected of you and me to have something *left over*. *Faithfulness* is the Essential Key to *maintaining* wealth. The widow had obtained wealth from her anointing. The "pot of oil" had *produced* for her. She paid off the debt. But, in order to *maintain* it, *Faithfulness* was required.

Let's look at Proverbs 13:22–23. God wants you to be free. He wants you to live in the *Blessing*, and then *pass it on* to your children.

> *A good man leaveth an inheritance to his children's children: and the wealth of the sinner is laid up for the just.*
>
> *–Proverbs 13:22*

This means that a "good man" or woman leaves an inheritance, not only to their children; but also to *their grandchildren*. This state says, "You did a *good job* at being *faithful* over what God gave you. You were a *good steward*. You were a *good steward* over what God invested in you." It is the *anointing!* It is your *Purpose*. It is that thing that God anointed you *for*. You produced *wealth* from it. And, you were a *good steward* over it. You provided for your children and it was enough to pass down to your *grandchildren*. God says, "That's a good man!" He or she did a *good job*! Elisha, the prophet, told the widow in 2 Kings 4:7, "Go, sell the oil. And, pay thy debt. And, live thou and thy children of the rest." The "rest" is the *inheritance*. Paying off the *debt* was what was necessary for *this lifetime*. However, the "rest" is the *inheritance*.

> A good man leaveth an inheritance to his children's children: and the wealth of the sinner is laid up for the just. Much food is in the tillage of the poor: but there is that is destroyed for want of judgment.
>
> –Proverbs 13:22-23

In other words, there is "much food" or "much increase" or "much wealth" in the *work* of the poor. You can believe the widow's husband, a prophet, was working hard. But he wasn't able to discover or *maximize* his wealth that was in his *anointing*. The *pot-ential* was in the *pantry*. The "pot of oil" was in the *pantry*. That was his potential wealth. He was working in *somebody else's field*. He was working in somebody else's field, but he didn't discover his *own* potential. He didn't *focus* long enough, or see clearly enough to discover his potential. We talked about the Essential Keys to the *release* of the anointing within you. The first was *Focus*. The second was *Purpose*. The third was *Passion*.

The widow's husband, the prophet, didn't focus long enough, or see clearly enough to discover the *wealth* that was in his *anointing*. He didn't discover the wealth in his *purpose*. God gives *gifts* and *callings*. The *calling* is the *assignment*. The *gifts* are the *source of wealth* for the assignment. The widow's husband didn't discover the *gifts* that were a part of his *calling*, and passionately pursue them. This is what was necessary to release him and his family from *financial bondage*. Proverbs 13:23 says, "Much food is in the tillage of the poor: but there is that is destroyed for want of judgment."

"Tillage" means "hard work." It means working in the *field*. However, "much food" is in *your field*, if you will work *your field*, if you will work *your ground*, rather than working someone else's *field*. "Much food is in the tillage of the poor: but there is that is destroyed for want of judgment."

THERE'S *WEALTH* IN YOUR *WORK*

It's not that there is not *wealth* in your work. There is *potential wealth* there. There is potentially *millions* of dollars in your work! There are po-

FAITHFULNESS–AN ESSENTIAL KEY TO MAINTAINING WEALTH

tential *millionaires* all around us! But, "there is that is destroyed . . . " or *pillaged*, or *wasted*, ". . . for want of judgment." There is often a *lack of wisdom, insight, guidance, judgment,* and *knowledge* to take possession of the wealth. One of the reasons the poor *remain* poor is because they won't *receive instruction*. They will not *give themselves* unto *knowledge* and *instruction*. Often, they won't *read*. And, if they do read, they don't *diligently apply* what they read. There is one Australian billionaire that said he didn't know *how* to read. His name is Peter J. Daniels. During his earlier years, he worked laboring jobs because that was the only kind he could get. But, he said he listened to a preached message that changed his life. Jesus said, "The Spirit of the Lord is upon me, because he has anointed me to preach the Gospel to the poor." (Luke 4:18) Peter J. Daniels said he listened to a message by Dr. Billy Graham. The *gospel* went forth. And he got saved. And he learned how to read, by learning how to read the *Bible*. This ignited in him a great *desire* to learn. He taught himself how to read. He said he read several *thousand* autobiographies. He read about men and women that had become successful. He didn't say he went to *college*. He *taught* himself because there were *enough books* and resources *available* written by different people telling their story of how they succeeded. But, he *disciplined* himself. He *bought* and *read* the books. Or, went to the library, then sat down and read for free. He began to discover *patterns* of how successful people succeeded. He discovered *patterns of success*. He discovered *laws of success*. For example, *they worked hard, they discovered one chief aim, they discovered their Focus, they discovered their Purpose, they Passionately pursued it*, and *they overcame obstacles*. He started to see certain patterns from reading book after book of successful people's autobiographies and biographies. And then, he became a *billionaire*. Not *only* a *millionaire*. Not a "hundred thousand-aire." He became a *billionaire!* That's *inspirational!* That encourages me to do more *reading!* Because, Proverbs 13:23 says,

> Much food is in the tillage of the poor: but there is that is destroyed for want of judgment.

We're looking at *Faithfulness* as an Essential Key to *maintaining* wealth. The scripture says "Much food is in the tillage of the poor, but there is that is wasted or destroyed for want of judgment." If you don't have proper judgment for how to *manage* what God has given you, you will *waste it*. You will not be "faithful and wise."

YOUR WEALTH IS IN YOUR ANOINTING

> *Who then is that faithful and wise steward, whom his Lord shall make ruler over his house, to give them their portion of meat in due season?*
>
> *–Luke 12:42*

To be "faithful and wise" is what's needed. *Faithfulness* is an Essential Key to maintaining wealth.

Based on the example of Peter J. Daniels, the saying is true which says, "Leaders are readers." When you read, you *learn how to do* and you *learn how to lead*. You grow in knowledge. You grow in understanding.

Let's look at 1 Thessalonians 4:11–12 to look more at *Faithfulness* as an Essential Key to *maintaining* wealth. We looked at the fact that a "good man leaves an inheritance to his children's children." The way that a good man leaves an inheritance to his children's children is by *managing* that wealth. He or she manages their wealth through increasing in knowledge. Getting the knowledge that's necessary is *good stewardship* and *Faithfulness*. In 1 Thessalonians 4:11–12 it says,

> *And that ye study to be quiet, and to do your own business, and to work with your own hands, as we commanded you.*

The word "quiet" means to come to a place of *rest*. The Bible tells us we should *labor* to enter into *rest*. We should be *laboring* to enter into *rest*, according to Hebrews 4:11. *Rest* is the *Blessing*. Rest is *Shalom*. Rest is *wellness, wholeness, soundness, safety, security, happiness, health, prosperity, nothing missing, nothing broken in spirit, soul, body, socially, or financially*.

God asked me a question several years ago when I was younger. I think I was sitting in my apartment thinking about my bills. The Lord said to me, "What would it be like not to have to think about money? What would it be like to be debt-free and have all your bills paid? And to owe no man anything, but to love them?" It shocked me that He asked me that. I was going to try to imagine an answer. However, before I could answer, He answered and said, "It would be peace." In other words, "It would be *rest*. It would be *quiet*." But, God didn't tell me *how* to get it at that moment. He just presented the *image* to my heart to give me an *appetite* for this *rest, quiet, peace,* and *prosperity*.

There was another time after that, that I felt like I wasn't quite doing everything that God wanted me to do. And I said, "Lord, how can I

FAITHFULNESS–AN ESSENTIAL KEY TO MAINTAINING WEALTH

please You? How can I bring You pleasure?" He said, "*Prosper!*" He said it like it was *up to me*. He said, "*Prosper!*" He was saying, "That would please Me. That would bring Me pleasure." How did I know it was the voice of God? Because, Psalms 35:27 says,

> Let them shout for joy, and be glad, that favour my righteous cause: yea, let them say continually, Let the Lord be magnified, which hath pleasure in the prosperity of his servant.

God has "pleasure" in our "prosperity." How do I know that's true? Because, 3 John 2 says, "Beloved, I wish above all things that thou mayest prosper and be in health, even as thy soul prospereth."

God is saying, "The thing that would give me the most pleasure for you is that you prosper, be in health, even as your soul prospers." *Soul prosperity* is *mental prosperity*. It includes *mental, emotional, personality,* and *intellect*. God wants you to grow and mature, and to become more *developed* and *refined* in your soul. How does that happen? Let's look again at 1 Thessalonians 4:11–12:

> And that ye study to be quiet, and to do your own business, and to work with your own hands, as we commanded you; That ye may walk honestly toward them that are without, and that ye may have lack of nothing.

We talked about the Australian billionaire, Peter J. Daniels. He didn't know how to read. But, he heard the gospel through Dr. Billy Graham. He got saved and started learning how to read the Bible. And then he started reading autobiographies and biographies of successful men and women. He learned how they became prosperous. He said he read thousands of autobiographies and biographies. He learned some principles. He started to recognize certain patterns, and laws of success. He *studied*. Again, 1 Thessalonians 4:11–12 says,

And that ye study to be quiet, and to do your own business, and to work with your own hands, as we commanded you; That ye may walk honestly toward them that are without, and that ye may have lack of nothing.

The *Strong's Exhaustive Concordance of the Bible* defines "study" like this:

STUDY

5389–philotimeomai

    1. to be fond of honor

    2. to be emulous (eager or earnest to do something)

195

3. labor

4. strive

5. study

God wants you and me to be *desirous* of the *honor* that comes with starting and succeeding in our own businesses. He wants us to "study" and become "emulous" of others that have succeeded in their businesses, and be *eager* and *earnest to do something* ourselves.

"Emulous" means to "imitate." It means "to imitate with the intent to equal or surpass" (Webster's). Again, to be emulous means to study and to imitate with the intent to equal or surpass. So that should be our goal in studying, reading after, or listening to successful people. Many Christians listen to and follow after successful pastors, teachers, and ministries. But God doesn't want you to just *listen* to what they *say*. He wants you to pay attention to what they *do*. Pay attention to the *skillfulness* in how they are *running* their ministry. Pay attention to the level of organization that is required for them to be successful. Pay attention to how they are writing their books. They take *time* to write those books. It takes *discipline*. We should *copy* and *imitate their discipline*. We should do what they *do*! That's a true *disciple*. A true disciple is someone that is *disciplined* by the same *manners, ways, words, and example* of their teacher. You should start *writing* something. You should discipline yourself. You should work on your *organization*. Listen to them tell about their life story, and how God raised them from not having anything to having success. There was a *process*. Discover those *keys to success*. You can do that from reading autobiographies and biographies. There are many that tell their story in their autobiography. They tell how they went from *barely* having anything, to having *more than enough*. The Apostle Paul is telling us here in 1 Thessalonians 4:11–12,

> *And that ye study to be quiet, and to do your own business, and to work with your own hands, as we commanded you; That ye may walk honestly toward them that are without, and that ye may have lack of nothing.*

Proverbs 13:22–23 says,

> *A good man leaves an inheritance to his children's children: and the wealth of the sinner is laid up for the just. Much food is in the tillage of the poor: but there is that is destroyed for want of judgment.*

FAITHFULNESS–AN ESSENTIAL KEY TO MAINTAINING WEALTH

Faithfulness is an Essential Key to maintaining wealth. But also, learning the *laws of success*, and faithfully working and maintaining those laws, so that you do not *waste* what you have, or so that what you have is not "destroyed." God wants you to be able to pass something down to your children and your children's children. That is the key. You want to pass down, not only the wealth, but also the *wisdom*. Look at Proverbs 12:11:

> He that tilleth his land shall be satisfied with bread: but he that followeth vain persons is void of understanding.

Your *heart*, your *soul*, your *mind*, and your *creativity* are your *"land."* That is your "land." The prophet Elisha asked the widow that came to him in the desperate situation, "What do you have in the house?"

> He that tilleth his land shall be satisfied with bread: but he that followeth vain persons is void of understanding.
>
> –Proverbs 12:11

"Vain persons" or *vain endeavors* are a *waste of your energy* that you should be *investing* in "tilling" your *own land*. If it's not contributing to the *Purpose* that God has called you unto, it's a *vain person* or a *vain endeavor*. If it's not going to make you money, and make you successful and prosperous, and take care of you and your family, then it's a *vain person* or a *vain endeavor*. If it's not the thing that is bringing *joy* to the Lord for you to do, because it's a part of why He created you, then it's a *vain person* or a *vain endeavor*. Ephesians 2:10 says,

> For we are His workmanship, created in Christ Jesus, unto good works; which God has before ordained that we should walk in them.

If what you are doing is not according to why He created you, it's a *vain person* or *vain endeavor*. I asked the Lord, "What can I do to please You? What can I do to bring You pleasure?" He said, "*Prosper!*" I know it was in alignment with the Word because He said in 3 John 2, "Beloved, I wish above all things that you prosper, and be in health, even as your soul prosper." **Your wealth is in your anointing.**

CHAPTER TEN

ABRAHAM: THE FATHER OF FAITHFULNESS

Your Wealth Is In Your Anointing is the name of this book and message, which God has put in my heart to share with you. And we've been looking at how *Faithfulness* is an Essential Key to *maintaining* wealth. The basis of this entire message is in 2 Kings 4:1–7, where we see the widow that came to Elisha the prophet in a desperate situation. Her sons were about to be taken into slavery to pay off the debt that her husband left behind when he died. Elisha the prophet helped her to discover that she had resources in her house to solve her problem. He helped her to recognize that the "pot of oil" which she had in her house was the anointing she needed to destroy the yoke of poverty off of her life and her children's lives. Elisha gave her a supernatural plan, and God gave her supernatural, extraordinary multiplication on her one pot of oil, and she was able to pay off the debt and have enough to live on for the rest of her life, and have something left for her children.

The woman's "pot of oil" in the story represents the *anointing*. You and I are anointed because we are *in* the Anointed One, the Lord Jesus Christ. The *anointing* is a special *issuance* of the "grace" of God. The Bible lets us know in 2 Corinthians 8:9,

> *For ye know the grace of our Lord Jesus Christ, that, though he was rich, yet for your sakes he became poor, that ye through his poverty might be rich.*

So, there was a special issuance of the "grace" of God to destroy the yoke of poverty. We were *bound* by poverty. We were bound by the *curse*. Poverty is a *spirit*, and it wraps up people for *generations*. It is a yoke of *slavery*. It is a yoke on the *mind* and *soul*, and it restricts people's ability to *excel*. It restricts people's ability to succeed. It restricts people's ability to *prosper*. It restricts people's ability to *abound*. It is a *yoke*. It has bands of bondage and slavery. But, the *anointing destroys* the yoke, and *lifts* the heavy burden! (Isaiah 10:27) Therefore, there was a special issuance of the anointing upon Jesus to destroy poverty, lack, depression, oppression, etc. Jesus came to "destroy the works of the devil" (1 John 3:8).

PARADIGM SHIFT: FROM *LACK* TO *MORE ON RESERVE*

Now, once again I am speaking of *Faithfulness* as an Essential Key to *maintaining* wealth. The basis of the message is the widow with the pot of oil that discovered her wealth in the oil or the *anointing*. Let's quickly examine that foundation once again in 2 Kings 4:1–7:

> Now there cried a certain woman of the wives of the sons of the prophets unto Elisha, saying, Thy servant my husband is dead; and thou knowest that thy servant did fear the Lord: and the creditor is come to take unto him my two sons to be bondmen. And Elisha said unto her, What shall I do for thee? Tell me, what hast thou in the house? And she said, Thine handmaid hath not any thing in the house, save a pot of oil. Then he said, Go, borrow thee vessels abroad of all thy neighbours, even empty vessels; borrow not a few. And when thou art come in, thou shalt shut the door upon thee and upon thy sons, and shalt pour out into all those vessels, and thou shalt set aside that which is full. So she went from him, and shut the door upon her and upon her sons, who brought the vessels to her; and she poured out.   And it came to pass, when the vessels were full, that she said unto her son, Bring me yet a vessel. And he said unto her, There is not a vessel more. And the oil stayed. Then she came and told the man of God. And he said, Go, sell the oil, and pay thy debt, and live thou and thy children of the rest.

Once again, the "oil" represents the *anointing*. The widow told Elisha that she didn't have *anything* in the house, "save a pot of oil." In other words, she only had the *anointing*. But, that was *enough*!

Elisha, the prophet of God, gave the widow a *strategy* of how to *utilize* the *anointing*. He gave her a strategy of how to utilize the anointing that was contained in her "vessel." He showed her how to utilize the anointing that was contained in her *pot-ential* to destroy the yoke of poverty off of her life and off of her children's lives. Her "pot of oil" was her *anointing* and it was her *potential* wealth.

He created a *paradigm shift* from her sons being seen as potential *slaves*, to being her employees and staff at her company. It was a paradigm shift that transformed her house from being a house that was about to be *foreclosed* on by the creditor, to being her *manufacturing plant*. It was a paradigm shift from her being just a widow in a desperate situation, to being a *business owner* with an *oil business*! It was a paradigm shift that transformed her perspective from that of *lack*—"save only a pot of oil"—to *abundance*—"borrow not a few." It was a paradigm shift from *not enough* to *more than enough*. She went from saying that she didn't have anything but "one pot of oil," to saying, "bring me yet a vessel." "And he said unto her, there is not a vessel more. And the oil stayed." She had more on *reserve*. The oil didn't *run out*, it was just *on reserve*. In the United States, we have the Federal Reserve. We don't spend *all* of our money. The purpose of the Federal Reserve is threefold according to www.FederalReserveEducation.org:

1. Monetary Policy - which refers to what the Federal Reserve, as the nation's central bank, does to influence and regulate the amount of money and credit that is in the US economy. They have impact on interest rates and determine how the US economy performs overall.

2. Supervision and Regulation – which includes monitoring the activities of US financial institutions and banks. They monitor their lending practices. They also monitor the borrowing patterns of customers, which impact their monetary policy decisions.

3. Financial Services – In other words, the Federal Reserve is the central bank from which all US banks, credit unions, and savings and loans institutions receive financial services, such as help with check collection, electronic funds transfers, and distributing and receiving cash and coins.

In other words, the Federal Reserve is in place as the nation's central bank to help *manage, regulate,* and *govern* the financial activities of the nation. Their purpose is to help ensure *stability* and *reliability* of the financial well-being of the US economy.

So, we see that the widow's *oil* didn't run out. It just "stayed." There was something *left over* on *reserve*. The prophet brought her and her sons into a new *paradigm,* from *not enough* to *more than enough,* and something *on reserve!*

YOUR WEALTH IS IN YOUR ANOINTING

> *Then she came and told the man of God. And he said, Go, sell the oil, and pay thy debt, and live thou and thy children of the rest.*
>
> *–2 Kings 4:7*

In other words, "Go into business. Work this thing! Take care of your areas of lack. Pay your debt. Come to a place of financial balance." And then, afterward, "live thou and thy children on the rest." In other words, "live thou and your children on the reserve." The "rest" is something that you have *left over*. Beyond what you used to *pay off your debt*, you have something on reserve or something left. The Federal Reserve regulates the financial system in the United States so that we can have something on reserve. Well, this section of the message is about *Faithfulness* as an Essential Key to *maintaining* wealth. The point of the Fed regulating the US financial system is so that we don't *run out*! They provide regulation in order to avoid *financial disaster* in our country. The goal is to avoid *recession* or *depression* in the financial system. They provide various stimulus efforts to *jump-start* the economy at times. The goal is for the country to have *long-term wealth, endurance,* and *stability*. The FDIC (Federal Deposit Insurance Corporation) guarantees up to $250,000 of money deposited in each bank for each account type. The purpose is to give wealth earners confidence to *deposit* their money in the banking system. Because, as long as your money is in the banks, it is able to be used by the financial system to make loans to individuals and businesses for the purchase of homes or automobiles, to finance education, to start and expand businesses, for equipment and projects, etc. This helps to keep the financial system *vibrant* and *functioning*. They don't want people to be *afraid* to put their money in the financial system. It's not a *total guarantee*, but it's some amount of confidence. Along with that, you can spread your money out into other financial instruments and investments in order to gain the greatest amount of security for your money to last and grow over time, such as *stocks, bonds, mutual funds,* etc.

FAITHFUL IN *NATURAL* AND *SPIRITUAL* FINANCIAL PRINCIPLES

So, I'm now talking to you *about Faithfulness*: an Essential Key to *maintaining* wealth. The first place I am focusing on is in God's financial system, from a *biblical* standpoint. And, of course, you have to have other *natural* financial wisdom in regards to maintaining wealth, particularly once you've *obtained* it.

ABRAHAM–THE FATHER OF FAITHFULNESS

So, we are in a place in our message where the widow has *obtained* her wealth. She's *paid her debt*. Now, she has to have a level of *faithfulness* to God's principles, and other sound financial principles, in order to *maintain* the wealth so that she will have enough to live on for the rest of her life, and for her children to be able to live on the "rest."

In this section of the message, let's look at an example of someone that was faithful to God and His principles: Abraham, the *father of faith* or *Faithfulness*. We are the *just* and we *live by faith*. Therefore, as members of the Body of Christ, we are studying biblical financial principles. We are not, at this time, teaching natural financial principles. However, if you understand *biblical finance* and obey the principles, God can protect the rest of your *natural financial affairs*. We, as Believers, operate according to biblical principles, which impact our *spirit, soul, body, social, and financial life*. In other words, honoring God's principles profits us in every area of life. This is what we believe.

We are looking at Abraham, who is the *father of faith* as an example to us of how a *principle* was *established* in his life in regards to *tithing*. Tithing is a principle, which we have to be faithful toward while we are seeking to enter into our wealthy place. And after we have obtained wealth, we have to *maintain* it.

You could become blessed, but you could be tempted to stop honoring God with your finances. Some people will give a tithe on *$10*. They will give a *dollar*. Or, they will give a tithe on *$100*. They will give that *$10*, and maybe an additional *$2 or $3* as an *offering*. But, if they start making *$1000*, they may find it a little more difficult to *get up off* that *$100*. Or, they may start making *$10,000*, and they may not want to give up that *$1000*. And, don't let God bless them with *$50,000*! They won't want to give up that *$5,000 tithe*. Why am I considering this *increase* at this point? It is because you and I are *wealthy* people. God wants to *increase* us. You've read this message on **your wealth is in your anointing**, and you are about to *increase* in wealth. Yet, I want you to be established in God's principles regarding increase, so that you will *maintain* the wealth and continue to increase. I want you to have something to *pass down* to your children and loved ones. You ensure lasting success and prosperity by honoring God's principle of tithing. God has abundance in store for you. He's raising you up to *much more* than you've ever experienced before. Therefore, He wants you to have *Faithfulness* at this *level*. He wants you to be faithful where you are right now. It's because God has much more in store for you. God wants you and me to exercise the principles of *Faithfulness*.

THE *FATHER OF FAITHFULNESS*

Let's examine the legacy of Abraham as an example of this principle of *maintaining* wealth. Let's start at Genesis 14. We are going to look at quite a bit of scripture in order to layout the example of Abraham as a *tither*, and the resulting *Blessing* which rested upon his life. God *reinitiated* the *Blessing* of Genesis 1:28 into the life of mankind, through *Abraham*. We lost the *Blessing* because of the sin of *unbelief*. God reinitiated the *Blessing* back to all mankind through *faith*. Abraham ". . . believed in the Lord; and He counted it to him for righteousness" (Genesis 15:6). Through Abraham's faith, he was restored to the "right" to be blessed in the earth. He was delivered from the power of the *curse*. Therefore, whatsoever he set his hand unto *prospered*. He was once again empowered to prosper. (Deuteronomy 8:18) The favor of God was restored to Abraham through *faith*. He was deemed as *righteous* by faith. Therefore, Abraham is the *father of faith*. We are the *just*, we live by our faith. (Hebrews 10:38) Abraham was *blessed*. The Bible says, "Abram was very rich in cattle, in silver, and in gold" (Genesis 13:2). I believe if we *do* what those in the Bible did, we can *have* what those in the Bible had. We should believe God to be blessed in *biblical proportions*! We should not live our lives according to the *world's system* or the *world's limitations*. We should not be restricted to our *neighborhoods*, or *how we were raised*, etc. We should live according to the Bible. Let's look at Genesis 14. Abraham's name was Abram before God changed his name to represent that he would become the "father of many nations" through his faith:

> *And when Abram heard that his brother was taken captive, he armed his trained servants, born in his own house, three hundred and eighteen, and pursued them unto Dan. And he divided himself against them, he and his servants, by night, and smote them, and pursued them unto Hobah, which is on the left hand of Damascus. And he brought back all the goods, and also brought again his brother Lot, and his goods, and the women also, and the people.*
>
> *–Genesis 14:14-16*

So, we see that Abraham was able to rescue his nephew, Lot: "and he brought back all the goods, and also brought again his brother Lot, and his goods, and the women also, and the people." In other words, all the *spoils* of the battle, Abram was able to bring them back.

> And the king of Sodom went out to meet him after his return from the slaughter of Chedorlaomer, and of the kings that were with him, at the valley of Shaveh, which is the king's dale. And Melchizedek king of Salem brought forth bread and wine: and he was the priest of the most high God.
>
> –Genesis 14:17-18

COMMUNION AND THE *COVENANT* WITH GOD

This is an example to us of why we bring tithes and offerings to *church*. This scripture gives us the first *light* as to why we bring tithes and offerings to church. This is the Biblical first mention of a "priest". In today's setting, that would be the *pastor* of the church. Melchizedek was the "priest of the most high God." He brought forth "bread and wine," representing the *communion*. The "bread" represents the broken or torn body, and the "wine" represents the shed blood of Christ. "Without the shedding of blood is no remission of sins" (Hebrews 9:22). The communion and covenant between God and man was restored as a result of the *broken body* and *shed blood of Jesus*. After the fall in the Garden of Eden, God took an animal and sacrificed it to ". . . make coats of skins, and clothed them" (Genesis 3:21). The sacrifice of the innocent animals body and blood created a *covering* for Adam and Eve so that God could justly continue to interact with them, and still carry out His *ultimate* plan for their life. Sin had *separated* man from God. Man had "died" in his relationship with God (Genesis 2:17). The animal's broken body and shed blood created a *temporary* covering, until the *True* Lamb of God, Jesus Christ, the *Anointed One* would come and make atonement for all mankind's sin, *once and for all*. John 1:29 says, "The next day John seeth Jesus coming unto him, and saith, Behold the Lamb of God, which taketh away the sin of the world." Revelation 13:8 says, "And all that dwell upon the earth shall worship him, whose names are not written in the book of life of the Lamb slain from the foundation of the world."

Therefore, Melchizedek was *administering* a *service* of the covenant between Abram and God. A pastor *administers* a church service. It is a spiritual *service* between God and man. When we go to church, we are going to meet with God. God sets forth a pastor and a pastoral staff, and ministry team, in order to help to *administer* a spiritual *service* to God's people. That's the purpose of a church. The purpose of a church in a community is to administer a spiritual service to that *community*, and to the people that come to meet in that church. A local church provides *spiritual* and *practical services* to the community at large. That's why a pastor is called a *minister*. They *administer*. They are a part of an *administration* of a spiritual service to a community.

We are a *spirit*. We are *spirit* at our *core*. We came out of God. We are a *spirit*, we live in *a body*, and we have *a soul*. The *soul* is our *distinct mind, will, personality. emotions, and intellect*. These are the personal things that make us *different*. Yet, we are all *spiritual* at our core. We came out of God, and now we live in an earthly, physical body. The body is *not* the person, but we live *in* the body. However, the spiritual service that is administered in a church, ministers to *every part* of your life: *spirit, soul, body, socially,* and *financially*. It is because the *Blessing* is *released* over all parts of you. When God administers the *Blessing* over our lives, *every area* is blessed. This is why we give of our tithes and offerings, because it helps to administer the *Blessing*. So God calls the *minister* or *priest* to *administer* the *Blessing* of God upon the people.

ADMINISTERING THE *BLESSING*

In Genesis 1:26–28, God initiated the *Blessing* over all mankind:

> *And God said, Let us make man in our image, after our likeness: and let them have dominion over the fish of the sea, and over the fowl of the air, and over the cattle, and over all the earth, and over every creeping thing that creepeth upon the earth. So God created man in his own image, in the image of God created he him; male and female created he them. And God blessed them, and God said unto them, Be fruitful, and multiply, and replenish the earth, and subdue it: and have dominion over the fish of the sea, and over the fowl of the air, and over every living thing that moveth upon the earth.*

A *minister, priest,* or *pastor* helps to administer the *release* of that *Blessing* over you and me, so that whatever we set our hands to prospers (Psalms 1:3). The *Blessing* administers *healing* to your body. It administers *peace* to your mind. It administers *prosperity* to your family. So again, Genesis 14:18 says,

> *And Melchizedek king of Salem brought forth bread and wine: and he was the priest of the most high God.*

ABRAHAM—THE FATHER OF FAITHFULNESS

The word "Salem" has the same meaning as the word "Shalom," which means *peace, prosperity, wholeness, wellness, health, healing, safety, soundness, happiness, strength, victory, and friendliness with God and man*. It means nothing missing; nothing broken; spirit, soul, body, socially or financially. Jesus is the *Prince of Peace*. He is the *Prince of Shalom*.

Therefore, Melchizedek was a priest and minister of the Kingdom of *Peace*. He was a minister of the *Prince of Peace*, the Lord Jesus Christ, who came to restore peace between God and man from the penalty of sin. Jesus was the sacrifice. He is the Lamb of God. "Melchizedek king of Salem brought forth bread and wine..." This represents the *communion*. That "bread" and "wine" for us under the New Covenant, represents the *broken body* and *shed blood* of Jesus Christ, our Lord and Savior. It represents the reestablishment of the *Blessing* through our covenant with God. Melchizedek brought forth bread and wine, in order to administer the *Blessing* of Abraham's covenant with God. This is like Abraham's *church service*. After Abram (which is Abraham) came back with the spoils of war, or after he *got paid* at the end of the week of battle, he brought in his *increase*. Melchizedek carries out a service, through which he administers the *Blessing* of God unto Abram.

> And he blessed him, and said, Blessed be Abram of the most high God, possessor of heaven and earth: And blessed be the most high God, which hath delivered thine enemies into thy hand. And he gave him tithes of all.
>
> –Genesis 14:19-20

Melchizedek administered the covenant of the *Blessing*. He was the minister that represented God's side and Abram's side. Abram's response was to give God "tithes of all." The covenant of the *Blessing* was administered and brought into remembrance through Melchizedek, and he received the tithes on God's *behalf* for his service. It was his *responsibility* to administer the *proper use* of the tithe. However, his *position* was to receive the tithes on God's behalf for *his service*. Some may ask, "Why do we bring the tithes and offerings to the church?" It is because the minister, priest, or pastor is in a *position*, *ordained by God*, to *administer* the *Blessing* between God and the people. That's why we bring the tithes.

WE *BLESS* GOD THROUGH *SERVICE*

> And blessed be the most high God, which hath delivered thine enemies into thy hand. And he gave him tithes of all.
>
> –Genesis 14:20

YOUR WEALTH IS IN YOUR ANOINTING

Abram had been carrying out *God's service* by fighting the enemies of God. He *blessed* God by carrying out God's service. The way that we can *bless God* is by carrying out God's *service* in the earth. We don't really bless Him by giving Him anything. He already owns everything, including us. However, we do *honor Him* with the *tithe*. The scripture says that Abram "gave him tithes of all." So, when you go to work, you're carrying out God's service. He has to have someone to do that kind of work that you're doing. He has to have someone to carry out that *responsibility*. God created the earth. God created the Garden of Eden, but He gave Adam the *responsibility* to "... dress it and to keep it" (Genesis 2:15).

God didn't make it rain upon the earth at first because "... there was not a man to till the ground" (Genesis 2:5). When God created Adam, He gave him a service to carryout. Therefore, your service on your job, or whatever area of service you are carrying out, is needed in that particular area. The focus of this message is **your wealth is in your anointing.** Your *wealth* is in the *service* that you've been anointed to carryout. There is something specific that you have been *anointed* to carryout. Your wealth and increase is there. Whether it's on your job of being a *doctor*, a *teacher*, or even *a parent*, because someone has to raise those children and teach them in the "nurture and admonition of the Lord"(Ephesians 4:6). They won't learn about God if you don't *teach them*—that's a part of your *service*. Your wealth is *connected to* that. Payday may not come every *Friday*, particularly in the area of raising children, but it's *going to come*. We honor God in our *service* to Him.

We are in *covenant* with God. We're *Blessed* of the "most high God, possessor of heaven and earth." And we are *blessing* Him by helping to make His enemies "His footstool" (Hebrews 10:13). Jesus is sat on the right hand side of God the Father, until His enemies be made His footstool. You and I are helping God take "dominion" in the earth. God is increasing in every area of the earth realm, *through us*. Each of us has been given an area of responsibility. Each of us has been given an area of *dominion*. Each of us has been given a *domain* to have *responsibility* over.

When I was a boy, my mother would tell my brothers and me to "Clean your room." She said, "Make your bed." That bed was my area of *responsibility*. That room was my *domain*. She said, "Clean your room. Make your bed." That was my area of responsibility for *helping* my mother. She said, "Do your lesson in school." As a child in school, that was my *do-

ABRAHAM—THE FATHER OF FAITHFULNESS

minion. Do my lesson, clean my room, wash the dishes on my day, etc.; and then I could get an *allowance* when she got paid because my mother was the *Blessed* and *possessor of all the money that came in the house!* God is the "Blessed . . .most high God, possessor of heaven and earth." As we carry out our responsibility, He *blesses* us.

My grandfather told my brothers and me to "Always give your mama some of your money." My mother told us, "Always pay your tithes."

In looking at *Faithfulness* as an Essential Key to *maintaining* wealth, we've looked at Abraham as the earliest biblical mention of tithing.

PASSING ON THE *BLESSING* THROUGH *FAITHFULNESS*

Now let's look at Genesis 17. We will see how the *Blessing* continued on and was *passed down*. Abram was blessed. One of the key principles that Abram maintained was that of *honoring God* in tithing his increase. With all of his increase, he *honored God*.

The reason we are examining the principle of *tithing* is because it is the *chief biblical financial principle*. Of course, you should *budget* the 90% that you have left. You should give the first *10% to God in tithes*. You should also add an offering. You should then *take 10% and put in savings* for your future. And then, live off the remaining 80%. You should also *budget the 80%* for investing, as well as daily living. You should do regular *good sense* budgeting. God promises blessings if we will honor Him in that way. We're looking at the principle of tithing because that is the number one, chief biblical financial principle of *Faithfulness*, an Essential Key for *maintaining* wealth. The foundation of this message is based on the widow with the "pot of oil" that came to Elisha in a desperate financial situation. Her sons were about to be taken into slavery by the creditor to pay off her husband's debt. Elisha told her to go borrow empty pots and *pour her anointing into that which didn't have what she had*, and her oil *multiplied*. He then told her to "Go, sell the oil, and pay thy debt, and live thou and thy children of the rest." So her "pot of oil" or *anointing* contained enough to *get her out of debt*, and enough for her to *live on* for the rest of her life, and for her children to live "of the rest." In other words, there was something *left over*. In order for something to be *left over*, someone has to maintain *Faithfulness* in *money management*. There has to be management of certain financial and *lifestyle principles* for something to be left over to the "children and children's children"

209

YOUR WEALTH IS IN YOUR ANOINTING

(Proverbs 13:22). *Faithfulness* to God's principle of tithing is an Essential Key. Now let's look at Genesis 17:

> *And when Abram was ninety years old and nine, the Lord appeared to Abram, and said unto him, I am the Almighty God; walk before me, and be thou perfect. And I will make my covenant between me and thee, and will multiply thee exceedingly.*
>
> *–Genesis 17:1-2*

So we see, God was in covenant with Abram. We have a covenant with God through our Lord Jesus Christ. It is through the *broken body* and *shed blood* of Jesus. We have a covenant to be *blessed*. We read in 2 Corinthians 8:9:

> *For ye know the grace of our Lord Jesus Christ, that, though he was rich, yet for your sakes he became poor, that ye through his poverty might be rich.*

Jesus "became poor" on the cross. He took on *our* poverty on the cross, so that we "through His poverty might be rich." He took on the curse of poverty on the cross. Poverty is a *curse*. Poverty is not the *normal* state. Poverty is not what is expected. It is not what *should be*. Poverty is a curse. *Poverty is a result of sin entering into the world.* Failure, poverty, lack, etc., is the curse. *We were born to succeed.* You and I were born to succeed. We were created in the image and likeness of God to prosper and succeed. We were *blessed* in the beginning. Again, Genesis 1:26–28 says,

> *And God said, Let us make man in our image, after our likeness: and let them have dominion over the fish of the sea, and over the fowl of the air, and over the cattle, and over all the earth, and over every creeping thing that creepeth upon the earth. So God created man in his own image, in the image of God created he him; male and female created he them. And God blessed them, and God said unto them, Be fruitful, and multiply, and replenish the earth, and subdue it: and have dominion over the fish of the sea, and over the fowl of the air, and over every living thing that moveth upon the earth.*

Notice the scripture says, "God blessed them." We were made to *win* and *succeed*. God told the first man and woman to "be fruitful." "Fruitful" means to be creative; be productive; create something; do something. If you're *creative*, you *made something*. You *used your mind* and you *created something*. We were born to win. Genesis 17:2 says,

ABRAHAM–THE FATHER OF FAITHFULNESS

> *And I will make my covenant between me and thee, and will multiply thee exceedingly.*

So, it was a *restoring back* to the covenant of *Blessing* from the beginning. God said to Abram, "I will multiply thee exceedingly." That is what He said in the beginning, "Be fruitful and multiply."

> *And Abram fell on his face: and God talked with him, saying, As for me, behold, my covenant is with thee, and thou shalt be a father of many nations. Neither shall thy name any more be called Abram, but thy name shall be Abraham; for a father of many nations have I made thee. And I will make thee exceeding fruitful, and I will make nations of thee, and kings shall come out of thee. And I will establish my covenant between me and thee and thy seed after thee in their generations for an everlasting covenant, to be a God unto thee, and to thy seed after thee.*
>
> –Genesis 17:3-7

So we see that God created a covenant between Him and Abraham. Abraham was the *father of faith*. Let's look at Genesis 15:1-6.

> *After these things the word of the Lord came unto Abram in a vision, saying, Fear not, Abram: I am thy shield, and thy exceeding great reward. And Abram said, Lord God, what wilt thou give me, seeing I go childless, and the steward of my house is this Eliezer of Damascus? And Abram said, Behold, to me thou hast given no seed: and, lo, one born in my house is mine heir. And, behold, the word of the Lord came unto him, saying, This shall not be thine heir; but he that shall come forth out of thine own bowels shall be thine heir. And he brought him forth abroad, and said, Look now toward heaven, and tell the stars, if thou be able to number them: and he said unto him, So shall thy seed be. And he believed in the Lord; and he counted it to him for righteousness.*

God promised Abraham seed or children as multitudinous as the "stars of the heaven" and "the sands of the sea." However, they didn't come *only* out of his *physical* loins. No. These are the *children of faith*. That's why *we* are called *sons and daughters of Abraham*. Abraham was the *father of faith*. Abraham was an *example* of *believing God* and it being accounted unto "him for righteousness." And that's how we got saved. We believed that Jesus Christ is the Son of God, and that He died on the cross to pay for our sins, and that God raised Him from the dead for our salvation. We accepted that *by faith*. We accepted the free gift of salvation that God offered, *by faith*, that

Jesus died in our place and that we don't have to die for our own sin. We accepted the fact that Jesus "became poor" for us, that we might be rich. When you accept, by faith, that "I don't have to be poor. I can succeed. I can prosper. In fact, I'm supposed to prosper," and when you accept that "I was healed. Therefore, I'm not supposed to be sick. Jesus took my infirmities and bear my sicknesses" (see Isaiah 53:3–5), thus, you accept Him as your Healer; that's when you see a manifestation of it in your life. You *accept it by faith.* You receive it by faith, and *you are saved.* You are *delivered* from those curses. You're *delivered* from that bondage. And this is what Abraham did in Genesis 15:6: "And he believed in the Lord; and he counted it to him for righteousness." God "counted" or *accounted* to Abraham his *right* to the *Blessing.* Righteousness is your *right* to the *Blessing* that God intended from the beginning when He blessed us in Genesis 1:28.

TRANSFERENCE OF THE *BLESSING*

Now, let's look at Genesis 24. We know that Abraham is blessed. We know he has been exercising these principles of honoring God with his increase. He's honored God with all the wealth and increase that God blessed him with. God has changed his name to *Abraham*, and he has been honoring God financially with the *tithe*. We saw earlier where the principle of tithing was *established* and *observed* by Abraham. We saw in Genesis 14 that the *Blessing* was administered by Melchizedek, the priest of the Lord. Now as we begin looking at Genesis 24, we see that Abraham is *old*. He has lived out his life. And he's also *taught* his children. Now, I'm going to show you how the *Blessing* was *transferred*.

We looked at the widow with the "pot of oil." She had obtained her *Blessing*. She had gotten supernatural *multiplication*. The *Blessing* had been *restored* to her life, and she got supernatural multiplication. She was able to *pay her debt*, and it was enough for her to *live on*, and for her children to live on *the rest*. But, in order for it to be a "rest" left over, she had to *teach* her children. Abraham *taught* his children. The reason that God blessed Abraham is because He knew Abraham would *teach* his children. Before we look at Genesis 24, let's look at Genesis 18:16–19:

> *And the men rose up from thence, and looked toward Sodom: and Abraham went with them to bring them on the way. And the Lord said, Shall I hide from Abraham that thing which I do; Seeing that Abraham*

ABRAHAM—THE FATHER OF FAITHFULNESS

shall surely become a great and mighty nation, and all the nations of the earth shall be blessed in him?

—Genesis 18:16-18

God said "all the nations of the earth" *shall be blessed in Abraham.* How? *By faith.* It would be by the same *faith of Abraham.* It would be by the same *believing God* and it would be *accounted to us for righteousness.* That's how we are *blessed* in Abraham. Abraham "believed God and it was accounted unto him for righteousness" (Genesis 15:6). And that's how we are blessed: believe God, and it is accounted unto us for righteousness. John 3:16 says, "For God so loved the world, that He gave His only begotten Son, that whosoever believeth in Him, should not perish, but have everlasting life." We obtain righteousness by faith. However, verse 19 gives us the key to Abraham *maintaining wealth*:

For I know him, that he will command his children and his household after him, and they shall keep the way of the Lord, to do justice and judgment; that the Lord may bring upon Abraham that which he hath spoken of him.

—Genesis 18:19

The only way for God to be able to bring this enduring, *generational Blessing* upon Abraham, was for Abraham to *teach his children* these principles. We're looking at *Faithfulness*: an Essential Key to *maintaining* wealth. It is *Faithfulness* to God's principles regarding honoring Him financially that maintains wealth. We saw in Genesis 14, where Abraham won the spoils of war that "he gave tithes of all." Melchizedek administered the communion and remembrance of the covenant between Abraham and God, and he spoke the *Blessing* over Abraham by pronouncing the relationship of blessing between God and Abraham; and Abraham "gave tithes of all." Abraham taught these principles to his children.

For I know him, that he will command his children and his household after him, and they shall keep the way of the Lord, to do justice and judgment; that the Lord may bring upon Abraham that which he hath spoken of him.

—Genesis 18:19

God may have *spoken* the *Blessing* over you. He may have told you that you were blessed. He may have told you "I have big plans for you, and I'm going to bless you indeed. I'm going to open up the windows of heaven and pour you out a blessing that there shall not be room enough to receive. I'm going to bless your children. I'm going to bless whatsoever you set your hand to."

However, if you do not *maintain the principles of God*, you *negate* God's *opportunity* to *release* the *Blessing* on you. If you don't keep it going, by doing your part, you are negating the *flow* of the *Blessing*. Abraham honored God with the tithe, which *released* God's "hands" to pour out the *Blessing* on him. Abraham's obedience *authorized* God's Word to come to pass in his life.

Now, let's look at Genesis 24. Abraham taught his children. That was one of the keys. We're connecting this key with the widow with the "pot of oil." She got the initial blessing from her pot of oil, which was enough to pay her debt. However, in order for her to have enough to live on for the rest of her life, and her children during their lives, she had to maintain certain principles. Again, we're talking about *Faithfulness*.

> *And Abraham was old, and well stricken in age: and the Lord had blessed Abraham in all things.*
>
> *–Genesis 24:1*

So, we see the Lord had already blessed Abraham, according to His Promise to him. However, now it's not about Abraham anymore. The Lord had blessed him in all things. He had *experienced* the *Blessing*. But, God also knew that Abraham would teach his children. So, now the *Blessing* is not just about Abraham. It's about the *Blessing enduring* to the next generation.

> *And Abraham was old, and well stricken in age: and the Lord had blessed Abraham in all things. And Abraham said unto his eldest servant of his house, that ruled over all that he had, Put, I pray thee, thy hand under my thigh: And I will make thee swear by the Lord, the God of heaven, and the God of the earth, that thou shalt not take a wife unto my son of the daughters of the Canaanites, among whom I dwell: But thou shalt go unto my country, and to my kindred, and take a wife unto my son Isaac.*
>
> *–Genesis 24:1-4*

Abraham knew that in order for the *Blessing*, which God had blessed him with, to be *maintained*, his son Isaac would need a *certain kind* of

ABRAHAM–THE FATHER OF FAITHFULNESS

wife. He had *taught* his son principles of tithing. He had taught his son the principles of God. He had taught him financial principles. He did not want Isaac to get *hooked-up* with a wife that would lead him *astray* from God's principles. That's the *bottom line*!

It wasn't just a matter of Abraham not wanting Isaac to marry one of the Canaanite women. It was because the Canaanite women didn't honor God. The foreign women didn't honor God's principles. He didn't want Isaac to be *unequally yoked*. Because, when you're *yoked* with someone, and they are pulling one way and you're pulling another, they're going to pull you in the wrong direction. Both of you could be pulling *against* one another. Either you're not going to get anywhere, or they're going to be strong enough to pull you their way. It's possible that you will be strong enough to pull them your way: but it's going to be an *adversarial* situation. The Bible says, "Be not unequally yoked with unbelievers" (2 Corinthians 6:14). So if you are yoked with someone that's pulling in a way that is *opposite* of God's principles, they will *pull you out* of the *Blessing*.

Abraham had taught his son Isaac to give tithes. Also, you can believe that before Ishmael left the camp, Abraham had instilled in Ishmael the principle of tithing because God told Hagar that Ishmael would be *blessed*. He said Ishmael would have "great kings come out of him" (Genesis 17:20). So, the *Blessing* of Abraham even endured onto Ishmael, because of these principles of honoring God. So Abraham didn't want Isaac to be unequally yoked with someone who would pull him away from God's principles.

> But thou shalt go unto my country, and to my kindred, and take a wife unto my son Isaac. And the servant said unto him, Peradventure the woman will not be willing to follow me unto this land: must I needs bring thy son again unto the land from whence thou camest?
>
> –Genesis 24:4-5

Abraham was saying, "Not only do I not want my son to marry a woman from Canaan, but *I don't want you to take him back to how I was raised either*! I don't want him going back to that *mentality*. I don't want him *going back*. I want him going *forward*. I want you to get a family member that understands how we *think*. Yet, I want my son to *go forward*. Do not go back to the *family way* of doing things. Do not go back to the *limited mentality* before I got a chance to know God. No. I want him to hook up with a *sister* that he can relate to, and I want him to go forward and not backward. I want him to go forward according to what I have taught him about my relationship with the *One, true God.*"

> *And the servant said unto him, Peradventure the woman will not be willing to follow me unto this land: must I needs bring thy son again unto the land from whence thou camest? And Abraham said unto him, Beware thou that thou bring not my son thither again.*
>
> *–Genesis 24:5-6*

Abraham was saying, "Don't take him *backward*! I worked too many years to push us *forward*! We're not going *back*!"

> *The Lord God of heaven, which took me from my father's house, and from the land of my kindred, and which spake unto me, and that sware unto me, saying, Unto thy seed will I give this land; he shall send his angel before thee, and thou shalt take a wife unto my son from thence. And if the woman will not be willing to follow thee, then thou shalt be clear from this my oath: only bring not my son thither again.*
>
> *–Genesis 24:7-8*

Now, we understand in this story that this is where Isaac meets Rebekah. He found his wife Rebekah from amongst Abraham's people. She was the right wife for Isaac to *maintain* the *Blessing*.

THE GREATNESS OF THE BLESSING

Now, let's consider how blessed Abraham was. Look at Genesis 24:34–36:

> *And he said, I am Abraham's servant. And the Lord hath blessed my master greatly; and he is become great: and he hath given him flocks, and herds, and silver, and gold, and menservants, and maidservants, and camels, and asses. And Sarah my master's wife bare a son to my master when she was old: and unto him hath he given all that he hath.*

In other words, the servant was saying, "Your daughter is going to be blessed with wealth. She is about to be blessed with the wealth of Abraham. He's given it to his son, Isaac. He needs the *right woman* to walk through life with his son to *maintain* this wealth." Abraham had taught Isaac these principles regarding honoring God with his finances. These were the principles for maintaining this wealth. He wanted Isaac also to get with the right wife, so that she would not be someone that would be *pulling against him* in regards to God's principles. He wanted him to get with a wife that would also want to tithe on the money that God had blessed them with. That's *the bottom-line*! God had taught Abraham to "give tithes of all." Abraham taught his son Isaac to "give tithes of all." Abraham wanted his son to be married to a wife that would also honor God, and be willing to "give tithes of all." He didn't want Isaac to be with someone that would be pulling against him concerning the money. This *Faithfulness* was the Essential Key to *maintaining* Abraham's wealth. That was the only way that the wealth would be *maintained* from *generation to generation*.

> And he said, I am Abraham's servant. And the Lord hath blessed my master greatly; and he is become great: and he hath given him flocks, and herds, and silver, and gold, and menservants, and maidservants, and camels, and asses. And Sarah my master's wife bare a son to my master when she was old: and unto him hath he given all that he hath.
>
> –Genesis 24:34-36

So, we see that Isaac was blessed. He married Rebekah. She inherited this *Blessing*.

THE *PROGRESSION* OF THE *BLESSING*

Now, look at Genesis 25. I'll show you the *progression* of the *Blessing*. This demonstrates how *Faithfulness* is an Essential Key to *maintaining* wealth.

> Then again Abraham took a wife, and her name was Keturah.
>
> –Genesis 25:1

So, after Sarah died, Abraham was still *kicking*! He got him *another* wife. He got another wife from within the land of Canaan.

> And she bare him Zimran, and Jokshan, and Medan, and Midian, and Ishbak, and Shuah. And Jokshan begat Sheba, and Dedan. And the sons of Dedan were Assurim, and Letushim, and Leummim. And the sons of Midian; Ephah, and Epher, and Hanoch, and Abidah, and Eldaah. All these were the children of Keturah. And Abraham gave all that he had unto Isaac. But unto the sons of the concubines, which Abraham had, Abraham gave gifts, and sent them away from Isaac his son, while he yet lived, eastward, unto the east country.
>
> –Genesis 25:2-6

So, we see that Abraham had another group of children. Yet, verse 5 says, "And Abraham gave all that he had unto Isaac." Why? It's because

YOUR WEALTH IS IN YOUR ANOINTING

Abraham had *taught Isaac these principles*. The *Blessing* was on Isaac. It would be passed down through Isaac. *The Blessing is carried on through maintaining God's principles*. Abraham had taught these principles to Isaac.

> But unto the sons of the concubines, which Abraham had, Abraham gave gifts, and sent them away from Isaac his son, while he yet lived, eastward, unto the east country.
>
> –Genesis 25:6

Abraham "gave gifts" to the children of the other wife, and the concubines. They received *some* blessing from being associated with the *one* that was *blessed*. But he separated them away from Isaac, his *promised* son. Abraham didn't want the other children from his other wife and concubines to *distract* Isaac from *maintaining the principles* of God, regarding the *Blessing* that Abraham had taught Isaac.

> And these are the days of the years of Abraham's life, which he lived, an hundred threescore and fifteen years.
>
> –Genesis 25:7

Abraham was *175 years old*.

> Then Abraham gave up the ghost, and died in a good old age, an old man, and full of years; and was gathered to his people. And his sons Isaac and Ishmael buried him in the cave of Machpelah, in the field of Ephron the son of Zohar the Hittite, which is before Mamre; The field which Abraham purchased of the sons of Heth: there was Abraham buried, and Sarah his wife.
>
> –Genesis 25:8-10

Both of Abraham sons—that had the most time with him—were able to come back together. God had specifically said to Hagar, Sarah's maid and Ishmael's mother, that Ishmael would be *blessed* too. And, God had specifically declared to Abraham and Sarah, that Isaac would be *blessed*. So, you can believe that Ishmael also understood the principles of honoring God through tithing, as well as honoring his parents. That's why he was there to bury his father.

The *Blessing* was maintained through *keeping covenants*. Abraham passed his wealth that he had gained through the *anointing to get wealth*, or *power to get wealth*, down to his son Isaac. Ishmael was also blessed. Abraham passed his wealth to his sons, through the covenant of *honoring God*. He passed down the *Blessing*.

THE *BLESSING* TO THE *NEXT GENERATION*

Let's continue following the *Blessing* in Genesis 26. We will look at Isaac as he walked in wealth and blessing. He walked in wealth and blessing because his father Abraham passed down the *anointing to prosper*. Abraham had kept God's laws and he continued to honor God financially during his lifetime. He passed down the *anointing to prosper*, and his wealth, to Isaac.

> And there was a famine in the land, beside the first famine that was in the days of Abraham. And Isaac went unto Abimelech king of the Philistines unto Gerar. And the Lord appeared unto him, and said, Go not down into Egypt; dwell in the land which I shall tell thee of: Sojourn in this land, and I will be with thee, and will bless thee; for unto thee, and unto thy seed, I will give all these countries, and I will perform the oath which I sware unto Abraham thy father;
>
> –Genesis 26:1-3

In other words, God was telling Isaac that He had put the same *Blessing on him* that was on Abraham. Earlier in his life, Abraham had said to Lot, his nephew, when they were together and strife came between their servants, "Let's separate. Wherever you go, I will go the opposite way." (see Genesis 13:5–18) He said that because he was saying, "The *Blessing* is with me. Wherever I am is blessed. So, wherever you go, I'll go the opposite way, and it will still be blessed." And it did become blessed.

> Sojourn in this land, and I will be with thee, and will bless thee; for unto thee, and unto thy seed, I will give all these countries, and I will perform the oath which I sware unto Abraham thy father; And I will make thy seed to multiply as the stars of heaven, and will give unto thy seed all these countries; and in thy seed shall all the nations of the earth be blessed;
>
> –Genesis 26:3-4

The *Blessing* of Abraham was passed down to and *through* Isaac. The *Blessing* of Abraham is ours through Christ Jesus. Galatians 3:29 says "And, if you be in Christ, then are you Abraham's seed, and heirs according to the promise." Therefore, the *Blessing* of Abraham is upon you and me. In 2 Corinthians 5:17 it says, "Therefore if any man be in Christ, he is a new creature: old things are passed away; behold, all things are become new." We are "in Christ" and we are the Blessed of the Lord. We are *Abraham's seed, by faith*. Abraham is the *father of faith*. Abraham "believed God and it was counted unto him for righteousness." (Genesis 15:6) We believe God and the *Blessing* is restored to us, by faith in what Jesus did on the cross, the broken body and the shed blood of the Lord Jesus, and the Resurrection from the dead.

> Because that Abraham obeyed my voice, and kept my charge, my commandments, my statutes, and my laws.
>
> –Genesis 26:5

The *Blessing* was passed down to Isaac because of Abraham—because Abraham had taught Isaac these *principles* of honoring God.

WHAT THE BLESSING *LOOKS* LIKE

Now, let's look to see how this *Blessing looks*. Let's look at Genesis 26:12–14. We will see how the *Blessing looked* on Isaac, even in a land of famine.

> Then Isaac sowed in that land, and received in the same year an hundredfold: and the Lord blessed him. And the man waxed great, and went forward, and grew until he became very great: For he had possession of flocks, and possession of herds, and great store of servants: and the Philistines envied him.
>
> –Genesis 26:12-14

This is how the *Blessing looks* upon your life. If you will honor God with your *tithes* and *offerings*, giving Him the *first fruits* of all your increase, then God will honor your life. If you will honor God in your financial dealings and lifestyle, God will bless you, even in a land of famine. You will *grow great* and *go forward*, and you will become "very great"!

Isaac "sowed in that land"—*financially*, in *energy*, and *investing* in that land of famine. He didn't *withdraw* out of life. The only way that Isaac was going to receive the *Blessing* was for him to *sow* in that land. "They that sow bountifully, shall also reap bountifully; they that sow sparingly, shall also reap sparingly" (1 Corinthians 9:6). "Be not deceived; God is not mocked: for whatsoever a man soweth, that shall he also reap" (Galatians 6:7). If you don't sow, you can't reap, because there's no *seed* in the ground. The Lord *blessed* Isaac, because Isaac had given God *something*

ABRAHAM—THE FATHER OF FAITHFULNESS

to bless. "Isaac sowed in that land." The Lord *wanted* to bless Isaac, but he had to *sow* in that land. And you can believe that Isaac "gave tithes of all that he had" because his father, Abraham, had *taught* him to; "and the Lord blessed him."

> And the man waxed great, and went forward, and grew until he became very great: For he had possession of flocks, and possession of herds, and great store of servants: and the Philistines envied him.
> —Genesis 26:13-14

It says, ". . . and the Philistines envied him." In fact, look at verse 16:

> And Abimelech said unto Isaac, Go from us; for thou art much mightier than we.

Isaac was so blessed, that the Philistines could not stand it! The power of the anointing to prosper was manifesting in Isaac's life. Abraham had been faithful to God's principles, and had passed the *Blessing* to his son Isaac. The power of the *Blessing* was manifesting in Isaac's life, even in a land of famine.

The widow that came to Elisha the prophet, during a desperate situation, with her sons about to be taken into slavery to pay off her dead husband's debt, discovered the multiplying power of the anointing to get wealth. The anointing in her pot of oil multiplied, even in the face of lack. **Your wealth is in your anointing!** As you obey God's principles, the anointing will produce for you. You can pass it to the next generation.

FAMILY PRINCIPLES EQUAL FAMILY BLESSINGS

Now, let's continue with Genesis 27. We now will look at Isaac as he has gotten old. We looked at Abraham when he got old and passed down the Blessing to Isaac. Now we will look at Isaac. The *Blessing* now will be passed down to Jacob, Isaac's son. Again, from the foundation of this message, the widow lived on the *Blessing* from the "pot of oil," and her children were to live on "the rest." The *Blessing* is *sustained* by *maintaining Faithfulness* to God's principles. Let's look at Genesis 27 starting at verse 5:And Rebekah heard when Isaac spake to Esau his son. And Esau went to the field to hunt for venison, and to bring it.

Isaac asked Esau to go get him some deer or venison, and prepare it so he could release the *Blessing* on him. This was a *principle*. In order for the *Blessing* to be *released*, there had to be an *offering*. The offering was the *venison*. Isaac was saying, "If you present the venison; I can release the *Blessing*. If you release the *offering* of the venison; I can release the *Blessing*." So, even that was a principle that was being *passed down*.

> *And Rebekah spake unto Jacob her son, saying, Behold, I heard thy father speak unto Esau thy brother, saying, Bring me venison, and make me savoury meat, that I may eat, and bless thee before the Lord before my death.*
>
> *–Genesis 27:6-7*

Again, that was a part of the *transaction*—"you bring the venison; I release the *Blessing*." But Rebekah wanted the Blessing to be on *Jacob*. Therefore, she came up with a plan to help trick Isaac to release the *Blessing* on Jacob.

> *Now therefore, my son, obey my voice according to that which I command thee. Go now to the flock, and fetch me from thence two good kids of the goats; and I will make them savoury meat for thy father, such as he loveth: And thou shalt bring it to thy father, that he may eat, and that he may bless thee before his death. And Jacob said to Rebekah his mother, Behold, Esau my brother is a hairy man, and I am a smooth man: My father peradventure will feel me, and I shall seem to him as a deceiver; and I shall bring a curse upon me, and not a blessing. And his mother said unto him, Upon me be thy curse, my son: only obey my voice, and go fetch me them. And he went, and fetched, and brought them to his mother: and his mother made savoury meat, such as his father loved. And Rebekah took goodly raiment of her eldest son Esau, which were with her in the house, and put them upon Jacob her younger son: And she put the skins of the kids of the goats upon his hands, and upon the smooth of his neck: And she gave the savoury meat and the bread, which she had prepared, into the hand of her son Jacob. And he came unto his father, and said, My father: and he said, Here am I; who art thou, my son?*
>
> *–Genesis 27:8-18*

I'm taking time to relay this story to show the *progression* of the *Blessing* from *one generation* to *the next*. The *Blessing* is *transferrable*, even if circumstances are not ideal. The widow with the "pot of oil" had the key to the *Blessing* in her pot of oil. Her *wealth* was in her *anointing*. Once she discovered what she had, she had to *pass it down* to her sons. *Faithfulness* to God's principles was the key to that *transfer*.

ABRAHAM–THE FATHER OF FAITHFULNESS

In the story of Jacob and Esau, Isaac was old and he *sensed* that there was a level of *deceit* going on in regard to the *transfer* of the *Blessing*. Yet, he was *anointed to prosper*, and whoever he *released* the *Blessing* unto would be *blessed*. Let's look down to verse 26:

> And his father Isaac said unto him, Come near now, and kiss me, my son. And he came near, and kissed him: and he smelled the smell of his raiment, and blessed him, and said, See, the smell of my son is as the smell of a field which the Lord hath blessed: Therefore God give thee of the dew of heaven, and the fatness of the earth, and plenty of corn and wine: Let people serve thee, and nations bow down to thee: be lord over thy brethren, and let thy mother's sons bow down to thee: cursed be every one that curseth thee, and blessed be he that blesseth thee.
>
> –Genesis 27:26-29

He released the *Blessing* over his son Jacob. Now, we understand that when Isaac blessed Jacob, Esau was *angry* because of it. Yet Isaac had already *released* the *Blessing*, and he told him "I have blessed him, and he shall be blessed."

However, there is a main principle that I want to convey to you as I bring this book and message to a close. The principle of *tithing* started with Abraham. Melchizedek *blessed him* by administering the *Blessing* over him. And Abraham "gave tithes of all." That *Blessing* was *passed down* to Isaac. Isaac has now *blessed* Jacob. Now, look at Genesis 28:1-2:

> And Isaac called Jacob, and blessed him, and charged him, and said unto him, Thou shalt not take a wife of the daughters of Canaan. Arise, go to Padanaram, to the house of Bethuel thy mother's father; and take thee a wife from thence of the daughters of Laban thy mother's brother.

Just like Abraham didn't want his son Isaac to take *just any kind of woman* to be his wife—because he didn't want someone that would *take his heart* from God; Isaac didn't want his son, Jacob, to take a wife that would pull him away from God's principles. He wanted someone that would understand and follow God's principles along with him. So, he wanted to get the *right kind* of wife.

> And God Almighty bless thee, and make thee fruitful, and multiply thee, that thou mayest be a multitude of people; And give thee the blessing of Abraham, to thee, and to thy seed with thee; that thou

> mayest inherit the land wherein thou art a stranger, which God gave unto Abraham.
>
> –Genesis 28:3-4

So, Isaac *released* the *Blessing* over Jacob. Also notice, Jacob obeyed his parent's request. *This also was a key to him being blessed.* Look at verse 7 in the same chapter:

> And that Jacob obeyed his father and his mother, and was gone to Padanaram;

Jacob *obeyed his parent's* request for him not to take a wife from Canaan; but to go to Padanaram "unto Laban, son of Bethuel the Syrian, the brother of Rebekah, Jacob's and Esau's mother" to find his wife. This was also a key to him being *blessed*. *Faithfulness* is an Essential Key to *maintaining* wealth.

THE *INSTINCT* FOR THE *BLESSING*

Now, let's look at my final example of this principle of *Faithfulness*. Look at verse 10:

> And Jacob went out from Beersheba, and went toward Haran. And he lighted upon a certain place, and tarried there all night, because the sun was set; and he took of the stones of that place, and put them for his pillows, and lay down in that place to sleep. And he dreamed, and behold a ladder set up on the earth, and the top of it reached to heaven: and behold the angels of God ascending and descending on it. And, behold, the Lord stood above it, and said, I am the Lord God of Abraham thy father, and the God of Isaac: the land whereon thou liest, to thee will I give it, and to thy seed.
>
> –Genesis 28:10-13

God wanted to fulfill the *Blessing* in Jacob's life. However, in order for it to manifest, Jacob had to maintain God's principles.

> And thy seed shall be as the dust of the earth, and thou shalt spread abroad to the west, and to the east, and to the north, and to the south: and in thee and in thy seed shall all the families of the earth be blessed.
>
> –Genesis 28:14

God was getting the *Blessing* of Genesis 1:26–28 back *into the earth*, through *Abraham, Isaac,* and *Jacob*. And there are certain principles that you have to be *faithful* to in order to experience, fulfill, and maintain the *Blessing*.

ABRAHAM–THE FATHER OF FAITHFULNESS

> *And, behold, I am with thee, and will keep thee in all places whither thou goest, and will bring thee again into this land; for I will not leave thee, until I have done that which I have spoken to thee of. And Jacob awaked out of his sleep, and he said, Surely the Lord is in this place; and I knew it not. And he was afraid, and said, How dreadful is this place! This is none other but the house of God, and this is the gate of heaven.*
>
> *–Genesis 28:15-17*

The reason we come to church is because it is the "house of God" and "gate of heaven." You bring your *tithes* and *offerings* to the altar at church as a sacrifice to *ascend* up to God. It is a *tangible sacrifice* that is presented in a *spiritual environment*. When you present your tangible tithes and offerings into the spiritual environment of the Church, you release spiritual laws. It produces tangible results in your spirit, soul, body, and both socially and financially. **Your wealth is in your anointing!**

> *And Jacob rose up early in the morning, and took the stone that he had put for his pillows, and set it up for a pillar, and poured oil upon the top of it.*
>
> *–Genesis 28:18*

Jacob *sanctified* the place where he met with God. He *anointed* it with "oil." **Your wealth is in your anointing.** You must count the House of God as *holy*. The *tithe* is holy. It is a key to our *financial, spiritual, mental, emotional, social,* and *physical blessing*.

> *And he called the name of that place Bethel: but the name of that city was called Luz at the first. And Jacob vowed a vow, saying, If God will be with me, and will keep me in this way that I go, and will give me bread to eat, and raiment to put on,*
>
> *–Genesis 28:19-20*

The release of your anointing is because *God is with you*. The release of what God has put inside of you and anointed you to be and do in life will happen because *God is with you*. It is "Christ in you, the hope of glory!" (Colossians 1:27). That's why you will be blessed.

> *So that I come again to my father's house in peace; then shall the Lord be my God: And this stone, which I have set for a pillar, shall be God's house: and of all that thou shalt give me I will surely give the tenth unto thee.*
>
> *–Genesis 28:21-22*

YOUR WEALTH IS IN YOUR ANOINTING

Jacob was telling God, "If you will bless me, I will come to God's House, the church; and I will give tithes of all that you've given me." He said that "of all that thou shalt give me I will surely give the *tenth* unto thee."

We've been exploring the revelation that **your wealth is in your anointing.** The key to the widow's deliverance was in the anointing, which she contained in her vessel. The key to the restoration of the *Blessing* into her life and the lives of her sons would be the respect and maintenance of God's financial principles. Honoring God with our tithes and offerings is a key to the spiritual release of the wealth that is contained in our anointing. Operating in practical principles of diligence and *Passion* ensure that you release the wealth contained inside of your vessel.

We have just explored the last key and final *nail* in this message. The message brought us back to the "House of God." It is the place of *Blessing*. It is the place of the *Anointing*. It is the place of discovering "Christ in you, the hope of glory." As God blesses us now and in the future, let us covenant with God to always honor Him with our finances through giving of our tithes and offerings, that the *Blessing* may be *maintained* for you, your children, and your children's children. In Jesus Name. **Your wealth is in your anointing.**

FINAL WORDS

God has given each of us gifts and talents in order to succeed and prosper in life. Those that have received the Lord Jesus Christ as Savior are connected to the source of all prosperity and life. God wishes "above all things that you prosper, be in health, even as your soul prospers" (3 John 2). You were born to succeed. You were born to win in life. All you and I need to do is commit to releasing what God has put inside of you. We must release our God-given potential. Do not leave it in the "pantry" of your "house." You must begin to pour out of you, what God has put inside of you, into people and places that need what you have to offer. God will prosper you. God will put His *super* on your *natural*. Always focus on pleasing God with the wealth that He gives you, through giving of tithes and offerings into His Church and Kingdom. God will make sure that what you produce will endure to future generations. **Your wealth is in your anointing.** You now have the *tools* and *path* to maximize what God has given you. Now, release it! Share it! And teach it to your children and grandchildren. You will impact future generations.

— PRAYER FOR SALVATION —

Have you asked Jesus to come into your heart? Have you accepted eternal life through the shed blood of Jesus Christ for the forgiveness of your sins? If not, please know that tomorrow is not promised. You can only choose in this moment for sure. Psalms 90:12 says,

> *So teach us to number our days that we may apply our hearts unto wisdom.*

John 3:16–17 says,

> *For God so loved the world, that he gave his only begotten son, that whosoever believes in him, should not perish, but have everlasting life. For God sent not his son into the world to condemn the world, but that the world through him might be saved.*

How do you get saved? Romans 10:8–13 says,

> *But what saith it? The word is nigh thee, even in thy mouth, and in thy heart: that is, the word of faith, which we preach; that if thou shalt confess with thy mouth the Lord Jesus, and shalt believe in your heart that God raised him from the dead, you shall be saved. For with the heart man believes unto righteousness; and with the mouth confession is made unto salvation. For the Scripture saith, Whosoever believes on him shall not be ashamed. For there's no difference between the Jew and the Greek: for the same Lord over all, is rich unto all that call upon him. For whosoever shall call upon the name of the Lord shall be saved.*

So now, if you've never asked Jesus to come into your heart please repeat this prayer with me:

> *Jesus, I believe you are the Son of God. I believe you died on the cross to pay for my sins. I believe God your Father raised you from the dead for my forgiveness. I accept forgiveness. I accept you as my Lord and Savior. Thank you Lord Jesus. I am saved. Amen.*

If you repeated that prayer from the sincerity of your heart, you are now born again. You are a Christian. You are in Christ Jesus. You are anointed to prosper and succeed in every area of life on this earth, and you are prepared for Heaven as your eternal home when you leave this earth. God loves you. Continue to seek Him by reading the Bible daily. Read through the Gospels to find out more about Jesus Christ, your Lord and Savior. Go to church in your local area, where you can be taught the principles for living the Christian faith and lifestyle. Read this book over again, so that you can be further established in the principles of wealth and prosperity for your Christian life. God bless you! Welcome to the family of Christ!

ABOUT THE AUTHOR

PASTOR TERRANCE L. TURNER is the senior pastor of Faith Country Holiness Church in Gallatin, Tennessee. Pastor Turner completed an MBA in Finance and Supply Chain Management from Tennessee State University. He also has a Bachelors of Speech Communications and Theater, with a concentration in Mass Media from Tennessee State University. Terrance is a prolific author. His books are available at www.TerranceTurnerBooks.com. Terrance started his communications company, Well Spoken Inc., which focuses on audiobooks and professional speaking, in 2005 with his wife. For more information, email WellSpokenInc@bellsouth.net. He also is an accomplished singer, songwriter, and recording artist. He and his wife, Avis, sing and record together. His music is available online as well as on his website www.FaithCountryProductions.com. He continues to serve the community and Body of Christ through service, music, preaching, and teaching of the Word of God.

A SPECIAL NOTE

Thank you so much for taking the time to read *Your Wealth Is In Your Anointing*. I hope you found inspiration, direction, and hope within as you take your own journey to discover and release the wealth potential from your relationship with the Lord Jesus Christ. Thank you for going on this journey of exploration with me. I pray it has given you insights and opened your heart to discover your passion. If this book helped you in some way, I would deeply appreciate your help in spreading the message so other believers might also find it. You may not realize how important positive reviews are to authors, but they can make a difference in who discovers the treasure that you have just explored. I would really appreciate hearing from you. Please share your feelings about this book on Amazon.

To increase in your discovery of God's wisdom for your wealth, please visit my website where you will find other books and resources to help you, like my book series Distinguished Wisdom Presents… "Living Proverbs"—Volumes 1 and 2. Each contains over 500 Wisdom Nuggets to Enrich Your Life. You would also be blessed in your relationship with the Lord Jesus Christ through the anointed, contemporary worship music from Terrance & Avis Turner. Visit FaithCountryProductions.com to find out more. Be sure to sign-up to receive announcements of when I will be coming to a city near you to preach this message live and worship God together: TerranceTurnerBooks.com.

www.ingramcontent.com/pod-product-compliance
Lightning Source LLC
Chambersburg PA
CBHW021123300426
44113CB00006B/263